The River Within

THE RIVER WITHIN

LOVING GOD, LIVING PASSIONATELY

Jeff Imbach

NAVPRESS
BRINGING TRUTH TO LIFE
NavPress Publishing Group
P.O. Box 35001, Colorado Springs, Colorado 80935

The Navigators is an international Christian organization. Our mission is to reach, disciple, and equip people to know Christ and to make Him known through successive generations. We envision multitudes of diverse people in the United States and every other nation who have a passionate love for Christ, live a lifestyle of sharing Christ's love, and multiply spiritual laborers among those without Christ.

NavPress is the publishing ministry of The Navigators. NavPress publications help believers learn biblical truth and apply what they learn to their lives and ministries. Our mission is to stimulate spiritual formation among our readers.

© 1998 by Jeff Imbach

Library of Congress Catalog Card Number: 98-10837
ISBN 1-57683-045-4

Front cover design: Digital illustration by Steve Eames
Back cover photo by Kevin Morris
General editor: Dallas Willard
Senior editor: David Hazard

Some of the anecdotal illustrations in this book are true to life and are included with the permission of the persons involved. All other illustrations are composites of real situations, and any resemblance to people living or dead is coincidental.

Unless otherwise identified, all Scripture quotations in this publication are taken from the *HOLY BIBLE: NEW INTERNATIONAL VERSION* ® (NIV®). Copyright © 1973, 1978, 1984 by International Bible Society. Used by permission of Zondervan Publishing House. All rights reserved; and the *King James Version* (KJV).

Imbach, Jeff, 1945-
    The river within : loving God, living passionately / Jeff Imbach.
        p.   cm.
    Includes bibliographical references.
    ISBN 1-57683-045-5 (pbk.)
    1. Christian life.
BV4501.2.I473 1998
248.4—dc21   98-10837
                                       CIP

Printed in the United States of America

1 2 3 4 5 6 7 8 9 10 11 12 13 14 15 /03 02 01 00 99 98 97

FOR A FREE CATALOG OF
NAVPRESS BOOKS & BIBLE STUDIES,
CALL 1-800-366-7788 (USA)
or 1-416-499-4615 (CANADA)

Contents

This book is dedicated to
Miriam
with whom I have shared my passion
most deeply for more than a quarter century.

Getting In and Getting Wet

This book stands at the confluence of two great themes — the life of God within the Trinity and our passion in daily life. It is not a theological discussion of the Trinity nor a general exploration of passion. It explores our passion for life as the river of God's life within us.

The flowing of love within the Trinity shows us that God is passionate. The stream of passionate desire that runs in us reminds us that we, too, are part of the great river of God's life.

This meeting place can be a risky place to stand. The Trinity is essentially grounded in mystery. Passion is grounded in the muck and beauty of everyday life.

It's hard to write about the Trinity in the specific, earthy terms that passion demands. Each statement, if taken by itself, could sound lopsided. If we talk in isolation about how our intimacy with God encompasses our desire to be respected as unique persons, we can quickly sound cheap — or worse, self-centered. If we talk in isolation about our desire to abandon ourselves and surrender into union, spirituality can easily degenerate into quietism — or worse, into a lifeless spiritual conformity.

Despite the difficulty, neither theme — the Trinity nor Passion — allows for the cool detachment of armchair analysis. The Trinity invites us into the intimacy of shared love. Passion invites us to get living.

These can be explored but never mastered. I have had to jump in and get my feet wet.

As I have worked on this book, I've gradually realized the book itself is an example of what I'm trying to say. It is a risk, an attempt to express my passion. It gives voice to the truth that has become profoundly transforming in my own spiritual life and in the lives of many with whom I have talked over the years.

The writing has shaped me. I have had to face my own biases and open up more fully to the spectrum of God's life. Through the choice to offer my passion to the world, I have come to enjoy God more deeply and depend on God more profoundly.

The audience has also shaped the writing. I care deeply for those who have a hunger for spiritual intimacy, who are at home in their relationship with God, and for whom this book offers new ground to explore.

My heart goes out to the growing number of people who feel empty, frustrated, disappointed, or just plain disillusioned with what they have been given as spiritual food. Some have lived with this ache for years; others are just beginning to realize they have questions they wouldn't have dared to admit just a short time ago.

Finally, I have purposely chosen to write with as little religious language as possible so that those who have no faith background might find a hopeful and, perhaps, even an alluring invitation to get into the river for themselves.

I pray this book will give people permission and courage to find a way forward in their spiritual pilgrimages. Like plants, all books emerge from their own soil. *The River Within* has grown in the soil of my life, in my marriage and family, my friends, and within the church community of Barnabas Christian Fellowship. I owe a deep debt of gratitude to all those who have stood with me and who have explored the vision together.

I have been blessed to have David Hazard as my editor. I cannot imagine an editor wrestling with the content and style more deeply and more sympathetically than he has as he approached the material out of the richness and breadth of his own life and wide learning. It has been of immense help. I want to thank Steve Eames for a magnificent cover and all the staff at NavPress for their very caring support.

Finally, I would like to express thanks to my wife, Miriam, and to Bonnie Tarchuck, Heidi Grogan, and Art Norris for their helpful contributions as they read and marked their way through the material.

General Introduction

BY DALLAS WILLARD

The Spiritual Formation Line presents discipleship to Jesus Christ as the greatest opportunity individual human beings have in life and the only hope corporate mankind has of solving its insurmountable problems.

It affirms the unity of the present-day Christian with those who walked beside Jesus during His incarnation. To be His disciple then was to be with Him, to learn to be like Him. It was to be His student or apprentice in kingdom living. His disciples heard what He said and observed what He did, then, under His direction, they simply began to say and do the same things. They did so imperfectly but progressively. As He taught: "Everyone who is fully trained will be like his teacher" (Luke 6:40).

Today it is the same, except now it is the resurrected Lord who walks throughout the world. He invites us to place our confidence in Him. Those who rely on Him believe that He knows how to live and will pour His life into us as we "take His yoke . . . and learn from Him, for He is gentle and humble in heart" (Matthew 11:29, paraphrased). To take His yoke means joining Him in His work, making His work our work. To trust Him is to understand that total immersion in what He is doing with our life is the best thing that could ever happen to us.

To "learn from Him" in this total-life immersion is how we "seek first his kingdom and his righteousness" (Matthew 6:33). The outcome is that we increasingly are able to do all things, speaking or acting, as if Christ were doing them (Colossians 3:17). As apprentices of Christ we are not learning how to do some special religious activity, but how to live every moment of our lives from the reality of God's kingdom. I am learning how to live my actual life as Jesus would if He were me.

If I am a plumber, clerk, bank manager, homemaker, elected official, senior citizen, or migrant worker, I am in "full-time" Christian service no less than someone who earns his or her living in a specifically religious role. Jesus stands beside me and teaches me in all I do to live in God's world. He shows me how, in every circumstance, to reside in His Word and thus be a genuine apprentice of His—His disciple indeed. This enables me to find the reality of God's world everywhere I may be, and thereby to escape from enslavement to sin and evil (John 8:31-32). We become able to do what we know to be good and right, even when it is humanly impossible. Our lives and words become constant testimony of the reality of God.

A plumber facing a difficult plumbing job must know how to integrate it into the kingdom of God as much as someone attempting to win another to Christ or preparing a lesson for a congregation. Until we are clear on this, we will have missed Jesus' connection between life and God and will automatically exclude most of our everyday lives from the domain of faith and discipleship. Jesus lived most of His life on earth as a blue-collar worker, someone we might describe today as an "independent contractor." In His vocation He practiced everything He later taught about life in the kingdom.

The "words" of Jesus I primarily reside in are those recorded in the New Testament Gospels. In His presence, I learn the goodness of His instructions and how to carry them out. It is not a matter of meriting life from above, but of receiving that life concretely in my circumstances. Grace, we must learn, is opposed to earning, not to effort.

For example, I move away from using derogatory language against others, calling them twits, jerks, or idiots (Matthew 5:22), and increasingly mesh with the respect and endearment for persons that naturally flows from God's way. This in turn transforms all of my dealings with others into tenderness and makes the usual coldness and brutality of human relations, which lays a natural foundation for abuse and murder, simply unthinkable.

Of course, the "learning of Him" is meant to occur in the context of His people. They are the ones He commissioned to make disciples, surround them in the reality of the triune name, and teach to do "everything I have commanded you" (Matthew 28:20). But the disciples we make are His disciples, never ours. We are His apprentices along with them. If we are a little further along the way, we can only echo the apostle Paul: "Follow my example, as I follow the example of Christ" (1 Corinthians 11:1).

It is a primary task of Christian ministry today, and of those who write for this line of books, to reestablish Christ as a living teacher in the midst of His people. He has been removed by various historical developments: assigned the role of mere sacrifice for sin or social prophet and martyr. But where there is no teacher, there can be no students or disciples.

If we cannot be His students, we have no way to learn to exist always and everywhere within the riches and power of His Word. We can only flounder along as if we were on our own so far as the actual details of our lives are concerned. That is where multitudes of well-meaning believers find themselves today. But it is not the intent of Him who says, "Come to me . . . and you will find rest for your souls" (Matthew 11:28-29).

Each book in this line is designed to contribute to this renewed vision of Christian spiritual formation and to illuminate what apprenticeship to Jesus Christ means within all the specific dimensions of human existence. The mission of these books is to form the whole person so that the nature of Christ becomes the natural expression of our souls, bodies, and spirits throughout our daily lives.

Introduction

BY DAVID HAZARD

Many Christians are wondering why they have not experienced the life of depth, fulfillment, and happiness promised by Jesus. "Whoever believes in me, as the Scripture has said, streams of living water will flow from within him" (John 7:37).

We know as adults that demands and duties have a wearing effect. But beyond that, many believers come to a point where they question their understanding of the Christian spiritual life at a very fundamental level. Great numbers of men and women are saying, "The type of Christianity I was introduced to seems to me now to focus on rule-keeping. On being correct, and always knowing and doing the right thing. But the problem is, I don't always know what's right . . . and I don't always do what's right. And I usually feel either worn out from trying, or guilty if I don't try to be a better Christian."

Quite a number of these sincere Christians secretly want to give up. Some do, and leave the church and Christian fellowship altogether. They cannot stand the sense of being deficient when they are with others who seem to be performing well in the Christian life. Others stay in the church, and experience cycles of trying hard and "recommitting" themselves to Christ and His service, only to fail or wear out from all their striving and give up. Time passes and, feeling a bit rested, they start up again, hoping that this time they will find the right set of disciplines or rules to live by, the right set of performance standards that will make them feel like they are better Christians. But they seldom find life in any new program of self-improvement that they try.

All the while they meet other Christians who encourage them in these fruitless and painful cycles of striving and quitting. Few seem to have the courage to stop gutting it out long enough to admit their soul feels fairly dead, or at least listless and unmotivated. Fewer want to voice these feelings to other Christians, because they are more concerned with how they will sound to their friends than with standing before God in soul-naked honesty. At the bottom of it all, they may be afraid that God will pronounce them defective after all, unfit to be His son or daughter.

The questions that want to bubble up from inside are, quite often these: Is the Christian life all rule-keeping, and struggling to live and act and speak "the right way"? And what about these drives, ambitions, dreams, and goals—my will, the force that really pushes me from within? What do I do with these drives, if I'm supposed to be the fulfillment of God's will in my life—even if I knew for sure what that was?

As Jesus said, however, those who ask, seek, and knock are the ones who find their way. And so it is to the brave in spirit—the ones who refuse to let stagnation and discouragement win—that answers and vision and entry into the fuller Christian life come.

Jeff Imbach is one of those brave spirits, one who is unafraid to ask honest questions and to open his spiritual struggles. All in the interest of getting more light on the question, does our new life in Christ come from living carefully, timidly, between the confining "banks" of Christian morality and mission—or from riding out the "current" of drives and impulses that make us feel fully alive? How do we live as spiritual beings in human bodies? He has delved into Scripture, into the nature of God, into the peaks and chasms of human life, and into the wells of ancient Christian wisdom in search of answers we can all live with.

For these reasons, NavPress is pleased to offer as part of our Spirituality and Spiritual Formation Line *The River Within*.

DAVID HAZARD
Senior Editor

PART ONE

THE LIFE OF PASSION

■

You carry a whole world within your soul always.
It surrounds you and you are impregnated by it.
It has become part of you and since you are its
creation and moulded by it, it lives in you.
It is God Himself.

ABBÉ DE TOURVILLE[1]

CHAPTER ONE

THE RISK OF GROWTH

■

C AN WE LOVE GOD WITH ALL OUR HEARTS AND LIVE LIFE PASSIONATELY? This single question catapults us to the heart of the spiritual life. We often hold these two great desires — the longing to love God and the urge to live full, juicy lives — at arm's length, as though they were incorrigibly opposed to each other.

Are spirituality and passion mutually exclusive? Do we have to curb or kill our love of life to be spiritual? If we open up to passion, will we lose our devotion to God? We need to face these questions squarely.

Commitment to God without embracing the goodness of life leads to a soulless, fanatical spirituality. Passionate living without the undergirding of a deep commitment to God leads to dissipation and death.

As men and women throughout Christian history have discovered, life filled with devotion to God and full, robust passion calls for choices that are the very essence of discipleship. It demands reconciliation and healing at the very heart of our spiritual lives.

WHAT IS PASSION?

Do you sometimes feel as though you are dying rather than living? Does your spirituality seem to make your life feel smaller rather than making it feel larger? Do you wonder what to do with the simple urge to kick up your heels and live a full, rich life?

Passion is the torrent of desire that lives within us all. It propels us into life and, if we choose, to God. It is the inner craving for the rich, intimate exchanges of love — the drive to experience ourselves and our relationships deeply and fully.

Passion is not only the sinful cravings we experience. It is the whole of our desire lived in good or evil ways. C. S. Lewis put it clearly: "Wickedness, when you examine it, turns out to be the pursuit of some good in the wrong way. . . . Goodness is, so to speak, itself: badness is only spoiled goodness. And there must be something good first before it can be spoiled."[2]

Living passionately is about living wide and living deep. To live passionately as a Christian is to live wide — wide open to God and wide open to life. Living wide opens us up to receiving the fullness of God's life. It calls us to trust that God will be with us through the many twists and turns of our life journey. It challenges us to risk letting go of everything that detracts from the free flowing of God's life in us. At the same time it challenges us to embrace all the ways God comes to us. It keeps us from limiting our spirituality to a narrow range of acceptable religious activities.

Living wide with God and our passion opens us to the whole cycle of experience. The whole bundle of our longings — from sex to solitude, and from making money to studying the Bible — is part of our passion. All longings are a sign of God's life and a call to experience God deeply.

Living wide includes living with our desires and longings through the metaphor of each season — the anticipation of the first crocus, the vigor of summer growth, the many dyings of fall that slow and freeze us in the stark dormancy of the winter. The dormant times in our lives are as much a part of life as the seasons of lush growth and full fruit. Grief is as much a part of the cycle as praise.

Living wide includes accepting our sexuality, facing our fears and limitations, celebrating our joys, expressing our gifts, and in the end, still tasting the longing that sometimes seems like an all-consuming fire inside.

It means embracing and celebrating all that is good and enriching, all that brings us to fullness as human beings. It opens our whole being — emotions, intellect, and body — to embrace the vast sweep of life head-on.

To live passionately as a Christian also means to live deep. Passion takes us to the heart of life and calls us to live out of our souls. It challenges our facades, bursts through our nice, safe, petty expressions of Christianity and asks us to be real. It brings all our values, ambitions, and desires into unity with the Source and Current of Life, grounding the vast sweep of our lives in God.

Who wants to live a shallow, hollow existence on the surface of things? We get so focused on external appearances . . . on the trappings of holiness. Life becomes proscribed by all the things we should avoid, and prescribed by all the things we must be careful to do. We get so busy trying to demonstrate our spiritual correctness that we lose the art of living out of our souls.

We downsize our souls to achieve a safer bottom line of religious acceptability. We are left to live between the rock of crisp correct religious doctrines and rules, and the hard place of duty-bound activity as supposed proof of our spiritual fervor. To open up our souls and discover the fullness of who we are in the stream of God's love has not even been an option for many Christians.

OUR FEAR OF PASSION

This reductive approach to spiritual growth is not surprising. It is easy to fear passion.

Passion is a charged word. Living with robust passion touches us way down deep, dredging to the surface tremendous longing and fear. Our passion has the power to turn our lives into a tangled mess, much like the storm path of a hurricane. Yes, cut off from its source and goal in God, passion becomes ugly and destructive through our addictive, exploitative, narcissistic choices. Unbridled lust for power, status, acceptance, and sex distorts passion. So does spiritual pride, intolerance, and a condemning spirit.

It is so easy for desire, shaped by the bombardment of advertisements, to degenerate into greed or infidelity. It's easy for us to learn the need for boundaries in personal relationships only to turn them into barriers and become defensive and alienated from the ones we love.

We see evidence of the distortion of passion every day in our fractured and dying culture. In the name of wholeness, people are catering to their own egos. In the desire for fulfillment, people are greedily consuming themselves into oblivion. Families rupture, values get trampled, and life becomes a slavish drive for self-gratification.

With examples like these all around, a spirituality that embraces passion could easily degenerate into a justification for egocentric, compulsive behavior. It could be used to cover a lackluster commitment to God and an obstinate refusal to let ourselves be transformed into truly God-centered people.

I, for one, am not prepared to throw aside my Christian commitment so that I might live out of unbridled desire. To do so would be nothing more than self-indulgence, even if it is dressed up in religious language.[3]

Regardless of our uncanny ability to make a mess of things, our desire (as the ancients called it) is nothing less than the life of the triune God in us. With the gift of God's Son, it is the best gift we've been given!

God lives in a constant interflowing of love between Divine Persons in the Trinity. We get a glimpse of that love at Jesus' baptism when a voice from heaven boomed, "You are my Son, whom I love; with you I am well pleased" (Mark 1:11).

It is this Trinity of Outpouring Passion that has reached out to us in love and offered us reconciliation in Christ. We have been raised with Christ to new life (Ephesians 2:4-10). We are alive with the life of God. It is at the heart of our desires, even the desires we manage to distort into almost unrecognizable forms.[4]

Jesus said, "I have come that they may have life, and have it to the full" (John 10:10). If this is what Jesus offers, why should we, why *do* we, settle for less?

Why should we die by degrees, in lives of quiet desperation, because we're afraid to live? Why should we merely exist in our careers, our marriages, and our church life with a dull resignation? Why should we cower in ruts and traditions—sterile forms that are no longer life-giving? Why should we sell ourselves to spiritual conformity at the cost of our own souls?

Is this the kind of life Jesus promised to bring?

FACING THE CHOICE
This false dichotomy between Christian commitment and engagement with life afflicts many sincere believers today. It puts us into the impossible dilemma of having to choose between God and what we have begun to suspect is our real self.

Frank's story, which emerged with difficulty while on a camping trip with some friends, illustrates this dilemma. Frank admitted that he is slowly dying inside. At fifty-five, his life has been usurped by the church. His time is indentured to deacon duties, prayer rallies, men's group, and weekend seminars to learn how to be a more powerful Christian.

Frank gets the strange sensation, at times, that he is no longer a human being. He is disconnected from the natural world, from friends, and from life. Between family responsibilities, business affairs, and church commitments, his zest for life has eroded away.

Frank further admitted that he doesn't know any way out. The church men's group has called him to be even more responsible for his family duties. This only heightens his perception that the "Christian thing to do" is to sacrifice himself for the sake of others. He loves his family. He can't point to any one thing that is wrong. Yet, when he finally looks honestly at his life, it seems warped and rootless.

Is there life beyond duty? Is this kind of life what the Bible calls "life to the full"?

Fortunately, Frank has begun to look for a truer balance. He says he sometimes feels closer to God on a hike with his boys than he does at Bible study. Although he struggles with guilt feelings about that, he's determined to get real in his life, even if he has to fail his own expectations of what a "good Christian" should be like.

If he is going to study Scripture, he wants to do it in the context of real life. He's learned at least one thing: Consistently denying or squelching the desires inside him, as the price exacted for a narrow view of holiness, has not produced a vibrant life.

Frank had never heard anyone talk like this before. It scared him to admit these things. Yet when he did speak out, other men began to open up the hollow places in their own lives.

Sally's story illustrates similar themes. Her life is in turmoil. Outwardly, Sally looks like she's doing fine; inside, she's rumbling. A forty-four-year-old mother of three teenage children, Sally is deep into a life transition that seems foreign and frightening.

Until recently, Sally's life has been clear and stable; we might almost say, impeccable. She has a good Christian family, enjoys her part-time job as a nurse, and has more friends than she can keep up with.

But a growing restlessness within her feels like the stirrings of a volcano. She described it this way: "It feels as though something wants to erupt or like I need to molt. I want to become more myself, and that feels very selfish."

Is this good? Should she pay attention to her inner promptings? Or are they just her own sinful desires? A verse she memorized as a child, "The heart is deceitful above all things and desperately wicked" makes her afraid to trust inner urges, especially when they call her to stand up, speak what is important to her, and change accordingly.

So far, Sally has managed to cap this urge, fearing it will explode into crazy, destructive choices. But her old ways of coping don't seem to be working. She wants desperately to follow God, but Bible reading doesn't hold the same comforting reassurance, and her prayers seem confused between asking God to take away these urges and getting the distinct sense that they are here to stay.

Sally doesn't know how she got here. Whether this will be the ruin of her spiritual maturity or the unfolding of an important spiritual journey is not yet clear. About all she knows is that she can't seem to go back. She recorded these words in her journal:

> I don't know what to do with myself. I love my life and yet I have this tremendous longing that makes me feel like I'm going to burst. Sometimes the longing feels exquisite, sometimes it feels like I'll choke on it. I want to live to the full. Jack doesn't seem to know what to do with me. I know he loves me and wants the best for me, but I think deep down he would be happy if I were content to be nice and supportive, stay at home all the time and be there to ease the burden of his busy work life. Sometimes I feel totally at peace with life just the way it is. I think I'm finally becoming mature. Then the next thing I know, I have this urge to overturn the entire apple cart and start fresh. What am I going to do with this wonderful, terrible, insistent urge within me? If I tame it, will it die? If I let it loose, will it destroy me? I don't know!

In conversation, I asked Sally when she noticed these inner rumblings. She said, "Mostly, when I'm alone. When I get right down to facing myself. Then I try to read the psalms, like Psalm 46. You know, the one that says the Lord is our help when the earth quakes and the mountains fall into the sea."

Probing further, I asked, "Is it possible these rumblings are the promptings of God's Spirit in your life?"

The question frightened her. But as we talked, it became clear that the choices before her seemed to be less about whether she was going to allow them than how she was going to live with them.

Slowly we began to explore the possibility of saying yes to God's Spirit. She would need to believe she was being drawn into a deeper walk with God and to trust that she would learn what is self-centered and what is truly of God for her.

Whatever has prompted Sally's hunger for change and growth, she is faced with choice. Will she finally address the fact that her spirituality needs to open her up to life rather than protect her from it? Will she choose to continue to love God with all her heart and at the same time refuse to back away from life just to be safe?

This imposing shift challenges her entire spiritual framework. Life seems big and scary, bigger than the accepted Christian lifestyle she has learned to emulate. Up to this time her spiritual life has kept her in a little bubble of acceptability. Will her relationship with God and her own understanding of spirituality be strong enough to take these changes on?

For many of us the transition from duty to passion is a frightening one. Look carefully at what is at stake. Sally fears becoming self-centered. Anyone who has been grounded in biblical doctrine in a conservative milieu, as Sally has, will immediately know what I mean. We feel the massive pull that our narcissistic world exerts on us. And Sally knows how strong the temptation to self-indulgence can be, because she sees the trail of tragic consequences of self-indulgence in our culture. She fears, as many of us do, that if she pays any attention to her inner promptings, she'll lose the keen edge of her servant heart.

Sally also fears—it seems to me, unconsciously—that her Christianity cannot withstand the pressure of change. She fears that if she challenges the stereotype of "a good Christian" that she has learned to follow, her Christianity will fall like a house of cards. Intellectually, she might admit that her fear is absurd, but emotionally she has bought into a narrow view of what Christian acceptability looks like.

■ ■ ■

MOST OF US, if we could, would keep up the same exterior life, and silence the powerful voice inside, hoping to find a little happiness and fulfillment somehow. We would love to avoid the uncertainty of change. But life has a way of slipping past our defenses and changing the turf we thought was so solid. Sometimes the change grows gradually, but often we face these things only when the crises of changing circumstances— a death, breakdown of a marriage, trouble with teenage children—force themselves upon us and demand our attention.

Frank, Sally, and those of us with similar stories need a way to open up to a life that is bold, free, deep-running, and satisfying. We need careful footing *and* daring hearts.

Here is the challenge: Will we continue to repeat the same patterns over and over, hoping that the old and familiar will somehow satisfy or at least stifle the rhythm that drums in our souls? Or will we wrestle with our passion—letting the life of our desire and of our devotion to God fuse together into new steps, new circles, and graceful and gutsy new patterns?

How do we live in our bodies and, at the same time, live deeply spiritual lives? Dallas Willard's landmark book on spiritual disciplines makes a strong case for uniting the body with our spirituality as being the only true understanding of the spiritual life.

"Volumes could be written," Willard says, "on the harm done to human personality and to the practice of Christianity by the 'repressionist' view of spirituality. The spiritual and the bodily are by no means opposed in human life, they are complementary."[5]

He concludes with this tragic question, "How many people are radically and permanently repelled from 'The Way' by Christians who are unfeeling, stiff, unapproachable, boringly lifeless, obsessive, and dissatisfied?"[6]

I believe Willard takes us to the heart of the matter. When we deny or repress our passion, we turn Christian spirituality into a boring, insipid, religious piety largely unrelated to life. Life's richness is reduced to answers, slogans, exhortations, or warnings.

When passion gets diverted from its normal expressions and narrowed into religious zeal, the result is fanaticism. Without a full-bodied acceptance of passion, Christianity becomes insufferable, intolerant, and self-righteous.

We must accept the reality of our bodies, the goodness of passion, and the long journey required to learn how to live well with this jumble of desire. In so doing, we will become whole people. Our spiritual lives will become embodied in rich and powerful ways, and we will have something truly authentic to offer our world.

THE RISK OF GROWTH

Opening ourselves to a passion that goes far beyond a restricted, religious zeal to embrace the whole of life is both frightening and exciting. It challenges our faith and deepens our dependence on God.

If we are going to choose the risk of growth, we will need to be clear about several underlying things. First we must be anchored in our determination to grow into deeper intimacy with God in the nitty-gritty of life. In any given circumstance, we might not know how to follow God, but we have chosen to follow Him as best we know. It is an unabashed sellout—not to a narrow God but to a passionate God—who has lovingly placed us in a voluptuous world.

Second, I find it helpful to remember that we are not the first spiritually minded people to face this challenge. Throughout Scripture, from Abraham and Moses to the Israelite exiles and the band of frightened disciples in the Upper Room, God has promised to be with us through each uncharted adventure. God is with us when we face the barrenness of the desert and when we face giants in the land of plenty.

Finally, we must accept that stepping out of the security of our encased but sterile lives will include mistakes and ambiguities. Living passionately is like giving birth to children. It may be wonderful, but it's a handful. And it's also messy! In the midst of the mess, we will have to trust in God's transforming love and tender forgiveness to keep us heading in the right direction.

■ ■ ■

DOES FRANK'S SWAMP of quiet desperation or Sally's inner volcano of bursting change sound familiar? Like many people today, you may feel caught between stability and desire. You want to understand and follow God's will in your life, yet you have an undeniable thirst for a deeper, fuller experience.

Perhaps you get the sense that something strong and powerful exists within you—something you've ignored or suppressed. Maybe you feel as if you've given your life away to other people, to a performance list, or to what the Christian life "should" look like. You find yourself looking out at a world of people who seem to be running headlong into life and fully enjoying it, yet you've been taught to avoid life because it is dangerous and unspiritual and will take you away from God.

Or, maybe you've run headlong into life and banged your head against some hard walls. You've been so focused on the trappings of success, sexual fulfillment, power, or being admired by others that you've sacrificed the truly important things in your life—God, your family, your soul.

You have discovered the pain of distorted and destructive passion. You want something more integrated, but the pallid complexion of conformity, so characteristic of much Christian discipleship, doesn't appeal to you.

I believe there is an alternative to those who would either squander or bury their passion. There is hope for all of us who, quaking either with fear or with anticipation, want to experience a healthy, liberated, passionate life within a deeper, more integrated spirituality.

Jesus promised life to the full, a river of living water emerging from our souls and flowing out through us—a life in loving union with the Triune God. Is our spirituality robust enough to deal with this life in all its dimensions? That profound question is not for the fainthearted. It is not for those who want to avoid their passion and walk through life with a narrow, innocuous spirituality.

Learning to live in healthy ways with this cauldron of love and desire is the heart of our spiritual transformation. Can we come to believe that passion is not evil? Can we trust the richness of God's life in us? Are there ways both to affirm the current of God's life and make sure that this flowing current of desire doesn't become dissipated, distorted, or destructive?

We will seek to answer these questions and to apply those answers to crucial areas of our lives in the chapters that follow.

When the mother of James and John asks Jesus to give her sons a special place in his Kingdom, Jesus responds, "Can you drink the cup I am going to drink?" (Matthew 20:22).

"Can we drink the cup?" is the most challenging and radical question we can ask ourselves. The cup is the cup of life, full of sorrows and joys.

Can we have our cups and claim them as our own? Can we lift our cups to offer blessings to others, and can we drink our cups to the bottom as cups that bring us salvation? Keeping this question alive in us is one of the most demanding spiritual exercises we can practice.

HENRI NOUWEN[1]

CHAPTER TWO

Becoming "All Flame"

■

TEILHARD DE CHARDIN ONCE SAID, "WE ARE NOT HUMAN BEINGS SEEKING a spiritual experience, we are spiritual beings seeking a human experience."

What does it mean to be a Christian and a human being? How do we live as spiritual people in the real world? Frank and Sally are finding out. But the question is bigger than personal experience; it concerns our entire understanding of discipleship.

Christianity has often been reduced to a spirituality of restraint and withdrawal from passion. The twin biblical texts "If anyone would come after me, he must deny himself and take up his cross daily and follow me" (Luke 9:23), and "Come out from them and be separate" (2 Corinthians 6:17) have often become slogans of a discipleship that focuses on the avoidance of anything that even smacks of desire.

Many Christians do need to leave behind destructive lifestyles and relationships. They need to refrain from old patterns of lust and greed, overspending, and selfish behavior. But instead of helping Christians learn how to bring their physical, mental, and emotional urges back into balance and healthy expression, we teach self-denial and suppression. We have focused on external conformity. In so doing, we excise the guts of living and overlay a Christian "lifestyle." Then we call it maturity.

Perhaps I grew up in an unusually strict background. We were not allowed to ride our bikes or take pictures on Sunday. We were not allowed to talk to girls or walk with them to school, even in elementary school. We could not participate in community sports because it might capture us and take us away from God. Christian dedication was characterized by radical denial.

Touted as a spirituality of discipline and dedication to God's best, it became a spirituality of fear and avoidance. We were to give up our small ambitions[2] (which seemed to mean giving up anything we might enjoy) and give all to the service of God. And in my corner of the tradition, at least, that almost surely meant becoming a missionary.

I don't mean to disparage my background. If it was unusually strict, it only highlighted the spirit that has been endemic in so much of what we've called discipleship. The emphasis is focused on exhortation, performance, and the outward appearance of dedication and purity rather than on responding to the life of God within us.

Does God want us to enjoy life? Yes, of course. Paul says, "Command those who are rich in this present world not to be arrogant nor to put their hope in wealth, which is so uncertain, but to put their hope in God, who richly provides us with everything for our enjoyment" (1 Timothy 6:17).

If this is true, we need to discover the deep relationship between enjoying life and discipleship. We need to find a discipleship that touches us at the very core of life and includes the wide dimensions of life's goodness.

Bill's story illustrates the dilemma. Already a longtime Christian by the age of forty-five, Bill feels confused. He has lived in two universes: the world of church and the world of life. One night, in the middle of Bible study, he talked with tears streaming down his face about the impossibility of this split in his own experience. Finally he blurted out, "I don't know what to do. I don't know whether to 'come out from among them and be separate' or to 'go into all the world and share the good news.'"

Bill was tired of an artificial split that had been imposed by his understanding of holiness as withdrawal. Why do restraint and withdrawal wear thin? Why do people get discouraged with their spiritual lives and gradually slide from frustration to mediocrity just to get some relief?

AN ANCIENT PARALLEL

Early in church history, believers struggled with similar questions. Their wrestling, and the discoveries they made, can bring perspective to our own spiritual turmoil.

During the fourth and fifth centuries of the church, an amazing spiritual revolution erupted. Christianity was rapidly moving from being a small, persecuted sect to becoming a dominant force in the Roman Empire.

Suddenly, while Christianity was busy becoming "successful," people began flocking in huge numbers to the deserts of northern Egypt, Palestine, and Syria. They left the forums and theaters, the port cities and provincial villages, their positions of wealth and authority to live in solitude. There they practiced rigorous disciplines of physical deprivation and continuous prayer.

Why did they make this radical step? They wanted to protest a strange new social mix and to demonstrate a pure devotion to God. While Roman society was sliding deeper into a moral cesspool, Christianity, with the conversion of Constantine, was becoming acceptable, even fashionable.

Society was literally drowning in worship of the flesh. Robin Lane Fox, in his important book, *Pagans and Christians*, says, "In the second and third centuries, accepted sexual practice in the Roman Empire had a range and variety which it has never attained since."[3]

Boys, for example, were abducted and sold at auctions to become sexual playmates for men. Not that the men were oriented exclusively toward homosexuality; they had their wives at home. They were simply looking for new outlets to satisfy their lust. Kiddie porn and the tourist sex trade in Bangkok are perhaps our closest contemporary parallels to the moral and spiritual vacuum of Rome at that time. Whatever felt good to the human body was the norm.

How could people be Christians and maintain any sense of commitment to God in the midst of such blatant abuse of passion?

Thomas Merton says that those who went to the desert had come to regard society as "a shipwreck from which each single individual had to swim for his life. . . . The fact that the Emperor was now Christian and that the 'world' was coming to know the Cross as a sign of temporal power only strengthened them in their resolve."[4]

What drove these Christians to choose this way of "following

Jesus" single-heartedly? It was their passionate belief that their lives could become so focused that there would be nothing left in their vision but God alone. Why else would you leave the comforts of home in the city to live in a small hut or cave in the desert for the rest of your life? Why else would you give up regular meals, the company of friends, and career opportunities?

They founded their faith on Scriptures like Psalm 62:1, "My soul finds rest in God alone" or 1 Thessalonians 5:17, "Pray continually." To physically flee the stranglehold of moral corruption was a grand gesture, a sign of new possibility in the church's young history.

To those of us who find this asceticism repugnant, I must say that the desert discipleship had a strong, positive side. It gave believers a clear vision of what radical commitment to God might look like. Dedication of will and heart was as obvious as one's cave, as specific as one's daily regimen of fasting and prayer.

The possibility of living in full and continuous intimacy with God fired their imaginations. They continually believed that Scripture passages like "follow me" and "pray continually" were literally possible. The vision was powerful enough to make everything else look cheap and worthless by comparison.

The rigors of this kind of discipleship also had a downside. It bred a kind of spiritual one-upmanship in which there was an unspoken contest to see who could be the most rigorous in discipline, the most restrained in passion. Spiritual maturity became identified with the greatest ascetic achievement.

By the middle of the fifth century, Benedict of Nursia was laying down the framework for a new order. He expressly intended to make Christianity "ordinary" again. Among other things, *The Rule of St. Benedict* was a protest against the extravagance of ascetic overkill that had become a mark of spiritual prowess.

I cannot help but believe this is the very dilemma surrounding our understanding of spirituality and discipleship today. For some, the emphasis on denial has been a life-giving, adventurous odyssey into a life of trusting God. But when it becomes unbalanced and is viewed as the core of discipleship, it becomes hollow and oppressive.

In the midst of this transition from the desert as the symbol of a fresh new way to love God with all one's heart, to the desert as a symbol of a dried-up spiritual dead end, an amazing and enigmatic story emerges of two spiritual leaders in conversation. Neither was a beginner in the spiritual way. Both were called "abba" because they were mature spiritual mentors, like fathers in the faith.

This story has become one of my favorites from early Christianity, and it goes like this:

> Abba Lot went to see Abba Joseph and said to him, "Abba,
> as far as I can, I say my [daily] office, I fast a little, I pray and
> meditate, I live in peace and as far as I can, I purify my thoughts.
> What else can I do?" Then the old man stood up, stretched his
> arms toward heaven. His fingers became like ten lamps of fire
> and he said to him, "If you want, you can be all flame."[5]

WORKING HARD TO BE A GOOD CHRISTIAN

"What else can I do?" says Abba Lot. Frankly, the question haunts me. I can feel the desperation in this early disciple's heart. I sense the humiliation of admitting he doesn't have the answers, and I admire his courage to cry out for help.

I wonder how we would have answered Lot? I suspect most evangelical Christians would write off the entire desert commitment — one of the great formative streams of our Christian heritage — by pigeonholing Lot as a misguided, "works-oriented" ascetic. We might have said, "He should have invited Jesus into his heart and trusted the message of grace." End of story.

But how many of us feel, if we could admit it, that "Christian discipleship" means living a legalistic, achievement-oriented spirituality? Ted's story, which follows, is only one example, but one replayed in countless people's lives today.

Recently, Ted and I shared one of the great cinnamon buns in a bakery near my office. He seems to be an ideal Evangelical — dedicated, loves the Lord, attended Bible college and seminary, and has been deeply involved in church ministry. Ted has been "on course" as people in his circles consider a godly man's life should go. But now, at thirty years old, he feels empty.

During coffee, Ted blurted, "For years I've tried to follow the prescribed pathway for spiritual growth. I've given up my life for the sake of ministry. I've worked hard for Christian organizations, which have paid a pittance. I drive an old car and spend almost no money on entertainment. I've been gracious in my dealings with others, held my anger in check, and have been very careful not to indulge my sexual desires.

"But for the most part, it's just an exterior facade, a game. I'm sorry, Jeff, but I've just lost interest in the game. I'm doing all these things, but I'm not living."

I was immediately intrigued. Ted had mastered the evangelical lifestyle. People around him would never have guessed his plight.

"I don't even know who I am anymore," Ted went on. "A gaping hole exists between the real me inside and the 'me' of my spiritual image. The church expects me to live a victorious Christian life. I am to be enthusiastic, vigilant, one who lives above my problems, faithful to all the spiritual disciplines, and a testimony to others.

"Frankly, I'm tired of having to keep up the image. It isn't me. My spiritual life no longer expresses who I am deep down in my soul."

After fifteen years of offering spiritual guidance (or spiritual direction, as it is often called), I have heard similar stories scores of times. Ted has lost his passion. His spiritual life has left him exhausted rather than energized. Is it possible to gain the whole evangelical world and lose your own soul?

Did Ted misinterpret the ways and means of Christian growth? Possibly. I could have told him he was missing the point, that he should be grateful for the opportunity to serve the Lord.

But Ted is not alone. Unprecedented numbers of Christians today live with profound restlessness and thirst in their spiritual lives.

I read the report of a survey that estimated over three million people in the United States, who call themselves evangelical Christians, no longer go to church. That represents a great deal of disillusionment. And it doesn't even begin to tap the countless numbers of people who continue to go to church but are wearied by the demands and expectations to curb their passion in order to be fully committed to God.

Honesty forces us to ask questions about this kind of spirituality. Should Christian devotion suck the life out of us? It's sad to see people exhausted from trying to live their Christian life, be faithful to the disciplines, carry out some kind of ministry, drive their children to soccer, take time to be intimate in their marriage, and find time to nourish themselves—all at once.

Christianity should not be a miserable load to carry. Jesus said,

"My burden is light" (Matthew 11:30). And He warned against spiritual leaders who put heavy burdens of legalism and religious standards on them: "They tie up heavy loads and put them on [people's] shoulders, but they themselves are not willing to lift a finger to move them" (Matthew 23:4).

The desert fathers and mothers went into the desert with good biblical precedent. Like Moses, Elijah, John the Baptist, and Jesus they could trust they would meet God there and hear God's Word to them. They could read Isaiah and hear God promise:

> The poor and needy search for water, but there is none; their tongues are parched with thirst. But I the LORD will answer them; I, the God of Israel, will not forsake them. I will make rivers flow on barren heights, and springs within the valleys. I will turn the desert into pools of water, and the parched ground into springs. (Isaiah 41:17-18)

How is it that much of what we call discipleship today has turned the promise of Isaiah upside-down? How is it that the spiritual river of Christianity becomes a desert? We have turned the pools of water of promised life and joy into a desert, and the springs of enthusiasm for God into parched ground.

I believe we have forgotten that we are created beings fashioned by God, who thought the product was wonderful. If I tie up a new fly for fly-fishing, complete with special body shape, wings, and hackle, it's because I think this is the best way to fool the fish. When I'm done, I like the result. I especially like it when I fool a fish with it!

God created us with humor and sex, with delight and longing. Was this counterproductive? Why has God filled the world with such exuberance if we were not meant to enjoy it? Like a full spectrum of color, God's passion fills all of life. Perhaps we have opted only for infrared.

In our idea of Christian discipleship, have we forgotten how to deeply embrace God and the life God has for us? It would seem that the best we've been able to do is to create and recreate the emphasis on restraint and denial. We warn people about the dangers of life but never invite them to go out and face the danger bravely. It appears we would rather people stay away from sensuality to keep from being tainted by it, with the mistaken assumption that restraining ourselves from life will create spiritual passion in us.

Instead, we cut ourselves off from life as God has richly given it. And in so doing, we have "forsaken [God,] the spring of living water, and have dug [our] own cisterns, broken cisterns that cannot hold water" (Jeremiah 2:13). We have idolized the forms of Christianity and have separated them from, life for which they were devised.

Without a right understanding of God's life in us, restraint in the spiritual life is mostly dry, dead legalism. God invites our passionate embrace, not a zealous clinging to the symbols of denial in our discipleship.

When we limit our Christianity to a narrow range of acceptable experiences and activities, it cripples something in us and quenches our spiritual vigor.

Should Abba Lot hold on to his vision of total commitment and try harder? One obvious way to understand Abba Joseph's response is to suggest that if Lot would just "keep on keeping on" he would eventually become full of spiritual fervor. Lot, we might say, is on the right track; he just isn't fully committed yet.

For those who are already spiritually weary, this way of understanding the challenge to become "all flame" is demoralizing. It becomes one more mirage in the great desert of spiritual performance. It only widens the split between people's real selves and the expectations of spiritual growth.

The only difference between Lot—the desert father—and many of us is that we have learned to keep our mouths shut and to keep our questions to ourselves. We've learned that to open our mouths about our spiritual disappointment and inner restlessness would court a volley of exhortation or censure. Those who dare to name their frustrations are flooded with exhortations to dig into Scripture, pray with more power, or give up their own desires to be more fully dedicated to God. Then, when they aren't "fixed" by the exhortations, they begin to experience a quiet but clear message of disapproval and ostracism.

Continued exhortation to be more committed just doesn't cut it. So if more doesn't work, maybe less is better.

Should Lot leave the desert and go back to the city? Should he abandon his desire for total commitment and quietly slide back into a life of spiritual mediocrity?

Disappointment with their Christian upbringing has pushed many people into cynical withdrawal. It is a response of cold anger to the damage inflicted by a spirituality that focused on restraint.

When these people get together, they swap stories about the ludicrous rules and expectations of their religious past. But their laughter rings hard. They have been hurt badly, and they plow on through life, adamantly refusing to risk spiritual vitality again. Openhearted desire to follow God becomes encased in bitterness and trapped, unseen and unnoticed, deep in their souls.

Bitter resentment and rebellion are not solutions. Long ago Cicero observed that rebellion is the most exquisite form of slavery. As long as we react to our religious past, we remain slaves to its view of the world and God. As long as God seems like life's greatest spoilsport, we are not able to open up to Him in positive, life-giving ways. Cynicism is as much a dead end as legalism.

Another way contemporary Christians deal with Lot's dilemma is to dilute the vision. Many people let go of both the legalism of withdrawal and the vision of radical devotion. They uncritically embrace the world again. They choose the enjoyment of life and almost unconsciously begin to let go of the commitment to God.

The result is a Christian veneer over a life captured by consumerism. The desert, a voluntary choice to have God above all things, is abandoned for the city, the choice to have all things with less and less thought about God.

In the end, as in the story of the parable of the sower and the seed, the heat gets to these people, too. Lacking the roots of deep commitment to God, their spiritual devotion withers and Christianity becomes a dull routine with just enough commitment to stave off the questions that tug at their souls. It leads to a lethargic spirituality.

We can easily let our disappointment keep us from moving on. We can sit in our weariness like victims and fail to address the great split in our spirituality. We can drift into a comfortable accommodation to the world around us, much like the people in Constantine's day. But these responses are as fatal to our spiritual passion as the split that drove us there in the first place.

Frankly, although I have flirted with both cynicism and lethargy, neither response satisfies me. I am not willing to remain captive to my past by continuing to rebel against it. Nor am I willing to be lulled to sleep by a spiritual vision that is nothing more than accommodation to our consumer culture.

Is there any other option? Can we allow the disappointment and the disillusionment around spiritual expectations to speak to us?

WHY NOT BECOME "ALL FLAME"?

In the story from the desert, Abba Joseph offered a totally unexpected response to Lot's question. Lot asked, "What else can I do?" hoping for relief. Joseph answered, "You can become all flame." It is a powerful, picturesque response. And an intimidating one.

If we hold on to the call to love God with all our hearts and insist on learning how to live passionately in the world, we can discover a deeper, integrated spirituality. I think this is the point of Abba Joseph's challenge.

It has been almost fifteen years now since I stumbled onto the words of the wily abba, and I must confess that I have often been angry with what seemed to be his gross insensitivity. I didn't even want to get back into the game, let alone compete to be as dedicated, as spiritual, as full of spiritual passion as this story seems to imply. I'd had enough for one lifetime of trying to become all flame for God. I didn't need another person telling me that if I was dedicated just that extra bit more, I could be really on fire for God.

Still, I was intrigued enough that I couldn't get away from the abba's challenge. Slowly the story began to shimmer in new ways for me.

What did Joseph mean? Was he talking about a zealously pious but completely unearthly life? After all, he lived alone in the desert! Or was he talking about a life that is fully and freely alive?

Alive! Truly and freely alive. I cannot help but think that Joseph was pointing to an inner-directed, extravagant experience—alive to God, to oneself, and to the world. Alive with feelings and dreams and the ability to see and celebrate the goodness and dignity of all things.

Abba Joseph knew what it meant to be alive with God whether he lived in the desert alone or in the city. His life did not come from his ascetic practice or the spiritual expectations of others. Nor did it come from consuming life like an addict. Life came from the presence of God within.

Gradually, I began to hear the old mentor speak of our own spiritual growth as a process of transformation. The Orthodox church has, for centuries, understood our spiritual growth in the light of Jesus' dramatic transformation on the mountain.[6]

The gospel story of Jesus on the Mount of Transfiguration tells us that while Jesus was alone with a few of His disciples, "he was transfigured before them. His face shone like the sun, and his clothes became as white as the light" (Matthew 17:2). As the light of the glory of God shone through the whole of Jesus' person from the inside out, so our own lives can be transfigured by the life of God.

In this image, the focus of discipleship is to get in touch with the inner life of God and allow God to change us from the inside out. The life of God within us will finally shine through with such force and clarity that it is like flame.

Joseph did not condemn Lot's disciplines; dedication of heart includes these choices. But Joseph saw far beyond them. He recognized that conformity does not bring vitality. True spiritual vitality comes from expressing the inner fire of God in everything.

MY STORY

I have had a love–hate response to the spirituality of conformity. Throughout high school I hated the way life was systematically squelched on all fronts to convince us that we were crucified with Christ.[7]

I reacted against this regime and left home after high school, bitter toward Christianity and toward God. However, despite myself, my thirst for God continued. Eventually I came back to my religious roots with a vengeance.

I became rigorous and proud in my own ascetic achievement. I remember being critical of my brother who, as a pastor, didn't memorize verses regularly or have Bible study with his wife.

After Bible college and seminary, I found myself in Jamaica teaching in a Bible college. The spirituality of withdrawal, characteristic of so much North American Christianity, had been transplanted intact by the missionaries. I was again forced to deal with the split between life and religious conformity.

Some years later, I returned to Canada and became pastor of a church in Calgary. In that transition I discovered, to my chagrin, that I had no more words with which to pray. It was awful to admit that I was in church leadership and didn't know how to pray anymore. I was overwhelmed with guilt—a prayerless failure, facing into a terrible silence.

Was I losing my faith? It became a wilderness of loneliness and isolation.

I entered a period of "darkness" for which I had been given little preparation. For five years, I lived with almost no internal awareness of God. I criticized myself for my sins, I questioned whether my expectations were too high, and I prayed for some supernatural event or visitation to reassure me. I had no end of desire for God, but I had almost no sense of contentment. My lack of fulfillment seemed proof that I was somehow doing it wrong, that the darkness was somehow my fault.

During this time, I read Chaim Potok's powerful novel, *The Chosen*. In the story, Reb Saunders, the Hasidic rabbi, chooses to refrain from speaking to his son, Danny, for years. He fears that Danny's intellectual brilliance will keep him from becoming a humble and compassionate rabbi and so he wounds his son to make him compassionate.

I wondered if God were somehow perversely refusing to speak to me to make me humble. Then, abandoning that idea, I prayed, "God, maybe we are from two different cultures. Maybe you don't talk to your friends in your culture, but here in mine we think it's rude not to talk to our friends. I don't like this silence, but if this is the way it is, I will stay open to you till my dying day, even if you never reveal yourself to me again!"

Encouraged by Richard Foster's book, *The Celebration of Discipline*, I took to reading the spiritual classics. I needed to broaden my own understanding of spirituality in hopes of finding something that spoke to my deep hunger. I laughed at Teresa of Ávila's acerbic humor; anguished with St. John of the Cross as he expressed an intense longing for union in *The Dark Night of the Soul*; and felt rocked like a baby by the gentle reassurances of Dame Julian of Norwich.

One day, I stumbled across William of St. Thierry.[8] This reformer, theologian, and friend of St. Bernard of Clairvaux was well acquainted with his own longing and disappointments. His treatise, "On Loving God," encouraged me to bring all my longing—my desires both good and bad—to God. He spoke of long stretches of desire punctuated by moments of fulfillment and helped me realize that the longing itself was good.

William of St. Thierry had acknowledged the longing! That was a starting point for me. We were not to avoid passion. There was no dichotomy left between longing for spiritual things and longing to go fishing or have sex. All was the echo of God in my heart. Even unfulfilled longing was to be treasured as the sign of God's presence opening me up to God. As one nun said to me, "There is no virtue in a nun who, afraid of her passion, refuses to live."

William's words catapulted me into a whole new universe.

THE *UP* SIDE

My world became transfigured. I couldn't explain it completely, but I knew I was embraced by God, passion and all. I was given permission to live. My longing for God, for the outdoors, for relationship, for recognition—all became part of my devotion.

Life burst with goodness. I felt like I was eleven years old again, staring with sweet longing at the dark, curly-haired girl sitting in the desk across the aisle.

Once, while hiking in the mountains, I became so full of joy and longing that I wanted to rip open my chest and let God's glory in those craggy peaks and the pungent spruce needles invade me. I was infatuated with God. I could risk being myself. I could open up to life. I could be passionate.

THE *DOWN* SIDE

Life, however, was not solved like a puzzle. What was I to do with all this newly legitimized desire? It did not infallibly produce goodness. Rather, I had landed squarely in the crucible of choice.

In the process of opening to life's fullness, I also became more vulnerable to sin. Would I continue to hold this wonderful passion openly, as part of my love for God, or would I get possessive and addictive? Would I learn to love God more deeply through my passion, or would it surreptitiously destroy my devotion?

I was more open, for example, in my relationships with women, yet at the same time more vulnerable. I deeply loved Miriam, my wife, and didn't want this newly awakened energy to drive me into an affair. *God help me*, I prayed. It was my worst fear and a painfully real possibility. I was forced to choose in ways I had never experienced before.

I was less judgmental and more affirming. Would this lead me to a compromised sense of holiness? I was free to "waste time" hiking and cross-country skiing. Would these hobbies take me away from the "important" things of God's kingdom?

Life bolted out of the gate before I had fully climbed into the saddle. I found, to my chagrin, that when I tried to backtrack and bury my passion, I shut down everywhere, including my new love for God.

I slowly came to the conclusion that I would not be able to get my life together first and then move toward embracing my passion. It would have to be all part of the same journey.

Once, on a silent retreat, I struggled with sexual fantasy throughout the day. I felt frustrated and guilty at my inability to concentrate on prayer. I was scheduled to meet with my spiritual director at the end of the day, and I wondered how to tell my mentor I had spent the day struggling with sexual fantasy instead of focusing on prayer!

To make matters worse, my spiritual director was a woman— a sixty-year-old nun!

You must understand that when I first met Sister Nora, an encyclopedia of stereotypes were challenged all at once. To begin with, when I'd knocked at the door of the retreat center to ask about retreats, I was petrified. I needed solitude in a spiritual atmosphere. But what was a good Protestant boy like me doing at a Catholic retreat center? I'd been steeped in all the arguments against Catholicism, yet I didn't even know any Catholics on a personal level.

To say nothing about the fearful barriers between myself and women other than my wife. I'd been brought up with the belief that you don't talk about sexuality, especially with someone of the opposite sex.

So there I was, wondering if I could trust this nun to give me a faith-filled, devoted-to-Jesus kind of reply.

As it ended up, the question of talking to a woman about my sexuality may have been a moot point. Her response to my struggle was one of the most significant healing moments in my life.

Part of me expected Sister Nora to be horrified—to say, "Tsk! Tsk! You need to get beyond your sexual desire so that you can be present to God."

Instead, she looked at me with a level gaze and said, "Jeff, people often try to avoid the passion by shoving it under the rug and hoping it won't interrupt their prayer. Sometimes people see it as the work of the Devil and get embroiled in confronting the Devil to take the temptation away."

Then she opened a new door for me. "Your sexuality is not foreign to your life with God. You can bring your sexual feelings into prayer.

You can open them up in God's presence and say, 'God, you have created me for love. You are wanting to speak to me in my desire. The very intensity of my feelings is a measure of how deeply you want to speak to me of your love for me.'"

I will never forget that moment. Any distinction between loving God with all my heart and living passionately melted. Both had been integrated without compromise.

I do not offer my experience as the norm. It is simply one witness to the poignant integration between our spirituality and the whole of our lives. Each person faces his or her own unique way of opening to passion. Though our stories will differ, we will all be called to face and make the choices that open us up to transformation and spiritual wholeness.

In the uncertainty of my own journey, I chose to stay open to God and open to my desire. All I could do was continually reaffirm my desire to follow God and at the same time open myself to the ongoing experience of passion. It was a pivotal turning point for me.

■ ■ ■

It's hard to write these things. I don't want to be unfairly critical. I have struggled with my own spiritual conformity and I've listened to the struggles of enough people to believe that we are in this together.

I truly believe that many people already know, intuitively, the shallowness of their spiritual lives. They're afraid to admit it—to themselves and to others. My desire is not to be critical but to get the truth of our experience into the open. I want to offer permission for people to be honest and to begin to discover a way of discipleship that heals the split between their image and their souls.

We *can* become "all flame." We can experience the integration of our passion with the depths of our life with God.

For many of us, this passage from an external spiritual conformity to living from the inside out will be the most important transition we will make. It is a radical reorientation of our hearts and minds. If we are relying on our own strength to live this well, we will fail. We can't possibly get it right.

But we can trust God. We will need His wisdom, strength, and forgiveness. And we can count on God's presence. It is God's life we are seeking to open ourselves to, not simply our passion but an intimate presence that, like a flowing river, will never cease (Matthew 28:20, John 14:16).

We can afford to trust that God is interested in this business of life—far more interested than we are. God is bringing life to us, and God will see us through.

O God, hope of my youth, where were you all this time? Were you not my Creator and was it not you who made me different from the beasts that walk on the earth and wiser than the birds that fly in the air? Yet I was walking on a treacherous path, in darkness. I was looking for you outside myself and I did not find the God of my own heart.

St. Augustine[1]

CHAPTER THREE

Jesus' Invitation to Fullness of Life

■

ONCE WHILE LEADING A WORKSHOP ON PRAYER, I SAID TO THE GROUP, "The psalmist talks about directing his prayers to God. Where," I asked them, "is God? Where do you direct your prayer? Do you pray to God up in heaven? Do you pray to God beside you or in front of you — like someone you have a conversation with? Do you pray to God inside you or outside you?"

Clearly, God is beyond us. Solomon admitted at the dedication of the temple, "The heavens, even the highest heaven, cannot contain you. How much less this temple I have built!" (1 Kings 8:27). Yet, just as God chose to dwell in the temple, so God is at home in our hearts as well.

I went on to suggest that our deepest and most intimate experience of God is the presence of God we discover at the core of our being. We have the privilege of praying deep within us — from the "bottom of our heart"—directly to the One who has taken up residence as neighbor to our deepest desires and fears.

After the session, someone came up, obviously irritated. She accused me of being new age because I spoke of God within. I was troubled by her vehemence; I don't like being accused of abandoning the faith I care so much about. But her response didn't take me by surprise.

It's not a common practice in evangelical circles to take the presence of God in our souls seriously, regardless of what we say we believe about it in our theology.

We're like the people Teresa of Ávila described in the opening of her book *Interior Castle*. Our soul is a magnificent castle, like a beautiful crystal or single great diamond. It is the castle where God lives, yet we make little or no attempt to discover what this means. We have "a vague idea, because we have heard it and because our Faith tells us so, that we possess souls." But we have almost no concept "as to what good qualities there may be in our souls, or Who dwells within them, or how precious they are."[2]

GOD WITHIN: AT THE HEART OF EVANGELICAL TRADITION

Viewing our spiritual experience as a movement from the inside out is a threatening thought to many Christians. It sounds too subjective to think that the locus of our experience of God could be within us.

How could we trust such a spiritual experience? How do we know whether or not we are just indulging our own twisted, egocentric notions and calling them God? And anyway, the new age writers talk about the God within. *Ipso facto*, the whole notion is suspect.

One morning, while visiting my mother, we followed her custom of reading from a well-known devotional booklet after breakfast. The topic of the day was "the God within." Speaking against the new age movement, the author held that any notion of God within is unbiblical and dangerous.

I was dumbfounded! How could any serious Christian writer suggest such a thing? Yes, the notion of God within has been co-opted by new age writers, who often twist it into a self-centered notion. But the promise of God's indwelling presence has always been at the heart of Christianity. To call it "a dangerous new age doctrine" gave witness, to me, to how little we really believe it or live as if it were true.

The understanding of God within is not only part of Christian teaching in general, it is at the very heart of evangelical Protestant thinking. We have flown the idea of inviting Jesus into our hearts, and being born again, like a flag on our evangelical ship. None of this is new to anyone who has been brought up in Sunday school in an evangelical church. We cut our teeth on it.

Yet strangely enough, few things have been more foreign to

evangelical spirituality than serious exploration of God's inner presence. Central as it is to our statements of belief, it has not been a serious part of our worship or discipleship.

One of the great focal points of our intimacy with God is deep within our souls. Inside us, instead of outside or beyond us. Yet we have not helped people treasure what it means that God lives in them. We can pray there. We can enjoy God there. We can live from that place of life.

Coming to trust that God's life is in us and wants to flow out of us is central to a healthy spirituality. It is the great antidote to conformity. The question is not, Where is God? We know that God indwells us. The question is rather, Where are we? God is at home within us and, as St. Augustine admitted, we are everywhere else. We are outside ourselves, trying to satisfy the deep needs of our hearts and constructing ourselves from the outside in.

Does the Bible support such a view? Let's look at some of the evidence in Scripture that demonstrates our spiritual life is to be lived from the inside out.

We will see that Scripture teaches we meet God in the depths of our souls and God's life becomes like a river flowing out of us into life. Jesus' teaching, the transition from the *Old Testament* to the *New*, and the teaching of the apostles all carry this same emphasis.

THE TEACHING OF JESUS

The revelation that God is present within us is central to the teaching of Jesus. He spoke of our thirst for life that could only be quenched by an internal spring. And He spoke of our lives as being like branches that receive life like sap from the vine.

This inner life meets the deep need of our hearts. It also overflows through us as a gift to others.

In John 4, Jesus offered an amazing message of tender hopefulness to a Samaritan woman who had no reason left to hope. It is a beautiful story of how Jesus dealt with the passion—especially with the failures of passion—that seemed to engulf her.

The story tells us of a woman for whom life had been bitterly disappointing. Like any human being, she looked for two major things in life: a place to belong and an experience of intimacy.

In the culture of the day, the Samaritan woman's only place to find significance and security was marriage. She had no voice, no place to belong in society, without a husband.

Picture the anguish and disappointment as those hopes and dreams for intimacy and security slipped through her fingers like soup dripping through the bare hands of a starving person. No matter how hard she tried, she couldn't grab it and hold on.

She had experienced at least five failures as she tried to find some semblance of life in relationship after relationship. The sixth try sounded like she was just settling for crumbs.

It's easy to label her a sinful, promiscuous woman. Perhaps she was. She could also have been a woman whose biggest sin was to be caught in a continuing cycle of linking up with losers.

Perhaps her promiscuity and her poor judgment with men was the result of sexual abuse as a child. The kind of entanglement she lived is one of the classic scenarios of sexually abused women. That doesn't excuse the sin, but it sheds a different light on what the real issue might have been.

Jesus may have been the first man to take her seriously without also trying to take her sexually. Jesus did the unthinkable. He treated her as a full person, speaking directly and unabashedly to her.

Even the woman acknowledged this was something that simply wasn't done. She said, "You are a Jew and I am a Samaritan woman. How can you ask me for a drink?" (John 4:9). She had two counts against her: She was a Samaritan and a woman. We sometimes add a third: She was "fallen."

In light of the excruciating disappointment of her deepest longings, Jesus offered her something radically new and different. He promised her life from the inside out.

Jesus said that the water He would give her would become within her a "spring of water welling up to eternal life" (John 4:13-14). Not even a cistern, but an artesian well!

Trying to find life on the outside had been a dismal failure. Now she could find life on the inside. At the center of her soul she would find a well of water — the living presence of God.

What an incredible gift! Eternal life! Not just a life extended forever, in the distant future, but the very life of God. Life from God was to become a spring of water inside her very being.

Imagine! Not structure, not a formula, not the denial of her desires. Not better accountability. Jesus offered *God's life from within*.

This was not an isolated promise to one woman. In John 7, Jesus proclaimed an almost identical message. At the great feast in Jerusalem, just as the passage from Isaiah 12 was being read about drawing water from the wells of salvation, Jesus stood up in the crowd and said, "If anyone is thirsty, let him come to me and drink." Then He added, "Whoever believes in me, as the Scripture has said, streams of living water will flow from within him" (John 7:37-38).

These are graphic images of life bubbling up from within, like an artesian well. What is it like to make the transition from looking for life in external experience to claiming the promise that life comes from within?

Imagine what it must have meant for this Samaritan woman to realize she had internal dignity. She was no longer the victim of circumstances or even her own failures. She didn't have to seduce intimacy or cling to crumbs. She could live with boldness, knowing that whatever the circumstances, her life came from within.

In John 10:10 Jesus made the same offer in another way, this time to a group of devoutly religious men, the Pharisees, who had just driven a man out of their fellowship because he had not followed their rules. Jesus proclaimed that He had come that we might have life and that we might have it to the full. There is no explicit image of water in this passage, but the Greek word translated by the phrase "to the full" carries the word picture of a container that is overflowing.[3]

Jesus made this offer of fullness of life *in direct contrast* to the burdensome life demanded by the religious leaders of His day. He called them thieves of the full life (John 10:8-10).

Like vampires, the religious leaders fed on the lives of the people. They forced others into strict conformity to the legalism they had prescribed. Criticism against the deadening influence of these religious leaders abounds in the Gospels. Jesus chastised the religious leaders for displaying external piety while forgetting to do the important things like show justice and mercy and loyalty (Matthew 23:23).

In Luke 5, Jesus offered a wonderful image to express the uselessness of this kind of "controlled" conformist spirituality. When asked why His disciples did not fast, Jesus replied that there would be times when they did, but now was not the time for fasting. It would be like putting new wine into old wineskins.

Jesus suggested there was a new movement afoot. It wasn't about abstinence as a show of religious zeal. It wasn't, first of all, about control. This fresh good news of God, proclaimed by Jesus, was not a spirituality of performance and acceptance by keeping all the right rules. It wasn't a dead spirituality that simply conformed to the old wineskins of external religious expectations at the expense of real life.

Jesus offered, and still offers, a river of life that cannot be dammed, a flame within that cannot be quenched. It's a fullness of life that boils over into our souls and out into the world.

So when Jesus said that He had come that we might have life and that we might have it to the full, we understand this life to be His very presence within us that brings to us a rich, fully textured, direct experience of life.

Life to the full is not merely thinking good thoughts about life. It isn't saying the correct things about life.

Anthony de Mello said it well, "No one ever became drunk on the word *wine*."[4]

Life from God, bubbling up like a spring, is not the power to conform to a spirituality that has become dead performance. It is the reality of actually living — in fullness and with passion. It is an inner spring that opens us to living God's life fully in the present moment through all the faculties of our being — body, soul, mind, emotions, and will.

Whatever we choose to call it, this is what I want. I don't care about the label, I want to live openly, honestly, directly. I don't want to talk about life, I want to live fully awake to the life Jesus offers me in my very soul.

This message of the inner presence of God as the fountain of life isn't limited to images in Jesus' teaching. It forms the very heart of Jesus' final, most intimate moments with His disciples on the eve of His crucifixion.

Jesus opened the evening by washing the disciples' feet (John 13). It was an act of great external intimacy. From there He began to make the great passage from external intimacy to internal intimacy. He was preparing the disciples for the profound change in relationship they would come to enjoy.

As they talked together over the meal, Jesus spoke directly about the coming transition. He gradually revealed the truth to them that this external relationship wouldn't last.

A time would come when they would no longer be with Jesus as they had become accustomed. They would discover a new way of being together — an even greater intimacy with their Lord.

They were clearly troubled. The thought that Jesus was going to leave wasn't a happy thought for the disciples. It probably seemed to them like the height of poor timing.

They didn't want Him to go. But if He was leaving they wanted to go with Him. Thomas reminded Jesus that they didn't know where He was going, so how could they know the way, implying that it would be nice if He would let them in on what was going on (John 14:5).

In that confusion, Jesus stated there was a new time coming. He said, "I will not leave you as orphans. . . . On that day you will realize that I am in my Father, and you are in me, and I am in you" (John 14:18,20).

Having promised His own internal presence, Jesus gave the heart of the message by using the analogy of the vine and the branches (John 15). Jesus explained that this new relationship with Him would be one in which His very life flowed in them, like sap in a grapevine, so that they would be alive and fruitful.

This was the great new transition Jesus had been moving toward all along. They would no longer have Jesus as their external leader, but they would have Him within, giving them life. That life would flow up within them so they could carry on the life of Jesus in the world.

They would embody Jesus' life from that time on. Jesus would not do the talking, they would. Jesus would not fix everything, He would empower them to live with courage in the circumstances in which they found themselves.

THE APOSTLES' TEACHING ABOUT GOD WITHIN US

This transition from God outside us to God inside us is also found in the teaching of the apostles.

The apostle John takes the theme of "birth into God's family" and offers it as a statement of privilege and a promise of transformation. He said, "How great is the love the Father has lavished on us, that we should be called children of God!" (1 John 3:1).

That privilege becomes the basis of a new transformation that shows itself in the way we act. "No one who is born of God," John goes on to say, "will continue to sin, because God's seed remains in him" (verse 9).

We might struggle with what that passage specifically means in regard to sinning, but two things are clear. We are born of God; God's seed (of life) is in us. Secondly, this new life of God is a transforming reality in our lives.

John closed his letter by stating succinctly, "And this is the testimony: God has given us eternal life, and this life is in his Son. He who has the Son has life" (1 John 5:11-12).

Peter said we have been made "partakers of the divine nature." That's one of those time-bomb statements. It looks so innocuous and can be easily passed over. Then the statement explodes with profound significance when we consider that we share in God's very nature.

Paul continually talked about God within us. "Christ in us" and "we in Christ" are two of Paul's signature phrases. Perhaps one particular passage will be enough to indicate Paul's understanding of the inner presence of God as the locus of our spirituality.

Ephesians 3:14-17 contains a great climactic summary prayer following what may be the greatest exposition ever given about the incredible richness of the good news of Jesus. We are God's inheritance, Paul said. We were dead but have been made alive with Christ and have been given a place in the heavenly realms.

In the coming ages, Paul said, God will show the incomparable riches of His grace expressed in His kindness to us in Christ Jesus. We have been brought into unity and made one in Christ, despite our ethnic and religious and social barriers. Even the Gentiles are heirs together in one body in Christ.

At the end of this great section, Paul, as was his habit, paused to pray. He prayed that all he had been saying would become real in the lives of the Ephesian believers.

He wrote,

> I pray that out of his glorious riches [God] may strengthen you with power through his Spirit *in your inner being*, so that Christ may dwell *in your hearts* through faith. And I pray that you, being rooted and established in love, may have power, together with all the saints, to grasp how wide and long and high and deep is the love of Christ, and to know this love that surpasses knowledge — that you may be filled to the measure of all the fullness of God. (Ephesians 3: 16-19, emphasis mine)

In this incredible passage, Paul locates the center of our experience of salvation in our "inner being." We experience the full dimension of love in the depths of our souls. It is there we are brought into all the fullness of God.

THE TRANSITION FROM THE OLD TO THE NEW

This emphasis on an internal experience of God is one of the central distinctions between the Old and New Testaments.

In the Old Testament, for example, the temple was located on Mount Zion within the city of Jerusalem. This external temple was the home of the presence of God.

In the New Testament, the image changes. No longer is there an external temple in which God dwells. The dwelling place of God is now in the community of faith, and more particularly within our physical bodies as individuals.

In 1 Corinthians 6:19, Paul says, "Do you not know that your body is a temple of the Holy Spirit, who is in you, whom you have received from God?"

Psalm 46:1-5 provides a good illustration of the profound difference this change makes. The psalmist expressed trust in Yahweh: "God is our refuge and strength, an ever-present help in trouble." Then, in a fashion typical in the Psalms, the psalmist described the present chaos of his situation.

He used the images of tidal waves and earthquakes—images of monumental upheaval—to say that his world was crumbling all around him. He wrote, "We will not fear, though the earth give way and the mountains fall into the heart of the sea, though its waters roar and foam and the mountains quake with their surging."

Externally, the community was on the edge of collapse. In the face of all this calamity and danger, what was their hope? The psalmist explains his opening statement of trust in God. "There is a river whose streams make glad the city of God, the holy place where the Most High dwells. God is within her, she will not fall."

The psalmist plucked up courage to face the calamity because God was present in the temple. God was resident in Jerusalem. In the light of this profound reassurance the psalmist was at last invited to relax and "know that I am God" (verse 10).

Do you sense the enormous importance of this truth?

Our assurance is not in an external temple but in the indwelling presence of God! Rather than looking outside ourselves for help, we are now invited to look within our very beings, where the Holy Spirit dwells in the temple of our bodies. We might paraphrase the psalm, "There is a river whose streams make me glad. . . . God is within me, I will not fall."

IMPLICATIONS FOR DISCIPLESHIP

Take a moment for a quick check. When you opened your heart to Jesus, did you open to the inside or to the outside? Did you think of Jesus coming from outside your body into your soul?

When you ask the Holy Spirit to come and fill your life, do you think of it like pouring liquid from the outside into a cup? Or is it more like a spring of water filling the cavern from the inside?

I suspect that most people usually think of opening their hearts to Jesus like opening a door outward. Perhaps a more scriptural image of what happens when Jesus enters our lives is not that of a door but of a spring of water.

God breathes life into us in creation. Then the fullness of God's life is made available through the work of Christ. It is as though the hard ground is opened and a well begins to flow, and a way is found for the life to emerge.

Thus, to pay attention to the life within us is to pay attention to God. Rather than distracting us from God, it is the means of drawing us to God.

We get farther and farther away from God when we try to control our lives and to ignore the passion that burns brightly within us. We get further into religious conformity rather than real intimacy with God by denying ourselves and the life that longs for expression within.

Does it matter whether we speak of God as the life present in our souls at the center of our being? Is it important for us to see our spiritual experience rooted in the life of God within us?

Without being rooted in our union with God within us, we will always have difficulty accepting ourselves and our passion as good. As long as we think that God's life is some other life imported from the outside, the life we live and breathe will always be something suspect; perhaps even something alien to the life of God.

We will try to contort ourselves into some other "life" and conform to some other standard. We will wonder why we feel so out of touch with God, so starved for intimacy.

If God is not within us — breathing life into us — then our whole life is suspect at a fundamental level. This is what has been so damaging in much evangelical spirituality.

There has been little or no room to accept the fact that our lives are God-breathed and God-loved. We are in touch with God inside, and the fundamental outworking of our Christian growth is from the inside out.

The Eastern Orthodox understanding of prayer is so very helpful here. For the Orthodox person, to pray is to descend with our mind into our heart and there stand before God.[5] In our inner being we touch Life and are touched by Life.

It is this inner transformation that brings about integration — integrity. Like a reversal of continental drift, the great inner rift is healed. We are unified at the source of life, and it enables us to enter life whole rather than alienated.

True, we need to learn how to live this life in healthy ways. But we also need to affirm that it begins from a place of union and purity.

Further, as we realize that our life with God comes from within instead of without, it makes a great deal of difference in the way we approach our problems. Much of our petitionary prayer is the attempt to get God to act in the externals of our lives. We want God to fix our marriages, to protect us from evil people, to change our circumstances, to make life easier.

When we accept the fact that God lives within and is emerging into our experiences, it changes the way we pray. We change from insisting that God fix things to realizing that God may be giving us the courage to act. Rather than becoming dependent on changing circumstances, we can act in a way that expresses God in our marriages, in our work, and in the whole of our lives.

Much of our prayer for guidance is externally oriented as well. Guidance is perceived as a path we must follow. In some circles it's a tightrope we must walk! When we discover the significance of God's life emerging from the inside out, guidance is more like a river we are learning to paddle. We learn to go with the flow of God.

Finally, to celebrate the inner presence of God, alive and well in our *joie de vivre* — in the keen edge of our intellect, in the kaleidoscope of our emotions, and the generosity of our compassion — is to become grateful for every moment of life. Every mundane and every juicy moment is sacred, because God is alive in us and is coming to birth through us.

When I was a child, an ex-gangster spoke at a Bible conference I attended. He would hook himself up to a generator that put out thousands of volts and then turn off the lights. When he turned on the juice, sparks would fly from every part of his body.

It was a spectacular sight for a young boy. Even though I have no recollection now of the point he was making, it's still a graphic picture. God's life is seeking to emanate from every cell, every pore of our being.

The phrase "all flame," from the old abba, comes back to us. We have moments of awareness and joy when it feels like we're aflame with the life of God.

"God is within her . . . be still and know that I am God."

Batter my heart, three-personed God;
For you
As yet but knock, breathe, shine,
And seek to mend;
That I may rise and stand, o'erthrow me,
And bend
Your force, to break, blow, burn
And make me new.

JOHN DONNE[1]

CHAPTER FOUR

THE THREE-IN-ONE SOURCE OF OUR PASSION

■

NEW LIFE FROM GOD — LIKE A RIVER RUNNING WITHIN US. WATER TO drink and water to share. *Do we have the least idea what this means?*

Jesus promises God's life to us as an internal gift. An amazing offer! But like an unopened birthday present, we have to unwrap it to get the full picture.

What is it like, this inner flowing river of life? How do we live with a fountain that wants to bubble up in our souls — your soul and mine — and spill out into this planet of ours?

God's life coursing through our beings is both wonderful and disturbing. It is tumultuous and beyond our control. It is nothing less than the infinite life shared by God — Father, Son, and Holy Spirit — an ocean of love that has come to indwell us![2]

Passion runs deeper than the burning desire we happen to feel at the moment. Passion is God's life flowing through us. It is not merely a gift from God, it is the presence of God. The vibrant, flowing, love-filled life of the Trinity.

These are very strong words. Have you really, truly opened yourself to this "river of life" that wants to flow from within you? Have you ever truly considered the enormous implications for your spiritual growth to believe that God's indwelling life is a life of vibrant, loving communion? Have you ever contemplated what that means for the way you live your passion in the world?

Thinking of God's life within us as the source of our passion is wonderfully radical. As one of my friends says, "It's enough to get your blood running!"

Take it one step further and suddenly it loses much of its vibrancy. To say that this inner river is the life of the Trinity can make it seem otherworldly and not very meaningful.

We need to take time to dig deeper, to appreciate the significance of the Christian view of God as Trinity. It is the life of God as Trinity, which is passionately relational, that gives rise to our passion. This flowing of love is the headwaters of the river that emerges from our souls and plunges us into life.

Practically speaking, we have lost the doctrine of the Trinity to the intricacies of theological speculation. Yes, we believe in the fact of the Trinity, but we may have little or no idea how a Trinitarian faith affects our spiritual lives. In the Western church, the Trinity has been a theological proposition, not a foundation of discipleship.

For the most part, even devout Christians tend to worship God as a single Being. Colin Gunton wrote that "the Trinity has more often been presented as a dogma to be believed rather than as the living focus of life and thought."[3]

Karl Rahner's now famous indictment puts it even more bluntly: He said that one could dispense with the doctrine of the Trinity as false and the major part of religious literature could well remain virtually unchanged.[4] .

For many of us, the idea of the Trinity seems too difficult to deal with. One God in three Persons. It may be an esoteric truth, but not one we can get our minds around.

In the end, it doesn't really seem to matter to most of us. We confine the notion of the Trinity to the mystery of God's internal life and then we don't have to deal with it. We still pray to God, obey God, and serve God, but practically speaking, we relate to God as a single Being. True to our Greek philosophical heritage, we focus on the "One God" at the expense of the "Three Persons."

Dividing God's action into discrete compartments is another way we sidestep the real power of the Trinity. We think of God the Father as the Creator, God the Son as our Redeemer, and God the Holy Spirit as our Comforter and Guide. That way we can give lip service to the Trinity without really dealing with the relationship between them. For all practical purposes, we believe in one God doing three different things. The heart of the Trinity as a relationship of love is obliterated.

Do three persons exist in profound unity and unique diversity simultaneously? And is this relationship of dynamic love the very essence of who God is? Or is the Trinity simply a way to describe three separate manifestations or activities of one God?

The first is orthodox Christian belief. The second is, in reality, heresy[5].

A fully developed doctrine of the Trinity was not worked out in the New Testament, but the raw data is there. The New Testament writers knew the Jewish creed, "Hear, O Israel: The LORD our God, the LORD is one" (Deuteronomy 6:4). Yet they insisted on expressing the revelation that Jesus is God manifested in the flesh.

At the baptism of Jesus we are given a glimpse into the relationship of love within the Trinity. While Jesus was coming up out of the water, the Spirit descended on Him and the Father spoke words of intimate love, "You are my Son, whom I love; with you I am well pleased," (Mark 1:9-11).[6]

Paul, in Ephesians 2:18, gives us the clearest summary of the Triune God in action for our salvation. He argues that both Jew and Gentile are brought into relationship with God in Christ. Paul said, "Through him [Christ] we both have access to the Father by one Spirit."

Expressions like these, along with the baptismal formula in Matthew 28:19 and the benediction in 2 Corinthians 13:14, became grist for later theological reflection and struggle.

It was left to the church to sort out the implications of what Scripture revealed. The great challenge to the church in the first few centuries was this: How could Jesus be God if there is only one God? If God is One, is Jesus somehow less than God? And if Jesus is God, is there more than one God?

The early church finally struggled with the language and thought forms of the day to express the truth that God exists in one essential nature[7] and in three co-equal persons.[8] Further, they said there is a mutuality of shared life between the persons of God. Each fully indwells the other in a loving intimacy.[9]

In essence, the early church was working out a new definition of reality. The Greeks believed that we exist first, and then we enter into relationship. By insisting that Jesus was the eternally begotten Son, in an eternally equal relationship with the Father, the church insisted that a kind of static "being" does not come first. Being is rooted in relationship.[10]

We cannot grasp exactly how God can be Three in One, but we can understand that the being of God (and hence all reality) is relational at its very heart. "There is no 'being' of God other than this dynamic of persons in relation."[11]

The emphasis on the Oneness of God was further complicated by the notion of God's infinity. If God is infinite and eternal, then God can't be subject to feelings and passions that change.

Moltmann maintains that although the idea that God is beyond feeling and passing is contrary to the truth of Christianity, it has often been central to theology. He argues that the Trinity is subject to suffering because it is a relationship of love within freedom. He wrote,

> The logical limitation of this line of argument is that it only perceives a single alternative: either essential incapacity for suffering, or a fateful subjection to suffering. But there is a third form of suffering: active suffering—the voluntary laying of oneself open to another and allowing oneself to be intimately affected by him; that is to say, the suffering of passionate love. [12]

Moltmann argues that it is in the context of suffering for our salvation that the Trinity is revealed.

In the opening pages of her landmark book on the Trinity, *God For Us: The Trinity and Christian Life*, Catherine LaCugna summarized this well. She wrote, in speaking of the Trinity, "God is said to be essentially relational, ecstatic, fecund, alive as passionate love. Divine life is therefore also *our* life."[13]

This dynamic relationship of love is the life Jesus has promised. This is the core of Jesus' great prayer to the Father in John 17, when He said, "I pray . . . that all of them may be one, Father, just as you are in me and I am in you" (verse 21). Dame Julian of Norwich summed it up,

The lofty goodness of the Trinity is our Lord, and in him we are enclosed and he in us. We are enclosed in the Father, we are enclosed in the Son, and we are enclosed in the Holy Spirit.[14]

Accepting the startling fact that God's life within us is a Trinity of swirling, passionate love changes forever how we understand Jesus' promise of "life to the full." In the Trinity, God has invited us to participate in the Divine Friendship.[15] This flowing love is the source of our life, our energy, our passion, and our spiritual awareness.

It makes sense, now, to say that our passion is the life of the Trinity within us. We can start unpacking the gift!

Let's take a good, close look at the passion of love that has invaded our hearts. It might capture you with its boisterous goodness and take you on a spiritual odyssey beyond your imagining!

Trinitarian Life Is a Hunger for Infinity

Passion is brewed in the cauldron of infinite love. It is a hunger that can never be quenched, a fire that ignites us and fires all our experience.

God's infinite life fills our finite, human frames. That's like trying to contain an atomic explosion in a thimble. No wonder it's disturbing. By definition it's more than we can handle. The author of Hebrews said, "Our God is a consuming fire" (12:29).

It's no accident that the most majestic and awesome descriptions of God in Scripture are those in which God is immanently present. Think back through some of the more famous descriptions: the burning bush, Mount Sinai, Isaiah's experience of swirling smoke and shaking doorposts in a vision of God high and lifted up, Ezekiel's vision of God's glory.

These are not descriptions of God far away. They are close-up portraits of God in real encounters with human beings.

Ezekiel's tumultuous vision of wheels spinning within wheels, with rims full of eyes and beasts with four heads appearing like burning coals of fire, is an unparalleled description of God's dynamic presence.

There is nothing static here! Ezekiel said, "Fire moved back and forth among the creatures; it was bright, and lightning flashed out of it. . . . When the creatures moved, I heard the sound of their wings, like the roar of rushing waters, like the voice of the Almighty, like the tumult of an army" (1:13,24).

Is this the picture of a compliant God who comes to impose a library-like pall on our souls? It's folly for us to assume that if the God of Scripture indwells us, life will be placid or conformist. The old desert master who spoke of becoming "all flame" was right.

One writer in church history graphically described what it means to be invited into this relationship of love. He described it as a craving for the immensity of the Infinite.

> Our spirit is buffeted as in a storm by the heat and restlessness of love. The more we savour, the greater becomes our hunger and desire, for the one is the cause of the other. This makes us strive without attaining satisfaction, for we feed on God's immensity without being able to consume it, and we strive after his infinity without being able to reach it.[16]

Ray, a thirty-year-old man who comes for spiritual direction, told me he had tried to take time during Advent to be quiet and simply wait in God's presence. "How did it go?" I asked. Ray replied, "It was really empty and sad. Real sad. So I just quit doing it."

We explored his experience. Was it really sadness? Or could it have been pure, aching longing?

Perhaps sadness was the closest familiar feeling he could associate with it. Ray had stripped away all his normal prayer supports and simply sat open to God. Perhaps he experienced a taste of the longing for infinity from which we often hide.

I reminded him of T. S. Eliot's memorable line about our experience of the presence of God, "Human kind cannot bear very much reality." Perhaps Ray's longing was something to be treasured but kept in small doses for now.

If the truth be known, I think most of us avoid God. We prefer religion. God's life is too hot to handle. It's too big, and we're afraid it will do us in. It will—in the best sense of the word!

The Trinity Is a Relationship of Flowing Love

We could be terrified of God. Left without any further revelation, the thought of a finite being coming into contact with Infinity would be overwhelming.

But God is not only infinite. Fortunately, God is also Trinity. The heart of God's life is a constant flow of love between Father, Son, and Spirit.

The God whose presence rattles doors and whose infinite energy cannot be adequately described—even in Ezekiel's straining vision—has promised to come live in us. But to our great relief, the God with whom we share life is already in loving communion and brings this loving communion to reside in our souls.

Thus, when asked what is the source of my life, I can answer that I am born in love, and the call to love God with all my heart is a call to enter into passionate, loving communion.

This takes away the fright of experiencing the infinity of God as a consuming fire. The Old Testament visions of God are brought into focus in Jesus' full revelation that this tumultuous God drenches us with love.

John, the apostle who lay against Jesus' chest, must have been electrified by the promises Jesus made that night: "I will ask the Father, and he will give you another Counselor to be with you forever—the Spirit of truth" (John 14:16-17). And, "If anyone loves me, he will obey my teaching. My Father will love him, and we will come to him and make our home with him" (verse 23). In this short span of verses, Jesus promised that all three members of the Godhead would find their home within our hearts.

Jesus' words were not just for John. As we open our hearts to Him, as John did in that moment of intimacy, He promises us the same.

Imagine Jesus looking deep into your eyes as He did with John and the others. Imagine Him praying for you as He did for them that they "may be one, Father, just as you are in me and I am in you. May they also be in us" (John 17:21).

John Main, late founder of a Benedictine priory in Montreal, described prayer in similar language.

> It is our conviction that the central message of the New Testament is that there is really only one prayer and that this prayer is the prayer of Christ. It is a prayer that continues in our hearts day and night. I can describe it only as the stream of love that flows constantly between Jesus and His Father. This stream of love is the Holy Spirit.
>
> Again it is our conviction that it is the most important task for any fully human life that we should become as open as possible to this stream of love. We have to allow this prayer to

become our prayer, we have to enter into the experience of
being swept out of ourselves—beyond ourselves, into this
wonderful prayer of Jesus—this great . . . river of love.[17]

To be alive unto God, as Paul spoke of it, is to share in the flowing
of love that is the very heart of all things. This love is the source of our
being and the vitality of our passion.

Trinitarian Love Flows in a Constant Yearning for Union

Perhaps more than any other writer in the church, John Ruusbroec, a
little-known writer of the fourteenth century, helps us grasp something
of this stream of love as a profoundly passionate, paradoxical movement.[18] His elaboration of this paradox is the heart of his great
contribution to our understanding of the Trinity.

One movement in the paradox is the drive toward union and oneness. The other movement is toward diversity. These two paradoxical
movements correspond to the two great aching hungers of our souls.
We want to belong, to be swallowed up in union; and we want to be
acknowledged for who we are as unique people.

True to the designation "one God," Ruusbroec described the flowing of love in the Trinity as a movement toward a profound and
unfathomable oneness. We cannot plumb the mysterious depths of this
union. It is so profound and full that we, along with the Old and New
Testaments, must proclaim that there is but one God.[19]

But we certainly know something of its power in our own experience. We all hunger for loving union. This hunger is echoed in the
ancient words of Scripture, "For this reason a man will leave his father
and mother and be united to his wife, and they will become one flesh"
(Genesis 2:24).

This is the passion so powerfully expressed in the poetry of the
Song of Songs. The loved one is literally drenched with longing for the
Beloved. And she is ecstatic with the delight of their shared union.

Marriage is one experience of union, but we also experience union
in many other ways. Have you ever found yourself so absorbed with
something that you literally lost yourself in the moment?

Perhaps you experience a momentary sense of union playing foot-
ball, or throwing a pot on a potter's wheel. Suddenly time stands still,
and you are lost in a profound sense of timelessness.

It may come in quiet moments by a lake, or over a cappuccino with a friend. It may come in prayer or while listening to the climactic themes of Rachmaninoff's *Second Piano Concerto.*

All of us have had at least one moment when we truly felt a profound oneness with life. This incredible sense of union may only last for a few seconds and then leave, but we are forever touched.

Longing for union within the Trinity is the source of the throbbing pulse of our sexuality. This same drive makes us long for God as the deer longs for the streams of water (Psalm 42). The longings are all of one piece.

Sometimes we experience this drive so powerfully that we feel raw with our aching. Especially these days, as we find ourselves lost and fragmented in an individualistic society, we desire to belong. We crave union.

This unquenchable thirst roiling up within us is the sign of God. We may not handle it well. We may distort it into lust and greed, but it is the flowing of the Trinity in our lives. It opens us up and drives us to find union beyond ourselves. What we want most deeply is to be consumed with God, to lose ourselves in God's fullness.

Sometimes in our spiritual walk we feel dissatisfied and restless because we don't feel as close to God as we'd like. We're restless for more. Often we criticize ourselves for not getting our spiritual walk right. Or we criticize God for not showing up.

Unsatisfied hunger may be a sign that we're being nudged toward new choices to open ourselves to God's presence. It may also be a sign that God has withdrawn the sense of presence to take us into a deeper union.

We can pay attention to these possibilities. But first of all, we need to celebrate the hunger itself. We can accept it as part of the Trinitarian love at work in our souls.

Rather than castigating ourselves for our hungry dissatisfaction, we should treasure the hunger as the sign of God's presence, one of the paradoxical movements within the Trinity.

Trinitarian Passion Flows in a Constant Yearning for Distinction
Learning to live well with the longing to lose ourselves in loving union could occupy us for the rest of our lives. But Ruusbroec insisted that another movement within the Trinity flows in the opposite direction.

True to the Trinitarian phrase, "God in three Persons," Ruusbroec understood the movement of Love as a blossoming into plurality and distinction. God's life is not a steady state of equilibrium. It is a fruit-ful union that bursts forth into the different persons of the Trinity. Trinitarian passion celebrates individuality as much as it craves union.

Ruusbroec wrote,

> This sublime Unity of the divine nature is both living and fruit-ful, for out of this same Unity the eternal Word is ceaselessly begotten of the Father. Through this birth the Father knows the Son and all things in the Son, and the Son knows the Father and all things in the Father.[20]

This blossoming into uniqueness has profound implications for our spiritual growth. In a spirituality dominated by self-sacrifice, our drive for uniqueness has not been well articulated. We have often been told to give up our life, not to celebrate its distinctiveness.

We have often focused our spirituality on one side of Jesus' rela-tionship within the Trinity—the side of self-surrender. He could offer His life as a gift, because He knew its unique goodness was already celebrated in His relationship with the Father and the Spirit.

Jesus gave Himself to the will of the Father and offered His life so that we could find life in Him. Yet, the portrait of Jesus in the Gospels is not one of wimpy self-abnegation. Jesus comes across as a strong, self-assured person who was aware of His own dignity.

He could claim freedom from the Sabbath laws and walk through the crowd, making statements that echoed with the "I Am" of Yahweh in the Old Testament. Jesus could also remain defiantly silent when questioned during His trial and then submit to being beaten.

We begin to get the strange sense that Jesus was fearlessly self-assured.

This movement toward diversity within the passion of the Trinity explains our own craving for uniqueness. We long to be joined in love, yet at the same time we passionately desire to be acknowledged as some-one unique and special. We want to be close and we want to have space.

These paradoxical movements create a tumultuous conflict that hounds us every day. In marriage we face the continual dilemma of wanting both union with our spouse and to be recognized as our own unique person. Too much union and we feel suffocated; too much uniqueness and we feel lonely.

Parents give birth in loving union, and the child who is produced
craves identity with the parents. Yet the child is also separate. When
healthy, the child naturally moves toward independence.

This same push toward uniqueness lies at the heart of all life. In
the political process, each state wants its own separate identity, yet it
wants the advantages of being part of a union. In our schools we
struggle with the important duality of letting a child think for herself and
helping her to master the accumulated knowledge of the society.
Regarding morals, we agonize over when we should act to care for ourselves and when to do so would be selfish.

The unquenchable passion for uniqueness is also the sign of God.
We may distort this passion into pride and self-centeredness, just as
we're apt to distort our longing for union into lust and greed, but they
are both the flowing of the Trinity in our lives.

Recognizing the Divine Source of these drives within us is a very
important step in our spiritual growth. The wise comments of Sister
Nora about dealing with sexual fantasy in prayer continue to be of
immense help.

We can learn to hear within our desire God's desire to love us, and
then we can embrace our passion as the life of God in us. We can surrender to God as the source of our passion and move away from the
many ways we are inclined to distort this great gift.

How often do we reject the heart of the desire because we're afraid
of expressing it in sinful ways? We don't want to be full of pride, so
we reject the passion that calls us to express our uniqueness. We don't
want to fall into sexual sin, so we reject the goodness of our own desire
for union.

Rob's experience illustrates how this tendency to reject passion began
in his relationship with his mother and then carried over into his marriage.

Rob grew up in a home in which his mother continually crowded
him. In her overbearing way she criticized him, dominated his every
decision, and then demanded that he take care of her emotionally.

As a married man, Rob began to discover that he needed to put some
boundaries in place to prevent his mother from being so invasive in his
marriage. This was hard work. Rob felt terribly selfish. Any act of caring for himself instead of his mother felt as though he were being untrue
to Jesus. After all, Jesus laid down His life even for His enemies.

Rob was tempted to reject his desire to establish his own space.

But by refusing to create boundaries for himself and his marriage, he would be rejecting the passionate movement of God within him.

Rejecting our passion is no answer to temptation. It disconnects us from life. Those who are able to achieve the split become spiritually proud, and those who can't, become discouraged. It's a challenge to accept the goodness of desire and to say no to sinful expressions of that desire, but this is the heart of our spiritual transformation.

The Life of God Is a "Storm of Love"

This pattern of paradoxical movement toward union and uniqueness within the Trinity is not a pulse. It is not a quiet, regular wave of inward and outward movement. If these two movements were sequential—inward toward unity, then outward toward distinction—we could come to terms with it as a nice, predictable rhythm.

We might even be able to control it! We might be able to schedule our marriages so that the pulses of the two partners would synchronize. As marriage partners we could schedule the longing for union and the need for space in nice harmonic intervals.

Instead of a predictable pulse, we experience God's life as an interminable storm of desire—in both directions at the same time. When my wife wants to be close, I don't. Or maybe I want to be close yet have my own space at the same time. It's confusing!

When your child wants to tell you something important, you're busy cooking supper. You go for a day retreat to get some much-needed space and spend half the day wishing you were back in town talking to someone.

Ruusbroec helps us understand this turmoil. He called it a storm, a maelstrom of love. He spoke of the collapse into unfathomable unity and the fruitful springing forth into plurality and distinction as a continual, simultaneous movement.

Here is the heart of the paradox: two simultaneous, continuous, and yet opposite movements. Both uniqueness and union are experienced together. Ruusbroec wrote,

> Here the Persons give way and lose themselves in the maelstrom of essential love, that is, in the blissful Unity, and nevertheless remain active as Persons in the work of the Trinity.[21]

In one place he described it as a heat "so extreme that the exercise

of love between ourselves and God flashes back and forth like lightning in the sky."[22]

If we could understand the life of God as either the longing for
union or the drive for recognition, we could learn to adapt ourselves to
the call of one or the other. It is the conflict we experience in wanting
both that seems so impossible to deal with.

Remember Sally and Frank from chapter one? If Sally could have
simply chosen to "find herself" without regard for others, she would
not have written in her journal. If Frank could have simply "lost himself"
in his self-sacrifice for family, church, and business, he could have concluded that this was the thing to do and lived with it. Instead, he faced
the simultaneous desires that seemed to almost pull him apart.

How is Frank to live both? How do we live both? This is the passion of the Trinity. The unified–diverse God lives in us.

Our natural instinct is to shelter ourselves from a storm. But this is
one storm to open up to. Its very intensity marks the power and vigor of
our passion. Can we afford anything less than the full life of God?

The Crucible of Our Existence and the Creation of All Things

This passionate longing toward the life of the Trinity is not limited to life
in the sky, far away. We, and the whole of creation, participate in this
mysterious pull toward uniqueness and union. All of created life finds
its being in the movement of love toward fruitfulness and union within
the Trinity. Ruusbroec put it well when he wrote,

> In this living, fruitful nature the Son is in the Father and the
> Father is in the Son, while the Holy Spirit is in them both, for
> this is a living, fruitful Unity which is the source and beginning
> of all life and all becoming. Here all creatures are therefore one
> being and one life with God. . . . But as the Persons proceed
> outward in distinct ways . . . [so] God has created and ordered
> all creatures in their own essential being.[23]

This continuous and simultaneous storm of movement toward union
and uniqueness is the center of creativity and passion. This is the richness that makes each fingerprint and snowflake so incredibly similar to
all the others and so beautifully different. This makes life the endlessly
changing pattern that it is. Within this storm, all creation is born. God's

Trinitarian life is the womb of all existence. "In [God] we live and move and have our being," declared Paul (Acts 17:28).

We can't look at the sky with its endlessly forming clouds, or look at the lavish diversity of tiny alpine flowers within the unity of creation, without realizing that this grand storm is at the heart of all life. Each expression of life shows itself as unique. Yet each is part of the whole.

The storm has become creation. What we thought was cacophony was the orchestra tuning up for the symphony.

This tension of togetherness and separateness creates the colors of a painting, the harmonies of a great piece of music, and the cantilevered beauty of architecture. Moments of shared joy and inevitable conflict create intimacy.

What, then, does all this mean?

To sum up so far, when we open ourselves to the life of God in our souls, we encounter a passionate God, living in a swirling movement of love that pulls us toward both oneness and distinction. We, along with all of creation, find the ground of our existence in that creative tension.

Through Christ we are restored, brought back into full participation in this intimate love. We become sharers in the life of God, the love that gives life to the universe.

We could go through life trying to find our spirituality apart from these great movements. We may want a spirituality that keeps the conflict under lock and key. But the love of the Trinity calls us out into the river. It calls us to get our feet wet and to embrace the passionate river that is God.

We want tranquility and we want creative power. We want to go to Bible study and we want to spend the evening playing basketball. We want our needs met, and at the same time we want to surrender to God.

We pray that God will give us a safe trip and yet we acknowledge that we want God's will. In that simple prayer the conflict rages. It's not wrong to want to have a safe trip. It's part of our longing for our own dignity. Yet we feel part of a larger union to which we want to surrender. And so our prayer echoes the Trinity.

Most of the time we don't even know what we want. We're a jumble of conflicting desires and impulses. We love the vibrancy, yet sometimes we feel guilty for the jumble. If you're like me, you might be tempted to think this is all somehow far from spirituality. Or worse, that it's the nemesis of our spiritual growth.

I find it both comforting and challenging to realize this conflict of emotion and desire is the heart and soul of our life in fellowship with the Trinity. It's comforting to realize that my vibrant, jumbled passion is not outside my experience of God. I don't have to get the mess cleared away to experience God.

To enter into the passionate life of the Three-in-One God gives us a way to embrace our deepest passion. We will experience the hungers and the contradictions that are part of that life, and we'll have to learn to live with it, but at least our passion has a home. It belongs.

I also find this incredibly challenging. It leaves me *uncomfortable.* That is not a word we use easily or happily when it comes to our deepest and most important relationship in life — our relationship with God. We would rather use words like *safe, happy, peaceful, protected.*

Much as I find this challenging, I also like it! Uncomfortable as it may be, this is what makes my relationship with God rich. This is what gives my spiritual life guts and turns it into an adventure.

I prefer this any day to a "rose-colored glasses" optimism, or psychological narcissism, or the rat race of religious performance. In so much new age and psychological spirituality, we remain in control and the process revolves around our own experience and process. In so much of what passes for Christianity, we have no significance or say, and the emphasis is on conformity rather than true personhood.

Trinitarian spirituality is more than either, yet it includes the richness of both. We are not in control but we're taken seriously for our own uniqueness. God is free and yet has so embraced creation that we experience God in all the varied facets of our lives.

Trinitarian spirituality is a life of loving communion. It is not a domesticated spirituality, it is passionate. God isn't just nice. In the words of C. S. Lewis, "He's wild, but he's good."

Sometimes I feel like I will never stop
Just go on forever
Til one fine mornin'
I'm gonna reach up and grab me a handfulla stars
Swing out my long, lean leg
And whip three hot strikes burnin' down the heavens
And look over at God and say
How about that!

SAMUEL ALLEN[1]

CHAPTER FIVE

EMBRACING THE GOODNESS OF PASSION

■

SEVERAL YEARS AGO, MY FRIEND AND I HIKED UP THROUGH LARCH VALLEY to the top of Sentinel Pass, eight thousand feet high in the Canadian Rockies. We sat on a boulder, drinking in the beautiful fall day. The alpine larch trees below were incandescent gold, and the pass itself was stark as a lunar landscape.

Looking out at the stupendous vista, we talked about our lives and about God at work in the things we were facing in our separate ministries. We "Oohed!" in awe of the beauty all around us and reveled in our gratitude to God for giving us these moments of wonder.

I pulled out the poem that precedes this chapter and read it aloud. It seemed to capture the thrill of being alive. Passion for hiking, for ministry, for creation, and for God were all one and the same.

When God's life bubbles up within us and spills out into life, what does it look like?

We're all familiar with many images of what religious zeal looks like. The media keeps us posted. We hear about violence in front of abortion clinics. Televangelists shout into our living rooms.

But the life of God is something far more than "religious fervor." It permeates every facet of our experience. It's alive when we sit on the beach or shuffle papers at the office. It doesn't recognize boundaries of secular and sacred. It's all God's life.

I can be a very self-conscious and introverted person. But this roiling life has bubbled up in me despite my natural inhibitions. I've felt the rush of creativity while preparing and giving a new course. Life has surprised me with joy when I've felt discouraged and gone for a walk by the river. It has held me when I've felt helpless in the face of circumstances beyond my control.

Passion has raged in my anger and in my devastating disappointment at feeling misunderstood. It has crept up shyly in moments of prayer and while I tied tiny Parachute Adams flies for fishing.

If passion is a river pouring out from God, we can wander close to the bank and look either upstream or down. In the previous chapter we peered upstream and looked at the headwaters. We saw the Living Source of passion at the core deep within us.

Passion flows out of the life of the Trinity—a powerful, pure, crystalline stream of shared life. It is Life celebrating itself in union and diversity in all created things, from guppies to angels.

Now let's turn and look downstream. We can begin to see passion as it is expressed in the vast range of everyday life. The water downstream is not so pristine. What poured from the fountainhead of God's Spirit now flows out of us in a mixture of purity and pollution. Some of our actions and attitudes reflect the Spirit whose life flows in us. Some reflect our fears and greed instead.

We need to be clear both about the *good news* of what passion looks like in our attitudes and behaviors and about the *bad news* of what it can be like when it gets muddied.

First, we need to recognize it as good. If we explore passion as it is expressed in wholesome ways, then we'll be prepared to deal with the ways we fear passion or distort its goodness. If we don't see its goodness first, we'll never get over our fear of its danger.

In this chapter we will sketch a basic description of some of the characteristics of passion in everyday life. Everyday life is almost always overlooked in discussions of spirituality. Spiritual exercises and spiritual growth are often seen as something we do beyond the everyday. But the truth is, we never get beyond our daily living.

Our spiritual lives as Christians are not meant to be lived apart from everyday life. Spirituality *is* everyday life, lived in tune with the Spirit of God. In tune, I say, to create and recreate, to enjoy and to grieve, to touch the world with glee and bring goodness to the world as God would, and as God flows through us.

There will be many times when our actions and thoughts need to be transformed. The ups and downs of everyday life will drive us deep into the heart of God. But transformation is never movement away from the simple passion of living. It is within the context of seeking to live fully—with mind, body, and emotions—that transformation is called for and deepens our life with God.

Perhaps we need a new beginning point for our spiritual growth as Christians. Instead of shunning the world, we could begin by understanding that *passion to embrace life is the true beginning*. In the end, our everyday life becomes the expression of the life that is deep within us.

What does passion look like when we live it on a day-to-day basis? How do we enter openly and fully into life? We can scarcely get more than a glimpse, a taste, a whiff; it can never be captured. But we can look and describe moments of life to the full. We can glimpse what wholesome passion might look like when we're eating a meal, when we're strenuously working, or when we're talking to someone we love.

Imagine for a moment that you and I have a common friend named Rick. Rick, an ice climber, was recently in a freak avalanche. He's now a quadriplegic.

Imagine with me the kind of qualities that made Rick's life so passionate before the accident. We might imagine Rick's courage to face his fears and overcome them. We might think of the enthusiasm that pushed him to live on the edge, or the focus to master the technical details of his skill. We might be touched simply by his profound enjoyment of life.

Imagine now what it would take for Rick, paralyzed and incapable of free movement, to live a rich, full life. These same qualities would be needed to sustain him in the awful transition he must face. Courage to face depression, focus to find new avenues of expression, humor to lighten the long hours of emptiness, and the ability to find enjoyment within a very restricted experience.

Joni Eareckson Tada and Christopher Reeve are wonderful role models of passion for life within a very restricted scope of expression. They remind us that passion is not the exclusive property of the rich and the mobile. It comes from within and infuses our lives even when we face great limitations.

Looking downriver at the way we experience passion in life helps us to understand the context of our spiritual growth, regardless of our circumstances. Whatever word we use to describe it, this is the way most people want to live.

EVERYDAY CHARACTERISTICS OF PASSION

Passion as Intensity

If passion is about anything, it's about intensity. The eyes of passionate people seem to burn brightly and their faces light up with delight. We say that they live passionately because their intense desire to live seems to leak, almost literally, out of their pores.

During one World Series game, the television camera zoomed into a close-up shot of Juan Guzman, staring down off the pitcher's mound. His face was impassive but his eyes were ablaze. This was embodied intensity, a picture that has stayed with me for years as an unforgettable image of tremendous passion honed like a laser to a single focus.

This same kind of intensity courses in the veins of a young corporate executive who is bound and determined to reach the top of her field. It moved the apostle Paul to forget the past and press on in his great missionary work (Philippians 3:13-14).

Intensity trembles in the fingers of a four-year-old child focused on learning to tie his shoelaces. You can see it in the teenager learning to drive or in a twelve-year-old girl on her first horseback riding lesson.

Intensity is the elemental force that drives us into life to suck its rich marrow and enjoy its stringent taste. We don't merely want to respond to life or become a victim of life. We want to take life on as a challenge, an adventure.

We love to feel the adrenaline that enables us to fight our way through life's challenges. We enjoy the rush of being just a little out of control on a ski slope. We feel that big "YES!" when things just seem to flow.

In the movie *Dead Poet's Society,* Robin Williams plays the role of an unconventional private school teacher. He has the class rip out the introduction to poetry in their textbooks and gets them to feel the power of poetry for themselves.

In one scene he takes on a frightened teenage boy and gets the boy to spill out the poetry that is locked up deep inside him. After dragging the boy to the front of the classroom, Williams gets him first to whisper and finally to shout a "barbaric yawp."

With coaxing, the boy stammers while the poetry he had thrown in the wastepaper basket in disgust the night before begins to leak through the dam of his own fear. Once he gets going, everything else just seems to fade before the intensity of his young raw art.

If God's life in us is anything, it's intense!

Passion as Potency

Another commonly understood characteristic of passion is the sense of potency or creative power. Passion brings newness to birth. It flows like a river into the world, bringing about growth and vitality, new creations and possibilities.

This characteristic is most obvious to us when we look at the incredible masterpieces created by the passionate genius of others. Vincent Van Gogh's *Sunflowers,* Michelangelo's *David,* George Lucas's *Star Wars,* or the poetry of St. John of the Cross overwhelm us with their power.

But the potency of passion doesn't have to be expressed on such a grand scale to be a central part of our lives. That same creative potency is expressed in the loving care a senior citizen puts into his garden.

Our family lives in Calgary, a city 3,500 feet above sea level, with only ninety frost-free days a year. Our neighborhood includes many post-war immigrants from Poland and Italy who are now senior citizens.

A walk down the back alleys of the neighborhood is almost a trip into fantasyland. If I peek over the fences I can spy tomatoes, apples, roses, and even melons. Those gardens are the creative accomplishment born of long and loving passion.

This same sense of generativity is expressed in the gifts of a friend who works in a classroom with learning-disabled kindergarten children. Under her passionate care they enjoy life and learn appropriate behaviors within a loving atmosphere.

It's the impulse within a nun who told me recently that she has a dream of moving to a new place and starting alone to build a new community of faith. "Since I never had children, this dream is part of my generativity," she said with deep feeling.

Conversely, the passionless person is someone who hides from the world, afraid or unable to bring his life into the open, to share his energies with others and thereby bring beauty and richness into the world.

One reminder: The product is not the measure of our passion. We may never be considered great by the world's critical evaluation. But we do have potency within us. The power to create, to generate life, and to bring goodness into the world is inevitably one of the great indications of passion and of the fact that we are caught up in the creative love of the Trinity.

Passion as Sensuality

Passion is deeply sensual. We think of someone who touches and feels life as much as she thinks about life. She loves the different textures of clothes on her skin. Her soul quivers at the sound of a Northern Water Thrush, and she waves her imaginary baton like a great conductor while listening to Beethoven's Fifth Symphony. She loves lighting candles when she has a bath. Whatever way she chooses, she revels in the delight of her senses.

Passionate people are not limited to their senses, but they include their sensory awareness as a vital and rich part of their experience.

In talking about our imaginary friend Rick, we might say that he lived in his own skin. He wasn't afraid to feel the bite of freezing weather, to get dirty, to be exhausted, and to laugh in the face of the wind.

The sensuality of passion has a sense of revelry about it. One of the most passionate movies I've seen is *Babette's Feast*. Set in a barren stretch of Jutland in Denmark, and focused primarily on one meal put on by a houseguest, the story appears to be a very staid movie. The house is owned by two older, unmarried women who are carrying on the traditions of a strict fundamentalist sect founded by their father.

These two sisters have lived their entire lives with the notion that pleasure is strictly forbidden and is anathema to spirituality. Yet, as the houseguest (an exiled Parisian chef traveling incognito) prepares and serves the dinner, the movie lingers over each sensual moment. Each movement, each delectable taste, each tiny contact between the people at the table becomes a rich, sacred experience.

Whether we love going for walks or getting a back rub, planting a garden or kneading bread dough, we can feel the passion in our bodily senses. We can revel in God's goodness and be grateful for these great gifts.

Passion as Courage

Passion naturally includes the idea of courage. We must be willing to risk the rough and tumble of life and to enjoy what comes to us. We must make choices in the midst of complex alternatives and have the courage to face the consequences.

It takes guts to live with passion. It takes courage for a man stricken with multiple sclerosis to keep opening up to life within the limitations of his own diminishing power.

It takes courage to risk the danger of being hurt. To say we cannot love without being willing to be hurt may be a cliché, but it's still a painful truth.

When our daughter, Julie, was younger, she had a run of bad luck with pets. At least one kitten ran away and another was run over in front of our house. Still, when a new kitty became available down the street, she wanted it.

That night, as Miriam went to look in on her before going to bed, she saw Julie lying in bed with Zeus, the new kitty, cradled in her arm and snuggled up by her neck. Julie and her kitty became a touching lesson of the courage of a child to open again to life and risk the possibility of being hurt.

Living passionately also calls for the courage to face the fact that we will make mistakes. This is one of the greatest difficulties many Christians have with passion. "Living passionately sounds great, but what if I screw up?" Fear of making mistakes gradually and inexorably shrinks the world until a narrow, insipid life is the only possible alternative.

We won't always know how to live or what choices to make. And the fact that we're willing to follow life fully and energetically, even though we don't have our act together completely, means that we will sometimes hurt others, even if we didn't intend to.

If we're going to live passionately, we'll have to choose to face these risks with courage. We'll have to choose to live with the consequences of those mistakes.

Courage is not the same as bullheadedness, however. We will have to choose courageously to say "I am truly sorry" as much as we choose to say yes to life in the first place. We learn to embrace our mistakes and make them a part of our learning and maturing.

Passion is nothing if it is not growing and changing. Only a passionless person maintains equilibrium. Passionate people, by definition,

brium simply because they inject the energy of their
x of the present.

Passion as Playfulness

Playfulness goes hand in hand with intensity as part of passion. Left to
itself, intensity becomes frightening.

Psychopaths can be intense, as can religious fanatics. But healthy
passion is more than serious intensity.

Playfulness keeps passion open, much like beaten egg whites keep
pancakes light and fluffy. Playfulness ensures that we can laugh at our
own foibles and absurdities and at the world at large.

Playfulness makes me think of a jolly old grandmother whose life
has been marinated with joy and sorrow, with success and failure. She's
no longer caught up with impressing others or proving herself. Laughter
comes easily as her oversized belly begins to shake and her eyes begin
to glint with mischief and joy.

My mother once remarked sagely, "In our twenties we are so wor-
ried about what others think of us. In our forties we get to the place of
not caring anymore what others think of us. When we reach our sixties
we realize they weren't thinking of us in the first place!"

Humor keeps passion supple and full of spirit and keeps it from
being so all-consuming that it eats away like acid in the soul.

Passion as Wonder and Devotion

To live passionately means to live with wonder. Passion takes us beyond
ourselves; it lifts us from the mundane and takes us into the realm of
amazement. When we live passionately we are ready to see things we
wouldn't otherwise notice.

Just as good Thai food includes the flavors of cilantro and chili
peppers, passion includes wonder. Wonder permeates the whole and
brings out a response of exquisite joy.

Annie Dillard, in her Pulitzer prize-winning book, *Pilgrim at Tinker
Creek*, wrote an entire chapter on learning to see. After describing a
time watching the flash of fish in Tinker Creek, she wrote,

> Something broke and something opened. I filled up like a new
> wineskin. I breathed in air like light; I saw light like water. I
> was the lip of a fountain the creek filled forever; I was ether, the

leaf in the zephyr; I was flesh-flake, feather, bone.
When I see this way I see truly. As Thoreau says, I return to my
senses.[2]

This ability to see beyond the normal and experience wonder is a learned art. We learn to hold back our preconceived notions about life and experience it for what it is.

One measure of the passion of Jesus' life was His ability to see the created world with such grace. He spoke easily about the ordinariness of creation: the lilies, the birds, the hairs on our head, and the planting of crops, linking them all to our experience of God.

Passion is the thermometer that gives us some measure of how full of wonder the world really is. It links us with life and makes us hum our own gravelly Louis Armstrong imitation of "What a Wonderful World."

Devotion is the child of wonder and the grandchild of all the other characteristics we have mentioned. As we experience something of God as the source of our life, the redeemer of our life in Jesus, and the presence of life all around us, we are filled with a desire to surrender to God and to offer Him our undying allegiance and trust.

This is worship. God brings life to us, and we respond with praise and devotion to the God we have come to experience with wonder and joy.

COMMON OBJECTIONS TO LINKING SPIRITUALITY WITH EVERYDAY PASSION

Is This Really Spirituality?

When we begin to feel the pulse of God's presence in the joy of an evening walk or doing the dishes or playing squash, then we can begin to speak of God's presence impelling us to great choices of faith.

We may still struggle with trust. We may often take life into our own hands and make a mess of things. But once we've come to rest in the fact that our life is the flowing of God's presence, we experience our spiritual life and our intimacy with God in a whole new way.

You may object, "This isn't spirituality, it's just life."

But where did the life come from? This is the presence of God in us—loving life into us and enabling us to live to the full. Life is not opposed to spirituality. It's what we choose to do with life that's the question.

The picture presented of Jesus in the Gospels shows Him at home and engaged in a wide range of circumstances: from debating in the temple to sitting with friends at a wedding. Brother Lawrence demonstrated to us that doing the dishes in a monastery (or in a suburban home) can be an experience of the presence of God.

It's wonderfully liberating when we begin to experience our lives as the presence of God within us. So many people feel distant from God; they feel that God is far away or not a part of their lives. In Pauline terms they can be described as "dead" and "alienated from God." These terms are not just for the heathen. They describe us all when we're shut off from the flowing of God's life within.

When we begin to celebrate our everyday, passionate experience as the life of God bubbling up within us, our awareness of intimacy with God is forever enlarged and transformed.

What About Spiritual Greatness?

The description of everyday passion might seem superficial or self-serving to you. You might be asking, "What about passion for God, passion for others, passion for great acts of devotion and self-sacrifice?"

When we come to celebrate all of life as flowing from God, we honor, respect, and love other people and all of life as God does. And these become places of love and praise to God. This way of seeing widens rather than narrows our understanding of God.

Passion for God is found in responding to the presence of God in all of life. As we learn to experience our lives as the surging presence of God in us, we can live with gratitude. We are part of the communion of the Trinity in the very act of living. This may be honed by Scripture and by our further choices, but it can never be ignored or superseded. When it is, we have nothing but religiosity left.

Authentic choices of great spiritual devotion and self-sacrifice emerge out of our gratitude for life at its simplest levels. When we see that our ordinary lives are filled with God, we can be at home with God, whether we are changing diapers or kneeling in prayer or cradling dying indigents in our arms.

Passion for greatness that is not grounded in the ordinary is dangerous. We see the destructive effects of such passion in a tyrant like Hitler, the disintegrated lives of so many rock stars, and the downfall of religious leaders.

Passion for greatness—even spiritual greatness—by itself can tempt us to focus on our "ideal" of greatness rather than on the presence of God in our lives. We do not have the power to predict what true greatness is. Whether it is greater for someone to lead evangelistic crusades or for another to raise a daughter in an environment of love and devotion is not for us to judge. That is God's responsibility.

Yet, when we focus on the presence of God in the way Brother Lawrence did, even the mundane becomes great and the true greatness of our created existence can emerge. In the language of Jesus, it can be said of us, "You have been faithful with a few things; I will put you in charge of many things" (Matthew 25:21).

This same passion, expressed in our ordinary lives, is the driving force that takes us beyond the ordinary. Our thirst for infinity creates in us an unsettledness and makes us want more from our lives.

The "more" can be expressed in many ways. For some it is the pull that compels them to develop their art as far as they can take it. Responding to the gift of God with gratitude includes taking responsibility for its stewardship.

Gratitude would be empty if we were to say thanks and then leave the gifts on the table untouched. It would be wrong for someone like Luci Shaw or Madeleine L'Engle to thank God for their writing gifts and then never do the hard work of writing.

For others, "more" can be the drive to study theology and learn as much as they can about God. It can be the hunger that calls forth spiritual disciplines that make us faithful during the dry times. It can be the urge within to trust that radical openness to God is like finding the "pearl of great price." This way of spiritual formation is characterized by the very things we described as ordinary. It is intense, playful, courageous, and full of wonder.

People like Eugene Peterson, Henri Nouwen, or Thomas Merton are examples in our own day of people who have found that the ordinary is filled with God. They have learned to experience "God in all things," as Ignatius of Loyola put it.

If we seek to be spiritually great, we will fail. Aunt Betsy, who never left the farm, and whose hands are wrinkled from hard physical work and the effort of mothering seven children, lives a life as significant as was Mother Teresa's. Each of us is called to attend to the indwelling presence of God in us so that our lives bring love to the world, whether we live in obscurity or fame.[3]

Responding to the deepest urges of our hearts becomes our vocation, our calling. We may not know where it will take us next, but we follow, whether it means to savor the moment, enjoy a day to ourselves, or lay down our lives for others.

Can it be possible that when we follow our deepest urges they lead us back to God as their source? Will they lead us from the ordinary to the extraordinary? Yes, if we truly follow.

The mom who loves her kids and keeps asking God, "How can I really love these children better and more truly?" will change and grow and deepen in her walk with God. She will be following the way of passion to discover how to follow God in her everyday experience.

The factory worker who seeks to discover and enjoy God's presence in a dehumanizing situation lives to the full. His spiritual life will deepen even as he enjoys small moments of humor or feels joy in a job well done.

In a book released just at the time of his death, Henri Nouwen revealed his journal through one of the darkest periods of his life. It was a time when he had opened up to love and then found that the intensity was so great that he and those around him were not able to live up to his expectations. As he spent time alone recovering from the collapse he experienced, he wrote to himself, "You are called to live out of a new place, beyond your emotions, passions and feelings." Then he corrected his own thinking a few sentences later in the words,

> Maybe it is wrong to think about this new place as *beyond* emotions, passions and feelings. *Beyond* would suggest that these human sentiments are absent there. Instead, try thinking about this place as the core of your being — your heart, where all human sentiments are held together in truth. From this place you can feel, think, and act truthfully.[4]

Nouwen had come to know through the pain of his own experience that he could not separate his passion from his spirituality. Opened passion, with the powerful enjoyment and the losses he experienced, drove him deeper into God at the core of his being. From that place, he could trust that his passion was "held in truth." He was learning, like all of us, to be passionate and to follow that passion into God.

My soul has come undammed.
And the grey stucco
bungalows of civilized propriety
collapse before the shock.
Rage and desire boil through the
musty cellars splattering
treasured resentments and
rusty cans of congealed longing
into the naked yard.
And in carefully prepared flower beds
the brown, swollen current has churned
my tender green shoots of life and hope
into foaming carnage.

JEFF IMBACH

CHAPTER SIX

Passion's Dangers

■

MARILYN WORKS AS AN ACCOUNTANT IN ONE OF CALGARY'S LARGE OIL companies. She makes good money, but she's been dissatisfied for years. What she would really like to do is run a hike-in lodge in the mountains. Her vision moves her so much that it sometimes keeps her awake at night.

She hesitates. She struggles with the financial risk and her ability to pull off the business. But the biggest struggle is whether her dream would be spiritual enough. She's nagged by uncertainty about what she wants and what is God's will.

What if the project consumes her? What if she loses contact with her Christian friends? What if she fails and blames God? Or succeeds and forgets God? What if this is her idea and not God's in the first place?

At present, she's still an accountant in the office tower.

If passion is so rich and vibrant, *why do we hesitate?* Why don't we just praise God and guzzle life?

I wonder if it's a consequence of the Fall—which separated us from God and His life in us—that we're stuck with this push-pull relationship between ourselves and our passion.

For those whose spiritual lives have become tedious and inconsequential, a spirituality of passion may be like pungent spring air. It conjures up dreams of new life deeply held through long, dormant years.

For one person, the treasured dream may be as small as finally being able to move a little to music. For another, it might be literacy work among New Guinean tribal people, or work for justice in the struggle for racial equality.

We have a powerful innate drive to drink deeply of life and of God—to come to the end of our lives saying that we've truly lived. That this urge belongs at the heart of a person's spiritual life makes the circle complete. Life is good!

There is, however, another side. While we long to live this way, most of us are actually terrified to do so. Confronted with the opportunity to dance with life, we cling to our inhibitions and fears and our little ways of skulking in the shadows of uninvolvement.

We may tap our toes, but we're firmly glued to our chairs. We aren't easily persuaded to get up and dance. Like Marilyn, unless we can justify our passion as something "spiritual" (which implies a false dualism between the material and the spiritual), we keep our passion tightly under wraps.

Ironically, we push away the very thing we want the most. Typical of so much of our experience of intimacy—even with God—we long for intimacy until it stares us in the face. Then we run in sheer terror of our own vulnerability from the thing we so deeply desire . . . the very thing that can unlock our prison.

Once, when I was feeling imprisoned by loneliness and isolation, I sought the help of a counselor. Finally in one session she commented, "Jeff, you talk a lot about longing for intimacy and about not feeling understood by others. Yet you won't let anyone get close enough to be intimate with you. You refuse to risk the very thing you claim to want. Then you blame others for the failure."

It was a wise comment and painful to hear.

Peering downriver in the previous chapter, we saw that passion is a mixture of purity and pollution. Now it's time to face the pollution directly and name the ways we distort or avoid the river of God's life emerging within us.

We can hinder the expression of God's life in us either through polluting the stream with our own sinful tendencies or by simply turning off the tap altogether.

THE DISTORTION OF PASSION

Those who are ready to follow God fully and live life deeply can't pretend naiveté. If we're going to learn to live well with desire, we need to face honestly our capacity for muddying the water. We must face the potential we carry to turn the life of God into sinful and destructive choices.

Each of the characteristics of passion named in the previous chapter—intensity, potency, sensuality, courage, playfulness, and wonder—can be warped into addictive and destructive behaviors.

A murderer can be intense. Sensuality can become a god. Even playfulness and humor can be warped into a game people play to escape facing life directly and honestly. People often learn to take on the clown role in families as a way of dealing with family stress.

Wonder can degenerate into a vagabond search for another hit, another high of amazement. It can become an addiction to titillation, a distortion rampant in so much of our contemporary worship experience.

Passion is often understood as craving—an unending thirst that can't be satisfied. Dante used the image of a starving wolf, always famished and never satiated, to describe the prospect of passion gone awry. This "constant craving"—as one contemporary singer puts it—threatens to drive us crazy or into addictive and destructive behavior.

Passion can be a dark, brooding power. It can be completely narcissistic—a ruthless, uncaring demand epitomized by the character, Howard Rourke, in Ayn Rand's novel *The Fountainhead*. Rourke refuses to submit to anything. He is his own measure and his own final court of appeal. His architecture is his life, unmitigated and totally egocentric. He insists on his own agenda at horrendous cost to others and ultimately to himself.

It's not surprising to discover that the destructive side of passion is nothing more than desire that has lost its mooring. The New Testament word for "lust" is *epithumia*. This word *family* is used in both positive and negative contexts in the New Testament.

It is used of the desires that choke out the Word, "the worries of this life, the deceitfulness of wealth and the *desires* (the noun, *epithumia*)[1] for other things come in and choke the word, making it unfruitful" (Mark 4:19). It is also used of Jesus' own anticipation of the final Passover: "I *have eagerly desired* (the verb, *epithumizo*) to eat this Passover with you before I suffer" (Luke 22:15).

Paul spoke of being dead in our transgressions and sins: "All of us also lived among them at one time, gratifying the *cravings* (epithumia) of our sinful nature" (Ephesians 2:3). Yet he also said that while he would like to remain on earth to help the believers, he *"desires* (epithumizo) to depart and be with Christ, which is better by far" (Philippians 1:23).

Desire is not wrong. But desire that is disconnected from its source in God's desire—and therefore, focused on our own ways of finding life outside of God—is *life destroying*.

Walt Whitman, whose sensuous volume of poetry, *Leaves of Grass*, revolutionized American poetry, sang "of Life immense in passion, pulse, and power." His poetry may even be a grand tribute to the powerful, healthy sensuality that is true for all of us. But as the theme song of autonomous individuals, without grounding in God, it certainly evokes legitimate fears of narcissism.

The many ways we can distort God's life into sinful choices can be summed up under two major headings. We can fall prey to the distortion of excess, in which we refuse to put boundaries on our passion. We can also fall prey to the distortion of idolatry, in which we turn the objects of our desire into gods.

THE DISTORTION OF EXCESS
Those who are serious about their spiritual lives may be legitimately concerned about the excesses of passion. They may fear that if they acknowledge their desire to be recognized as their own person, they will become egocentric. If they pursue their passion for art or politics or sports, they will get so involved as to lose their keen edge of devotion to God. If they truly celebrate their sexuality they will become promiscuous.

Like a river, passion is wonderful when it follows the banks, but, as the people in North Dakota and Manitoba have rediscovered, floods are unpredictable and devastating. It seems easier to stay away from passion and its potential excesses than to embrace passion and learn to live with it in a godly way.

For some, the very thought of living openly and freely brings up nightmares of being out of control. "If opening up to God means that I'll have to open up to my sexuality, then maybe I'll pass," someone said.

The specter of being completely overwhelmed by passion—losing control and ending up a spiritual and social wreck—is too frightening. Who, in his right mind, wants to live open to the wind if it's going to blow them so far out to sea they may never get back?

Passion becomes a Pandora's box, and those afraid of potential excesses sit on the lid as long as possible. Frankly, I don't blame them. This is my first reaction to passion as well. I would rather be safe than sorry!

The danger of excess is real. Scripture has no lack of dark, terrible lists of passion gone awry. In Colossians 3:5 we read, "Put to death, therefore, whatever belongs to your earthly nature: sexual immorality, impurity, lust, evil desires and greed, which is idolatry." Paul offers another list in Galatians 5:19-21, which reads, "The acts of the sinful nature are obvious: sexual immorality, impurity and debauchery; idolatry and witchcraft; hatred, discord, jealousy, fits of rage, selfish ambition, dissensions, factions and envy; drunkenness, orgies, and the like."

If we're standing at the top of a slippery slope, and the next step is on icy ground, maybe a step back is more prudent than a step forward! "Flee youthful lusts," Paul urged Timothy (2 Timothy 2:22, KJV).

Fear of excess, then, is a good thing. Like the ability to feel pain, it can be a way of warning us when the old wood stove is getting too hot to sit on.

THE DISTORTION OF IDOLATRY

The second danger is the possibility of turning our passion into idolatry.

The first and greatest commandment, as Jesus reminds us, tells it straight: "Love the Lord your God with all your heart and with all your soul and with all your strength and with all your mind" (Luke 10:27). And if we don't get the point, the first commandment in the Decalogue is, "You shall have no other gods before me" (Exodus 20:3).

If we're serious about our life with God, we can't afford to play fast and loose with idolatry. We can't risk anything that would jeopardize our commitment to put God above everything else.

Passion, indeed, has the potential to be all-consuming. It is a voracious appetite willing to find a meal almost anywhere. And like a hungry cat eyeing a mouse, passion can fixate on whatever object promises to alleviate the incredible hunger.

Passion tempts us to focus on the objects of our desire rather than on God, whose life is a gift. It makes us cling tightly to the things that seem to fill us with delight and power and give our lives meaning.

We're like the three-year-old child fascinated by a kitty. Instead of petting it softly, he clasps the kitty so tightly he begins to choke it.

We turn our goals into idols and bow down in worship to achievement, creativity, success, beauty, acceptance, marriage.

We long so deeply for our children to have a happy, unmarred childhood that they and their happiness become our gods. Everything in life becomes secondary to providing fulfillment for our children.

The classic issues of money, sex, and power illustrate this pull toward idolatry.[2] Money, for instance, is a unique way to quantify life. We work for wages that define how much one hour of our life is worth. Money holds out the illusion that it can buy us love, fulfillment, respect, attention, or security. We think that money will deliver what we so desperately want—life free of fear and full of goodness. We ignore the notion of being open and desirous of life with God in favor of a short-sighted fixation on the tangible object of money.

Sex as a means of experiencing and expressing union becomes an end in itself, and we become focused on a potential partner. We substitute our trust in the life of the Trinity and think that a person, or the sex act itself, will bring us the union and fulfillment we so deeply long for.

These experiences are potent. We find so much energy and meaning through the objects of our desire that we begin to worship them as the source of our satisfaction. This is the spiritual reality behind all addiction. James Houston says, "Addiction means being so completely possessed that one is enslaved, deprived of our inner freedom, and ultimately of our personal integrity. It is the ghastly process of 'losing one's soul.'"[3]

The idolatry of fixing our passion on some particular means of fulfillment is wrong, it turns out, exactly because it's reductive. It is really an exaltation of the object of desire into God, making God too small. It also cheapens our passion into something less than the life of God, making our passion too small.

WE CAN'T HIDE IN FEAR

Like the danger of excess, the danger of idolatry is real. Unfortunately, we can't hide behind our fear of excess or idolatry as an excuse to avoid dealing with passion. Passion denied becomes passion diverted and distorted into some other form.

Our life will emerge somehow, some way, even if it's warped almost beyond recognition. It will leak out in unhealthy and destructive ways.

We do not, for instance, escape idolatry by exerting a heavy-handed control over our passion. When spirituality is seen primarily as a means of control, we then focus on our spiritual denial to keep the "tiger in the cage."

We end up substituting one idolatry for another. Control becomes the means of fulfillment. We get fulfillment from feeling "spiritual" because of how well we're able to keep the rules and hold our passion under wraps.

Self-righteousness and debauchery are but mirror opposites on the same continuum. We feel good if we've memorized more verses than most people in our church. Or we get our high out of being free from vices. Perhaps we haven't struggled with immorality or addiction as others have. We haven't had an affair or gotten a divorce. We haven't . . . The list can grow long, but when we get right down to it, fulfillment is defined by the list of things we haven't done.

Too often, Christian spirituality gets focused on control in the name of holiness. We define our morality and spirituality in terms of things we don't do. Natural passion for life gets diverted into religious fanaticism, and we can turn into arrogant, critical, and lonely people.

When the natural passion for life gets denied or diverted into religious fear and fanaticism, something dark happens. We fall prey to the very idolatry we tried to avoid. Through self-righteous control we idolize our spiritual appearance.

The spiritual environment of my childhood was rife with a dark idolatry to control passion. Christians almost gloated over the fact that they didn't wear makeup, go to movies or dances, or do anything that might even have "the appearance of evil" (1 Thessalonians 5:22, KJV).[4]

We were the real Christians. Other people might be Christians, but they weren't fully dedicated to the Lord like we were. Anglicans, we were told, had one foot on a banana peel and the other in Rome. Lutherans supposedly had correct doctrine but "denied the power." We were the ones who were separated from the world and lived holy lives. Even Billy Graham's wife was suspect because she had the temerity to wear makeup!

As I look back now, I can see that these people legitimately feared disobeying God, but fear became the controlling impulse of their spirituality. In the name of holiness, they unwittingly bowed down to the god of fear. They imposed their life-sucking fear on others and became critical people who were vulnerable to spiritual pride.

They successfully dammed the outlets to passion, but the water went stagnant inside and became poisonous. They were unaware of the corrosive effect it was having on their insides and on the lives of others.

This is Jesus' argument with the religious leaders of His day. In Matthew 23 Jesus chastised the hypocrisy of the religious leaders. "Woe to you, teachers of the law and Pharisees, you hypocrites! You are like whitewashed tombs, which look beautiful on the outside but on the inside are full of dead men's bones and everything unclean" (Matthew 23:27). Outward conformity had turned passion in on itself. They became cruel and heartless to others in their own "spiritual" superiority.

THE AVOIDANCE OF PASSION

Not only is passion subject to distortion and pollution, it can also be suppressed or denied.

There may be any number of reasons why we avoid our passion and live closed, self-protective lives. Our fears may be irrational or they may be legitimate. Either way, they keep us from life.

Fear of Disappointment

Recently I heard on the car radio that research has shown people would rather appear lazy than incompetent. Therefore, they refuse to attempt to do things if they fear failure. It's easier to say I was too lazy to attempt a doctoral program than to actually attempt it and not make it. At least in the first case I can always say I would have succeeded if I had tried.

We may fear disappointment if we open up to passion. We may fear that we won't be as passionate as we thought, that our actual experience of passion may be something less than our dreams.

I suppose all of us are better lovers in our fantasy than we are in real life. Better at communication, better at compassion, better at celebration. We may be afraid to discover our limitations and inhibitions—to find out that life isn't what it's cracked up to be in our fantasy. It's safer to watch others from the comfort of the ski lodge than to attempt the hill ourselves.

Wounds from Others' Distorted Passion

We may live tightly controlled lives because somewhere along the way we were wounded by the hurtful choices of others. Those who have had to survive the distorted and invasive passion of another may see passion as a terribly destructive force. It may dredge up excruciating memories of being victimized and violated.

Some people have grown up in alcoholic homes or homes in which one of the parents became unpredictably and uncontrollably angry. Others have lived through sexual abuse as children. Many boys have grown up tortured by their fathers' projection of unreasonable expectations. One man I know continually undermines his life by quitting jobs and opting out of relationships. He could never live up to the expectations of his highly competitive father, and now he runs from life rather than get anywhere near feeling he's part of the pack.

Those who carry scars from the evil of someone else's uncontrolled passion may not be waiting breathlessly to embrace life with open arms. No one wants to be on deck with a loose cannon. Survival as children meant building great walls and retreating from life. Today these people may be more interested in control than in celebrating passion.

Fear That We Are Essentially Evil
Some people stay clear of living passionately because of shame. They falsely believe they not only do bad things, they *are* bad.

Shame is a deeply rooted trap. It is often the sad result of abuse. The victims internalize the sense of evil in the abuse, believing they must deserve the horrible things that are happening to them.

I would probably have remained hidden in my shame if I hadn't finally concluded that refusing to open up to God's life was as much a sin as distorting it. I've filled innumerable pages in my journal, gradually emerging from behind the rocks and allowing God to love me into life.

Learning to trust that God's life in me is deeper and more powerful than my sinful tendencies has been the greatest growth in trust I have had to go through in my Christian life.

Fear of Responsibility
We may fear the responsibilities of living passionately. Living deep and wide doesn't absolve us of responsibility for our choices. The goal is not just to live passionately but to live well with our passion.

If we never admit to our sexuality, we won't have to learn to live responsibly with a "hot potato." I've come to believe that it's better to be aware of my sexuality and live it responsibly than to deny it and discover I've unknowingly washed downriver and over the falls. I suspect that many pastors have affairs for this very reason. They fail to acknowledge their sexuality until they are way downstream.

To take up the journey is to assume the responsibility of facing the dragons and giants on the way. We must live our own Pilgrim's Progress, even though we may actually prefer a safe existence to risking the lessons of dealing directly with our passion.

Fear of the Unknown

The transition from a domesticated, predictable spirituality to a "wild," more unpredictable spirituality is frightening.

I choose the word *wild* on purpose. We could open up to passion after a lifetime of denial or suppression and become vulnerable, like domesticated animals who get lost in the wild. Everything is new; the rules have changed. They no longer know how to find food, and they don't recognize the danger of predators or know how to avoid the ones they do recognize.

There is a great unknown in moving from the narrow safety of tameness and domestication back to the wilderness.

In her book *Women Who Run with the Wolves*, Clara Pinkola Estes explores this image. "The word *wild* here," she says, "is not used in its modern pejorative sense, meaning out of control but in its original sense, which means to live a natural life, one in which the *criatura*, creature, has innate integrity and healthy boundaries."[5]

But Estes is not naive. She writes further about the dangers of leaving a domesticated lifestyle and returning to the wild.

> When [the feral woman] has opportunity to return to her original wildish nature, she too easily steps into all manner of traps and poisons. . . . No longer wary and alert, she easily becomes prey. . . . Feral women of all ages, and especially the young, have a tremendous drive to compensate for long famines and exile. They are endangered by excessive and mindless striving toward people and goals that are not nurturant, substantive, or enduring.[6]

Estes suggests that we can get into trouble by naively embracing our inner "wild" passion. After feeling pent up for years, we may react so strongly to our religious past that we binge on our newfound freedom. We can devour our passion. We may demand satisfaction and refuse to accept the necessary transformation.

This metaphor of moving from domestication back into the wilderness is a very fruitful metaphor for our spirituality.

One of the great tragedies in our Western civilization is that we've treated the wilderness much like we've treated our passion. We have pitted ourselves against the wilderness, taking on huge archetypal fears of "wild." Now we're beginning to see that taming the wilderness has had a devastating effect on the complex ecosystem of the environment.

Today we are having to change our opinion about "wild." We can no longer afford to see it as something evil, something to be eliminated or controlled.

The wilderness is a complex relationship of diverse but inextricably related plants and animals. It's not a chaotic threat to our survival. Rather, we need the wilderness to survive. Our artificial life of agribusiness and cities — with the infrastructure required to support them — simply doesn't have the diversity to support life by itself.

We must learn to treat passion with the same respect. Just as we must come to terms with respect for the wilderness as a great expression of wholeness, we are being asked to treat passion as something not inherently evil or frightening. Passion doesn't need to be eradicated or controlled for us to feel safe. It's the very thing that brings to us the fullness and complex beauty of life.

The answer, both to our fears of the wilderness and our fears of passion, is to face our fears directly and learn to live in harmony with what we fear so deeply.

I urge you to lay down your weapons and invite your passion out from its guerrilla position in the hills of your unconscious. Bring it to the bargaining table. Learn to embrace passion and to live with it in healthy ways. Start small, but start. Accept and respect the real dangers, but don't let them paralyze you.

Trust that the discovery and enjoyment of passion is an inextricable part of your intimacy with God. Savor the companionship of God's presence in your life and surrender to its flow.

Like a young, alienated, acting-out child who needs to be welcomed and held rather than jumped on, our passion needs to be embraced and freed to find its healthy place in the fullness of our lives. We can pray this way by holding the "child" of our passion with tenderness before God, or let God hold it for us.

We are now ready to face the call to choice and to learn to follow God by living in healthy ways with our passion. This is the great pathway to spiritual maturity within the Christian gospel. Eastern philosophy may tell us to supersede passion, but Christ, in the Incarnation, honors our passion and reveals to us that it is God's life in us to be lived with goodness.

· P A R T   T W O ·
Opening Up to Our Passion

■

I find it difficult to assign [music] its proper
place. . . . I realize that when [the hymns] are
sung . . . they kindle in me a more ardent flame of
piety than they would if they were not sung. . . .
But I ought not allow my mind to be paralyzed by
the gratification of my senses. . . . So I waver
between the danger that lies in gratifying the senses
and the benefits which as I know from experience
can accrue from singing.

ST. AUGUSTINE[1]

CHAPTER SEVEN

CHOOSING

■

SHALL WE ENTER INTO LIFE? IF WE DO, WE MAY SIN. IF WE DON'T, WE WILL wither and die.

Learning to live well with our passion is no easy business. Indeed, it will take a lifetime full of learning and choosing, but choose we must.

Say yes to passion. Say yes to trusting God with the process of growth and change, and get ready for the ride of your life . . . a canoe trip on a whitewater river.

Few experiences can match the thrill of sluicing down a runoff-swollen river on a bright day. Spring snow clings tenaciously to the mountains, and down along the banks the old cottonwood trees are fresh with new leaf.

Looming just ahead, and approaching too fast for comfort, lies a long set of rapids with huge standing waves. It's not impassable, but we'd better ferry to shore and take a good look first. We don't want to get swept into one of the boulders.

Two emotions fill the wise canoeist at that moment. The first is the thrill of the coming trip and the sense of freedom it brings. The second is a great sense of humility and respect for the water with its alluring riffles, its hidden boulders and swirling currents.

Choosing to live passionately is to live on the edge of discovery and adventure again. It requires both daring trust and humble respect.

Sometimes people tell me they're bored with their Christian life — bored with the same old answers that don't really touch life, bored with reading the Bible, and bored with prayer. For years I was careful to be sensitive and compassionate to these complaints. I would try to accept the feelings and probe as best I could to see what was causing this distress in their lives.

Were they knowingly being disobedient? Were they in some dark night of purification? Should they be concerned about this boredom, or should they just accept it as a natural season of life and learn to trust the Spirit through the dry times?

I still feel the same compassion. But now I have an initial response I try on for size when someone admits they're bored with the Christian life.

I simply say, "Try loving God with all your heart and living passionately at the same time. You probably won't be bored for long!"

I could add, even though I usually don't, "You'll be scared out of your bored little wits! You'll be dying for someone to tell you the way forward. You'll make mistakes and find out why forgiveness is important. You'll wonder if there will ever be a resurrection in the face of the deaths you must choose."

Guidance, forgiveness, faithfulness, death and resurrection, love — all these basic Christian themes will become real and urgent. They will come back into focus because we're alive again. Our spiritual lives will regain integrity because integrity comes when we're facing real issues, real struggles, and the thrill of real life — with a real God.

The joy of living from the depths of our souls and the deep integration that comes from the emerging transformation will be worth it all. At least, like white water canoeists, we won't be bored!

Eventually we're all faced with choice. Will we say yes to the life of God that is at the heart of our passion? And will we, at the same time, say no to a narrow, narcissistic indulgence of that passion?

Will we choose "life to the full," and will we refuse excess and idolatry? These choices are the heart and core of true spiritual growth.

The quote from St. Augustine's *Confessions*, at the beginning of the chapter, illustrates this dilemma. It's hard to imagine that Augustine would actually suffer over whether to ban music in church to avoid the risk of sinning. Yet we've always struggled between the flesh and the spirit, between a passionate, embodied spirituality and what has been termed "spirituality from the neck up."

This dualistic thinking is a crack that opened in the floor of the church ages ago and has run clear down to our day. Rather than choosing between opposites, the call is to choose both—to choose passion and to choose transformation.

A TWOFOLD CHOICE

Saying Yes

About fifteen years ago, I intentionally began to open up to my emotions. I had been growing toward a more well-rounded prayer experience for some time. My spiritual director was encouraging me to open up with my whole heart to God—with my emotions and not just my head.

It was scary stuff. I had learned through long years to be calm and dispassionate, to be reasonable, and to look spiritual by keeping everything in control.

I was so tightly controlled I couldn't admit to anger or to disappointment or fear. Nor could I express joy.

My spiritual director gave me a passage of Scripture from Isaiah to pray:

> I will lead the blind by ways they have not known, along unfamiliar paths I will guide them; I will turn the darkness into light before them and make the rough places smooth. These are the things I will do; I will not forsake them. But those who trust in idols, who say to images, "You are our gods," will be turned back in utter shame. (42:16-17)

I didn't fully appreciate it at the time, but praying that Scripture passage became a powerfully transforming experience for me. My familiar world was to be cool, in control, rational, and self-deprecating. To open my life to the fullness of God's passion, including my emotions, was an "unfamiliar path" so frightening that I could hardly contemplate it. But as I prayed the passage, the promise of God's guiding presence began to fill my soul.

I had come to the place in my life experience where I could no longer contain myself (otherwise known as the onslaught of mid-life crisis!). Things were going to open up one way or another. Just about all I could do was admit that I was the blind one and that I was unfamiliar with living with my emotions. Even so, I wanted to follow God with all my heart; I wanted to open up to Him with my whole being.

My spiritual director did her best to reassure me by saying, "The Spirit cares more deeply about this growth than you do!" Like a blind person, I had to trust that God would be there to help me cross the busy street of my own life.

Gradually I began to make specific choices to stay open to my emotions without being dominated by them. I began to take God's hand and trust that He would compassionately and faithfully open me up to my own emotions and passions.

Exploring my emotions in my journal became a safe first step. At least in my journal I couldn't hurt anyone! Then I had to risk choices to express my emotions to others. That was very difficult.

Once Miriam said to me, in the middle of a marriage conflict in which I had finally become angry, "I liked you better the old way." She wanted me to be steady and without emotion so she could range through her emotions at will!

We have to start somewhere. As Jesus' parable teaches us, we can't bury the gift of our passion and think that the Master will be pleased (Matthew 25:14-30).

The longer I live and become witness to other people's growth, the clearer it becomes to me that for many of us the "somewhere" of our choosing is that "blind," trusting willingness to take God's hand and welcome our passion.

Once we accept the fact that God's life is welling up within us, we're no longer free to say no to expressing that life. We can't say, "I want to be spiritual, but I don't want anything to do with living passionately, thank you very much." We're committed to the current.

We can't put out the fire and then expect to become all flame!

Let me put it as strongly as I can: *Denying the power of your passion through refusing to live fully and openly is one of the fundamental sins of the spiritual life. It is a refusal of the Spirit.*

Now, that's a turnaround worthy of the "upside-down kingdom!" Who ever thought that saying no to passion would be a sin? But in saying no to our passion we are literally saying no to God.

This may mean different things to you than it does to me. I may be passionate about helping people recover a sense of spiritual vitality, and about fly-fishing. You may be passionate about cellular development or classical literature or computers. You may experience the flowing of God's life in parenting, or space physics, or used-car sales, or church planting. These are all places where life happens—and all are potentially dangerous places of excess and idolatry. So be it.

We may need to be timid and careful. But if we refuse to open up to passion, we are denying the Spirit that brings us life.

The other side of the coin is just as startling. The welcoming of our passion as the expression of God's life within us is a step of obedience. Our feeblest attempts to live that passion with integrity are some of the greatest acts of devotion we can offer to God.

Choosing to say yes to our desire without demanding any particular fulfillment honors God's presence. It calls us to commit ourselves to live out God's life—despite our fears, despite our ignorance of the way forward.

As I am learning to be true to my emotional life without letting it dominate me, Miriam notices the difference. She likes the passionate person I'm becoming, despite the rough water she had to wade through with me at the beginning.

If the life of God-the-Triune-One is a river that wants to flow in us, then we must accept its power and step into the water like Ezekiel (47:1-6). We need to move past ankle deep and get in deep enough to swim!

In Galatians, Paul dealt with this very issue. He spoke harshly to legalists who forced people into a conformist spirituality. His opponents were more concerned about "the banks of the river," the controls, than they were about whether the water of life was flowing. They cared that the rules were followed, not whether anyone really lived.

Paul argued strongly and convincingly that this kind of controlled religion is not Christianity. The good news is lost if we are consumed with the cautions and the rules.

In Paul's day the issues were circumcision and the dietary laws of the Jewish religion—no longer burning issues for most of us. It's easy to skim over the text and miss the point.

But if we take a moment, we can put ourselves in the shoes of first-century Christians and imagine what might have gone through their heads and hearts. Our pondering might go something like this: "Maybe

Paul is right. Maybe eating pork or crustaceans isn't wrong. But then where will it lead us? If we 'get soft' on these issues, where will it stop? Soon we'll be ignoring all of the Old Testament, even the commandments concerning stealing and committing adultery."

Surely we've all heard this kind of suspicion. When I was first involved in home Bible studies in the early seventies, the argument was always, "Yes, it might be more personal if people met informally in homes, but where will it lead? We need to continue to meet in the church on Wednesday nights or people will lose their commitment to the church. The pastor won't be able to oversee these groups, and they might fly off into heresy."

Do these arguments rage in your soul? Have other people dumped them on you like a heavy burden? Are they keeping you from your passion? Do the old institutional patterns, the conformist fears, keep you from embracing the gift God has given you? If so, take heart!

At the rising climax of Paul's argument in Galatians, he urged the believers to live out their freedom in Christ. "It is for freedom that Christ has set us free. Stand firm, then, and do not let yourselves be burdened again by a yoke of slavery" (5:1).

Here is the call to passion. We have been justified by faith. We have been freed from the legalism of seeking to earn our acceptance before God by living a tight, rule-bound life out of fear we might do something wrong. We've been freed to live openly with Christ in all areas of life. In Him we are free to explore new, more egalitarian relationships because we've been freed to move out from under the tyranny of social roles for Jews and Gentiles, slave and free, male and female.

We are free to trust the life of God in us.

Galatians remains a closed book until we see the freedom Paul advocated as being very wide and wonderful. Justification by faith is more than being forgiven, it means we've been set free. Period.

Saying No
Once the fundamental truth of freedom is secured—even at the cost of calling anything less, alien to the Gospel—Paul then added, "You . . . were called to be free. But do not use your freedom to indulge the sinful nature" (5:13).

Here is the second choice we must make in learning to live with our passion. When we choose to live passionately as the expression of God's life in us, then we must also choose not to indulge our sinful tendencies.

Having once fundamentally chosen to live, we will continually face choices that call for discernment about what it means to live constructively with our passion. We need to be prepared to live through hard choices and sometimes even dark nights of struggle over what to choose.

We will choose to say no whenever we discover passion has become a twisted self-indulgence that denies God's presence in our lives. But we cannot deal with the question of discernment as long as we're afraid to deal with the welcoming of our passion.

The call to choice is not just a call to live out our passion; it is a radical call to surrender to the God whose life fills us with this mysterious power in the first place.

Some of the most tragic experiences I've heard about have been situations in which people felt that the call to life more abundant was simply a call to choose to live passionately, regardless of any call to surrender or transformation.

A realtor named Carla got increasingly good at what she was doing. She moved from residential real estate into light commercial and finally into the big leagues of heavy commercial sales. The stakes got higher as the commissions rose almost exponentially.

Carla loved it. She felt that God was blessing her. She felt alive and on top of the world. While Carla enjoyed the passion, she refused transformation. She wasn't openhanded in her prayer. She didn't consider the consequences of becoming wrapped up in her work.

Gradually, business became a game. She got caught up in beating the competition, in proving her competence. Her world began to wither and die on the edges. Family life became a burden. In the heat of business, she forgot to return her friends' calls.

What began as a gift, a passion that brought life to her, eventually became the rope that hung her. She ended up in divorce, lost custody of her children and, to medicate her pain, became increasingly dependent on alcohol.

Carla blamed everything else for the mess of her life. She never did pause to think that maybe the way she had demanded fulfillment was killing her.

Our surrender to the life of God in us includes willingness to embrace our passion yet forgo any expression of it that would be sinful. This basic choice underlies the myriad of specific choices we make every day.

For instance, a person could say, "I will learn to embrace the passion of my anger and learn to hold it in such a way that it doesn't become destructive to others."

When I began to explore my anger, any expression seemed to be destructive. I had to learn to express my anger in ways that didn't smear it all over others. But the fact that I was angry was not sin in itself.

I also had to learn that my anger is mine. I can't expect others to take responsibility for it. If I'm angry, it's my responsibility to face my emotion before God and learn from it.

You might need to say, "I will learn to be at home with my sexuality, even as I keep surrendering it to God so that I don't indulge it just to satisfy my lusts. I will learn to be at ease with women (or men) and remain faithful to my spouse."

A salesperson may need to say, "I will learn to enjoy the thrill of closing a deal as part of the intimacy of God's life in me. I will enjoy the companionship of God's presence. And I will keep surrendering it to God so that it doesn't become my idol."

A parent may need to say, "I will enjoy my children and hold them openhandedly with God so that I don't cling to them as the source of my happiness and fulfillment."

WHAT CHOICE DO YOU NEED TO MAKE?

Do you need to affirm your passion as God's presence in your life? Do you need to affirm your commitment to refuse its unqualified indulgence? The answer to these question will depend to a large extent on the context in which you are experiencing the choice.

Some people may be so closed to passion that their most difficult choice will be to embrace life. Their struggle will be to believe they are in the stream of God's love.

If this is your struggle, you will be tempted to believe that any expression of passion must be indulgence. You'll have a hundred reasons why it would be better to forgo passion on this particular occasion. The time isn't right; others around you will misunderstand; your desires will get out of hand; you might unintentionally hurt someone. You must address these excuses without allowing them to keep you from choosing.

You must consciously open up to God's life, even if you have to practice in a corner or in the safety of your journal at first.

If you're slow and timid about embracing life, open your timidity to God. When you pray, be honest about it without beating yourself up. Trust that God is offering to lead you, and commit yourself to following. After all, this is God's life, not yours. Ask God to lead you gently and graciously into a deeper experience of life.

You may also want to thank God for the gift of your timidity. You can be thankful that it has kept you out of some real messes.

But what if you naturally say yes to life? What if you're not very cautious by nature and you run pellmell into life, full of the juice of desire? Your problem isn't one of embracing passion but of keeping it within healthy boundaries.

You will then need to be clear about your choice to say no to indulgence. The gift of freedom, as Paul explained, is not license to gratify yourself at any cost. It is the freedom to enter into the mystery of passionate love with the Trinity. It is God's life, and God must be the One who calls the shots.

If you're impetuous about entering life, open your impetuosity to God. Be thankful that you don't have some of the baggage others have. Enjoy your love of life. Laugh with God about all the ways you've already drunk deeply of life's fullness.

Open your heart to any transformation God may call you to in living out your passion. Tell God you don't want to settle for anything less than His true presence. Reading the old masters or a contemporary book like Henri Nouwen's *With Open Hands* can form a helpful prayer guide to keep you honest about your tendency to control life for your own ends.

JESUS AND PAUL

We can see the relationship between opening up to passionate living and opening to the transformation process in a comparison between the ministries of Jesus and Paul. We could easily assume that Jesus and Paul had the same context and the same message. Both were first-century Jews. Yet there were fundamental differences.

Jesus spoke to people who were caught in a life of performance, unable to open up in the truest sense to life. Paul, for the most part, spoke to people who were caught in a life of dissipation. Much confusion is created by not seeing the difference between these two contexts. And Paul often gets the bad rap of being a moralist because of it.

Jesus lived His whole life within a culture of religious conformism and oppression. He spoke against it, He acted in ways to contradict it, and He paid the price for this reckless challenge.

He was a radical, calling into question the authority of the religious leaders. He associated with people who were marginalized and offered freedom to those who didn't fit in.

Jesus was free not only to go to sinners' houses, as in the case of Zacchaeus (Luke 19), He also welcomed religious outcasts to His own table (Luke 15). In Near Eastern custom, this was an act of acceptance and loyalty the religious leaders simply couldn't tolerate.

I believe we can begin to touch the emotional impact of that kind of radical behavior by asking ourselves if we would advise our children to associate with the kind of people Jesus associated with.

Jesus' portrayal of God was not that of an old man with a white beard, sitting on a chair of distant holiness. It was that of an old man running down the road to receive His profligate son. True, Jesus spoke of hell and punishment, but He never did to those who were the "sinners." Every time He spoke of hell it was in reference to those who, by their religiosity, refused the good news He brought.

In short, Jesus stressed the welcoming of life. He was willing to challenge the social taboos that created such oppression, even if He created havoc in the process. Jesus appears like a rebel in the face of a monolithic structure of religious oppression.

Paul may seem like the moralistic conservative by comparison. But Paul faced a very different scene. He did, indeed, have to struggle with the same religious oppression from the synagogue. And he was uncompromising in his challenge to spiritual conformity. The letter to the Galatians became the great magna charta of freedom as a result.

But Paul's converts came largely from a background that had no such moral structure. They were formed more by moral chaos than by religious conformity. He spoke to a situation that was rampant with the disintegration of personal agendas and unbridled passion. It's no wonder Paul speaks so much about the transformation process.

It's not surprising that Paul's letters call for moral choice and that he's so clear about the expressions of lust that are contradictory to the Christian vision. He stressed the welcoming of life with a big yes, but he also called for making choices that would lead toward transformation.

It makes sense that Jesus and Paul's approaches differ in emphasis. They spoke into different situations and tailored their message to the context of the people they addressed.

If we spent our lives working with street people, we might be much more emphatic about the dangers of passion and the need for structure than if we were talking to a group of orthodox Jews or fundamentalist Protestants. In those situations we might appear radical in order to speak out for and model the freedom that is possible.

Both Jesus and Paul offered the balance of choosing life and refusing self-indulgence. These are still the fundamental choices we are called to make. Will we choose to enter life as fully and deeply as possible and trust that it is indeed the life of God in us? And will we choose to surrender control of that process to the Holy Spirit?

Having secured the commitment to live with passion, the commitment to transformation makes sense and has a context in which to operate. There is now something vital, something essentially worthwhile, to tend and prune.

If we stay attached to the vine and let the sap run free and true to its nature, if we let the Gardener do the pruning where necessary, we have the promise of a rich harvest.

Neither choice can exist on its own. Bernard of Clairvaux alludes to this twofold nature of the commitment in his important dissertation, *On Loving God*. Speaking of finding fulfillment through the relentless pursuit of desire without transformation, he said with ironic humor, "You are like the one who is running on the right path, but you will die long before you attain your goal."[2] The affirmation of desire is good, but it is fruitless without accompanying transformation.

To choose passion without transformation is to choose eventual disintegration. It is the equivalent of choosing uniqueness without choosing union.

The unique fellowship of the Trinity would soon explode if diversity were to be held as the only reality.

Likewise, the grand display of different persons within the Trinity would implode if union were the only truth.

To choose transformation without the commitment to passion is to create a case without a diamond, a turtle shell without the turtle. Eventually we are reduced to the hard shell of outward conformity, whether or not there is life left at all. Jesus called it hypocrisy. It is the equivalent of choosing selfless union without choosing diversity.

Like the whitewater canoeist, we will choose to deal carefully with the rapids, but we have to choose to get into our canoes and get going.

The Three-in-One passion of the Trinity invites us to choose both—to choose the storm.

The wonderful thing, whether we [my husband and I] are together or apart, is to know that he is in the world and that we belong together. And what I must learn is to love with all of me, giving all of me, and yet remain whole in myself. Any other kind of love is too demanding of the other; it takes rather than gives. To love so completely that you lose yourself in another person is not good. You are giving a weight, not the sense of lightness and light that loving someone should give. To love wholly, generously, and yet retain the core that makes you.

MADELEINE L'ENGLE[1]

CHAPTER EIGHT

The Storm in Our Lives

■

How do we truly love another person? How do I "love with all of me, giving all of me, and yet remain whole in myself"?

This question haunts all our loves—our love of God, our love of another human being, our love of work or play.

We vacillate so easily between giving ourselves away in the longing for union and tightly clinging to ourselves and our own agendas.

John and Maria have four boys. They love their boys dearly, but they were raised with very different backgrounds and have different (or should we say opposite and conflicting) parenting styles.

In John's boisterous upbringing, the loudest person won the argument. He believes boys should be parented with a heavy hand to show who's boss. He thinks they will learn character and fortitude through submission to authority.

Maria was brought up to placate her alcoholic father. Busy tiptoeing around her father's rage, she spent her childhood repressing her feelings. As an adult, she has worked hard to trust that her feelings are important. She's had to learn to challenge the authority of others in order to escape being a victim.

John and Maria love each other deeply. They want to find ways to work out their differences, but they have some deep conflicts around the boys. John thinks Maria is too lenient. She's spoiling the children. She lets them say what they feel and ask questions about her parental decisions.

Maria is convinced that John is damaging the children. His autocratic authority is almost abusive.

When are John and Maria supposed to give in to the other? When are they to insist on what they think is important? What is important for their children—to grow up submissive or to grow up expressive?

Is their conflict—full of passionate feelings—a part of their life with God, or is it keeping them from God? Do they need to get over the conflict or go deeper?

These questions are not academic or trivial. We face them every day of our lives. When do we say yes? When do we say no? The Trinity brings a storm of love that we can neither master nor control. Our lives, fueled by the power of the Spirit, become the focal point of paradox that only the Spirit can handle.

The storm is good! It is the creative, life-giving breath of the Spirit. Life can be breathtaking in the moments when something new and precious emerges—when our struggles seem to melt and coalesce into something more than we could have thought possible. But the storm challenges our demand for control.

We don't want the storm. A manageable Christian life would be easier. But the storm keeps us from losing our vibrant, growing edge. This is the eye of the Spirit wind in our lives, the place of real new growth.

If we can't manage the storm of love, we can become aware of it in the midst of daily life. It helps to know that the tensions and conflicting desires are a sign of the Spirit, not a sign of our immaturity or failure.

Like the disciples in the storm on the Sea of Galilee, we may not be able to calm the storm, but we can trust that Jesus is in the boat with us. We can relax and surrender to the Spirit when we know the storm is normal.

The life of God-the-Trinity creates at least three conflicting movements or paradoxes that confront us every day. I believe they are the source of much misunderstanding and confusion in our spiritual living.

We can fight these paradoxes forever, or we can embrace them and gain power for our passion.

THE STORM BETWEEN "SELF" AND "OTHERS"

In learning how to live with this rivering life within us, one of the very first and most persistent conundrums of the spiritual life will be to sort out the pull between "self" and "others." At times this unresolved tension blows wild and furious.

Passion would be a simple topic if we lived alone! *Carpe diem!* It would be easy to seize the day and suck the marrow out of life if we had no one else to worry about.

No one would be hurt by our self-centeredness; no one else would suffer the consequences of our actions. One of the most frequent reasons passion is discouraged is because it affects other people.

The storm of love between the Persons of the Trinity—the tension between union and uniqueness—sounds lofty, exciting, and wonderful when we think about love and about God. It takes on a different hue when it comes to who's going to drive the kids to soccer.

We face conflict around finances and family goals. Work challenges us with choices about when to go along with the boss and when to stand up for what we think is important. The tensions inherent in friendships challenge us to either ignore or confront when something is bothering us.

When is it appropriate to insist on the things that are important to you? If you let go of them, will you create a positive sense of harmony or will you lose a bit of your soul?

We're invited to bring this storm into the loving intimacy of the Trinity. We don't need to avoid the storm, we need to go deeper. We can listen to our passion in order to find what God is saying to us in these difficult times.

When John and Maria look deeper into their parenting conflict, they might discover they have the same goals for their children but different ways of achieving them. Perhaps John will discover he's too narrow and needs to let go of his fears of losing control of his children. Perhaps Maria will need to surrender her own hurts from childhood so that they don't distort her parenting.

They would never discover these things by suppressing the passion of the conflict. By opening up to God in the face of the conflict they can grow and change and still remain passionate.

My wife Miriam and I have had to face this never-ending pull between "self" and "others" in a particularly poignant way. We have lived with her breast cancer diagnosis for fourteen years.

Five years ago, the doctors told us that Miriam's breast cancer had metastasized. This terrible news sent us both into isolated pools of pain and grief.

Our marriage has been a very special gift to both of us. Now it seemed threatened. Miriam likened it to going downriver in a canoe and suddenly being overturned. We had each fallen out on opposite sides of the canoe and were simply struggling to keep our own head above water.

I went to counseling at the cancer center. On my first visit, my counselor Jan asked if I thought these last years could be the best years of our marriage. The question floored me. No, frankly, I didn't think so!

But with almost twenty years of experience working with cancer patients, Jan assured me that it was possible to grow into even deeper intimacy in our final time together.

As we've lived through these past five years, Miriam and I have proved the counselor right in remarkable ways. But it didn't begin that way. I had two instinctive reactions. One was to focus on Miriam's needs; the other was to avoid the situation and take care of myself. Neither reaction, alone, was healthy.

When we first discovered that Miriam's cancer had metastasized, she was in a very vulnerable place. Emotionally, I wanted to withdraw. Her chemo treatments, loss of hair, her uncertain future, and my grief—all symbolized an ocean of pain I couldn't deal with. I didn't actually leave, but I became emotionally distant, and that was difficult for Miriam.

Over time, I began to come to terms with the diagnosis. My desire grew to take my counselor's words to heart. I wanted these next few years to be the best years of Miriam's life.

As Miriam began to experience bouts of profound pain and loss of energy, my attention and energy became focused on taking care of her and picking up extra work around the house.

Long-term, an orientation to Miriam's needs and the denial of my own didn't work either. In my determination to be caring and helpful to Miriam, I ended up losing my own place in the communion of our relationship.

I could easily have become more her nurse than her spouse, more her caretaker than her lover. Romantic passion gets confused in a caretaker role. It's hard to feel passionate about a patient, and I wanted to stay passionate.

My counselor kept pushing me to take time for myself. Gradually I was forced to follow her advice, but I felt terribly selfish and negligent in doing so. I've been learning to dance between two realities: when to focus on Miriam's needs and when to care for my own. There simply are no "answer" books to tell us how to make these decisions — no verse of Scripture that carries a generic application. It has taken me deeply into my dependence on God to continue to pray through these choices.

Sometimes I've had to choose to be alone, even when I was afraid I might disappoint Miriam. Sometimes I've had to choose to stay present to her in her pain when my whole being wanted to run as far away as possible.

Through the agony of these uncertain choices, I have grown and our intimacy has deepened. I'm learning to trust that God is with me.

Most important, I'm discovering that I'm not finally choosing between Miriam or me. All of these choices are really about how best to express God's life in my particular circumstances. They can ultimately be the best for both of us.

I can offer to God, in this storm, my desire to be true to the goodness of God's life in me—in my passion to live my own life and in my passion to be in loving union with Miriam.

Mothers feel the pain of this storm of tension between their own needs and the needs of their family. Perhaps in a more profound way than other people in our culture, they have been socialized to be nurturers at the expense of their own needs.

Often in the past, women became the passive, selfless wife. What they needed went unrecognized and they became slaves to the complex agendas of family and children, as though this was their God-given duty.

Today, the challenge is often compounded. Mothers find themselves strapped with impossible demands. Now the expectation is that they will raise brilliant, secure, happy children; maintain a magazine image of a gorgeous home; keep themselves looking like a seductive model; and succeed in a demanding career. Of course nobody achieves this, but the expectations make them feel bad about themselves! The thought of going back to school or taking an hour a day to do something as frivolous as being alone with their thoughts can create a family crisis.

Men often face the dilemma of self and others too, especially

Christian men. They feel obligated by the weight of guilt and duty messages that call them to self-sacrifice.

Between the demands of work and church and home they end up giving themselves away to other people's expectations. In the end, these normal places of passion become places of death by duty.

Ironically, two people in the same marriage can often feel they are each doing the lion's share of sacrificing for the marriage and getting nowhere. It's easy, then, to drift away into other areas of passion as a substitute: fitness, hobbies, or perhaps something dark like pornography or a critical spirit.

Must married people face the loss of self to keep the marriage intact? Must they slowly die to life in order to maintain union?

When we give up ourselves to keep tranquility at any cost, we lose the gift we bring to the marriage. A plain vanilla marriage experience, reduced to the lowest common denominator, is not a viable answer.

The alternative, repeated over and over like a road show these days, isn't viable either. Marriages break up as people break out of the suffocating trap of self-sacrifice. They clamor to "find" themselves, to resurrect their lives and become passionate again. They conclude that it was the marriage that killed them. Therefore, they must get out if they are to live again.

Let's be clear. The storm is real. We can try to avoid the storm by denying our needs for the sake of unity, or we can deny the mystery of unity by insisting on our own needs, even at the other person's expense.

Why is it that, almost invariably, we end up taking one side or the other? We vacillate between altruism in the name of Christianity and a self-fulfillment in the name of psychology.

Christian spirituality has often chosen the lopsided tack of negating self and choosing for others. There is good precedent for it. Jesus laid aside His garments, took up the towel and washed the disciples' feet, and told us to do the same to one another (John 13).

John comments many years later, "This is how we know what love is: Jesus Christ laid down his life for us. And we ought to lay down our lives for our brothers [and sisters]" (1 John 3:16-17).

In the telling and retelling, Christianity often became defined only, or at least primarily, as self-sacrifice — giving up oneself for the sake of others. In the milieu I grew up in, it was called "the crucified life." *Agape* was the paragon of love, not because it celebrates generosity, but because it was interpreted as self-abasement. We hear Jesus' command to wash each other's feet, but we don't read John's profound preface to the foot-washing scene. There, John says, "Jesus knew that the Father had put all things under his power, and that he had come from God and was returning to God" (13:3). Jesus' act of "self-sacrifice" was an act out of His own fullness. He could offer Himself to His disciples because He was secure in Himself and in the foundation of His person in God.

Not surprisingly, modern psychology has often championed the overthrow of altruism to crown a new monarch—"self." To some degree, this emphasis was an important corrective. It sought to redress the pathology caused by a distortion of Christianity that downplayed selfhood or even self-respect. But without understanding the reality of our Trinitarian life, the cure is at least as lethal as the disease.

Psychology has grown up within a model of the self as an isolated, independent unit of meaning.[2] The individual, and the importance of self-realization, self-actualization, and self-esteem have been its focus. In the end, psychology has often been little more than a worship of self in our individualistic culture.

James Houston penetratingly observed that our one-way emphasis on the individual has collapsed into a culture of narcissism.[3] And, we might add, victims.

When we try to resolve the storm between the self and others by choosing one or the other, we lose the wonderful, passionate interplay of relationship at the heart of the Trinity.

I don't know how you face the tension between self and others in your own life. I cannot say what you should choose. You might be tempted to give yourself away; you might be tempted to dominate others. I only know that God is with you in the uncertain choices.

The passion of the Trinity calls us to accept the paradox of both. When we choose self-sacrifice, the relationship is crippled because there's only one person—one pole—around which the passion can swing. Choosing for self at the expense of the other is just as detrimental. Either way there are no longer two people in the dance.

THE STORM BETWEEN "CONTENTMENT" AND "DESIRE"
A second great paradox, never fully settled in Christian spirituality, is the seeming contradiction between the craving that characterizes our

desire and the contentment that is so often seen as the paragon of Christian maturity.

Contentment gets equated with the loss of passion. If we could just get rid of desire, we would live a much more peaceful and holy Christian life. Paul spoke in Philippians 4:12 about learning to be content in all circumstances. He said, "I know what it is to be in need, and I know what it is to have plenty. I have learned the secret of being content in any and every situation, whether well fed or hungry, whether living in plenty or in want."

The desert Christians spoke of the goal of *apatheia*, the conquering of sinful passions. Often this has been understood as coming to the place of no desire. But the translation of the word, *apatheia*, should not be "without desire" but rather "freedom from the tyranny of desire."[4]

The idea of getting rid of desire denies the Incarnation. God chose to come into the world and take on a body with its desires. Ridding ourselves of desire as something evil is closer to a Buddhist notion than a Christian one. The answer to distorted desire is not to get rid of the passion but to discover the meaning of our desire in the presence of God.

Miriam and I often face this tension between contentment and desire. Miriam wants contentment. She likes organization and closure. She enjoys music like Mozart's that soothes her. I like openness and possibility. I want music more like Van Morrison's to get my heart going. In the mystery of marriage, we are finding a richer intimacy by honoring both desires.

People who thrive on change are often criticized for being malcontent. If they trusted God they wouldn't be so "antsy" about life. They would be content to settle into life and take it as it comes.

People who thrive on stability are often criticized for being a stick-in-the-mud. If they trusted God, they would be willing to risk growth and change.

In reality, these contrary movements are expressions of the flowing love of the Trinity. The need for contentment and stability echoes the inward movement into union. The need for flux and change echoes the movement outward into plurality and diversity.

As we grow spiritually, we learn to embrace both movements. Each is an expression of our desire for God and each is a part of our love relationship with God.

Our goal is not to be stable, or changing, but to experience God in each. Rather than focusing on one and rejecting the other as a threat, we are open to God, whose life includes both.

God may lead us to stop seeking the fulfillment of our desire, just as David had to relinquish his desire to build a temple for God. God may also lead us to stretch out in desire for something beyond us, like Paul, when he was counseled to stay in Antioch and insisted on going to Jerusalem anyway.

If we continually open our hearts to both, and hold each with an open hand, God will lead us. We may experience a growing contentment as the focus of our desires are brought into an integration with the life of God. We may also experience a growth of desire as we learn to be attuned to God's life bubbling up as a gift within us.

Often we will experience both at the same time!

THE STORM BETWEEN "RENUNCIATION" AND "AFFIRMATION"

Closely related to the paradox between contentment and desire is the seeming contradiction between two great emphases in the history of Christian spirituality. Some writers emphasize the need to renounce everything in order to know God. Others emphasize the fact that God comes to us in many ways and that we are to receive the presence of God through them all. It is another expression of the storm of Trinitarian passion.

The first is the way of renunciation; the second is the way of affirmation. These two major streams, known as apophatic and the kataphatic traditions,[5] have remained in tension in spiritual thinking throughout the history of the church. Both are central themes of our spirituality.

Charles Williams, a friend of C. S. Lewis, said,

> The one Way [kataphatic] was to affirm all things orderly until the universe throbbed with vitality; the other [apophatic] to reject all things until there was nothing anywhere but he. The Way of Affirmation was to develop great art and romantic love and marriage and philosophy and social justice; the Way of Rejection was to break out continually in the profound mystical documents of the soul, the records of the great psychological masters of Christendom.[6]

Should our spirituality be one of withdrawal or engagement? Which is more spiritual, to pray in a closet or cook meals for the homeless?

Everyday life raises an unending list of questions like these, and we can get caught debating whether one is more important than the other. Williams said that renunciation and affirmation are not contradictory. Rather, "Both methods, the Affirmative Way and the Negative Way, were to co-exist; one might almost say, to co-inhere, since each was to be the key of the other."[7]

Embracing both sides of the paradox is important to Christian devotion. We face the paradox because we are in loving relationship with the Trinity. In the mystery of God we experience God both ways. In our renunciations we experience God in union with our souls. In our affirmations we experience the variety of God's presence around us. Each is the key to the other because, by itself, either side of the paradox becomes a distortion.

Self without the other is narcissistic. Contentment without desire produces a dead institution. Apophatic detachment without the affirmation of God's presence in the created world becomes body-denying and world-hating.

When we realize that the life we're invited to enjoy is Trinitarian, we can embrace the fact that we will be caught up in the swirl. We won't need to resolve these paradoxes or choose one side or the other. We are called to express God's Spirit in ways that are unique to our own spiritual journey.

At times we will be called to choose one or the other. You might be facing such a contradiction of choices right now. Perhaps you're wondering whether it's right to quit your job and go back to school. It fits your deep desire, but how will it affect the family?

In these times, you can only trust that by holding on to the value of both sides of the paradox you are staying open to the Holy Spirit. If you stay open to God in these choices, and choose the best you can, you will live out the passion of the Trinity within the freedom you have been given.

What if we took the time to grow by following our passions with an open heart to God? What if we embraced the storm by refusing to choose one side or the other? We might find our spiritual lives more challenging. We wouldn't repress our passion, and perhaps we'd avoid the emotional eruptions that can scorch the landscape of our lives. Maybe some people wouldn't choose an extramarital affair, which is really a distorted attempt to find life again. Maybe others wouldn't condemn themselves for the way passion runs strong within them.

Maybe we'd recognize that we're truly free to choose self-denial in this moment because there will be other times when we rightly choose for our own needs.

What if we accepted Ruusbroec's vision of God as a storm of love, a turmoil of passions? What if you and I opened our hearts more and more to the God who loves us and lives in us? Could it produce fruit we hadn't dreamed of? Could it be the best thing that ever happened to us, providing life that is deeper and richer than we ever hoped it could be?

If we're going to participate in the life of the Trinity, we must embrace the tension of creativity, the turmoil of change and growth. We must learn to embrace the storm as good. Like the river Jesus promised, it breaks through the dams of our encrusted lives and brings newness and healing into the world around us.

God freely created us so that we might know, love, and serve him in this life and be happy with him forever. God's purpose in creating us is to draw forth from us a response of love and service here on earth, so that we may attain our goal of everlasting happiness with him in heaven.

All the things in this world are gifts of God, created for us, to be the means by which we can come to know him better, love him more surely, and serve him more faithfully.

As a result, we ought to appreciate and use these gifts of God insofar as they help us toward our goal of loving service and union with God. But insofar as any created things hinder our progress toward our goal, we ought to let them go.

ST. IGNATIUS OF LOYOLA[1]

CHAPTER NINE

Enjoying the Current

■

A MAN—I'LL CALL HIM RYAN—FOUND IT DIFFICULT TO GET UP EACH morning. He was afraid to go to work. Ryan enjoyed his work and was good at what he did. The problem was his boss, a bitter and vindictive man who had intimidated and bullied Ryan until he'd lost all sense of his own worth on the job.

Ryan wondered what he could do to fight through the fear he experienced every morning and get up with some sense of his own goodness. In talking about it, he mentioned that if he jumped right out of bed and began singing, it helped him to get out of the paralysis and get going. He felt silly saying it, but it was the only help he had found.

All of us have experienced small but important choices like this. We've said the big yes to God's life. We're on the way. What, now, are the choices that can help us say yes to the current in practical ways?

For Ryan, singing was a way to break through the incredible barriers that seemed to block God's life from emerging.

What choices can free up and support the life of God in your own experience? With this question we will explore the place of the spiritual disciplines in our lives.

SPIRITUAL DISCIPLINES

Many Christians might answer that the way to nurture the spiritual life is through Bible study, prayer, and service. Someone else, familiar with the spiritual writers of the past, might include disciplines such as silence, solitude, and fasting. A monk might add the classic monastic vows of poverty, chastity, and obedience.

What are spiritual disciplines? And how do they fit with a spirituality of Trinitarian passion?

In his book *The Spirit of the Disciplines*, Dallas Willard insists on a spirituality that accepts our bodies. Willard baldly asserts that Christianity, and especially Protestantism, lost much of the significance of following Jesus and living a transformed life when it let go of the importance of spiritual disciplines involving the body and retained only a mental faith.[2]

For some — often the people I end up working with — the term "spiritual disciplines" is enough to chill their blood. The spiritual disciplines of their experience, based in a spiritual culture of fear and control, seemed to focus on abstinence and withdrawal. Now these people have had their fill of being told what to give up to be a good Christian.

Willard defines spiritual disciplines in a broader and more healthy way. He says, "A discipline for the spiritual life is, when the dust of history is blown away, nothing but an activity undertaken to bring us into more effective cooperation with Christ and his Kingdom."[3] Spiritual disciplines are a matter of taking "appropriate measures," Willard says, "to bring our whole selves in cooperation with the divine order, so we can experience more and more a vision and power beyond ourselves."[4]

In developing his definition, Willard argues that our desires are fundamentally good, even though they are terribly skewed. Willard's sense of cooperation with the Divine order is simply another way of expressing the emphasis in this book on openness to the river of Divine Life.

A spirituality that embraces passion and the goodness of desire takes a rich, holistic view of spiritual disciplines. When our desires are considered fundamentally suspect or evil, spiritual disciplines can easily get focused on abstinence, withdrawal, or control. But when we accept the goodness of our desires, then we dare not focus exclusively on withdrawal. Cooperation with the divine order must include those practices that help us open up to and revel in the current of God's Life as much as they safeguard or control it.

Spiritual disciplines are not an end in themselves. They must be linked to the presence of Divine Life deep within us. They are valuable only to the degree that they help us celebrate and channel the Life of God rising in us.

Jean Illsley Clarke, who has done so much work teaching parenting skills, talks about both nurture and structure. If we're going to parent our children in a wholesome, well-rounded way, she says, we need to encourage our children and provide limits. We need to welcome children into life as well as say no to the things that are inappropriate for them.

Parenting a two-year-old toddler would be a very discouraging responsibility if it focused exclusively on limiting the child's activities. We want more for our children than control. We want them to flourish. Because we treasure our child's life for its incredible goodness, we put up with dealing with the ongoing struggle with limits.

The same is true of a person's spiritual life. Our passion needs both nurture and structure if it's going to be lived in a healthy and mature way. If we ignore the current and spend all our time making sure the banks are strong and secure, we won't have to worry about the flood. The current will have dried up while we were busy sandbagging.

Sometimes fasting is important. At times it may even be important to increase the length of time we fast. When the life within us needs focus, fasting can give us the freedom and clarity to sharpen the direction of our desire. When we become enslaved to our passion, fasting can free us up to remember that our life is far bigger than any specific fulfillment.

If we get addicted to reading, fasting frees us to discover the many ways that life is more than the intellectual stimulation or vicarious experience that comes through reading. Fasting frees us to touch life directly once again.

Yet, that's not the whole story. When the life within us needs encouragement to flow freely, fasting may be a hindrance. Then fasting may become a way of avoiding the very thing that will bring healing and integration to us.

Life is the issue here—cooperation with God's order. Fasting in itself is nothing. It has no inherent value. It is only valuable as it helps us to treasure and channel the life of God in us.

Silence is nothing. Bible reading is nothing. Jesus made that clear in John 5. "You diligently study the Scriptures because you think that by them you possess eternal life. These are the Scriptures that testify about me, yet you refuse to come to me to have life" (John 5:39-40).

Paul testified that his whole life of religious discipline ended up to be nothing more than garbage without a transforming experience of Jesus (Philippians 3:7-11).

When attuned to the life of God in us, the disciplines are of value. They prod us to be aware of God's life and to be intentional about how we're responding to the gift.

They ask us to be specific about our behaviors, not just sincere in our intentions. But they are only instrumental. Without the flowing of life, they are hollow.

When linked to the goodness of passion as the presence of God in our soul, Willard's definition of spiritual disciplines can be expanded to provide a balanced perspective that is so often lost. We can say:

> Spiritual disciplines are the choices we make to nurture and support the Life of God emerging within us *and* to resist becoming captive to the ways we can distort the power of this life.

We can nurture the goodness of life in many ways. We can say yes to God's life by meditating on Scripture. Colossians 3:15-17 encourages us to allow the peace of Christ to rule in our hearts, to let the Word of God dwell richly in us, and to sing to the Lord with gratitude in our hearts.

We can pause throughout the day to cherish a phrase from Scripture like "Abba, Father" or "Though a mother may forget her children, I will not forget you!" We can say yes to God's life by going for a walk or listening to music.

One woman I know lights a candle while she makes dinner. Although she's too busy to stop, she can remember, before God, the people she's concerned about that day.

These choices to say yes to God's life are as important as choices to say no to distortions like excessive eating or addictive TV watching. They are valuable ways of nourishing the life of God in us. They remind us of what is true behind the veil of everyday events. Scripture tells us the truth about God and ourselves that we wouldn't otherwise know, and our resultant gratitude keeps us openhearted to what God is bringing to us.

Perhaps, with all our overlays of religiosity, even the word *discipline* gets misunderstood. I often prefer instead to use the word *support.* I find it much more positive.

What choices can you make to support the emergence of God's life in you? What choices support the directing of this life in appropriate actions?

These are questions that go to the heart of our choices for spiritual transformation. The choices may be informal or formal. They may be occasional or habitual. A one-time choice to cherish the life of God in you by going for a walk and being grateful for the sheer pleasure of being alive is a wonderful "discipline."

You may make your choice every day, twice a week, or only occasionally. The number of times, or the consistency, doesn't qualify as better or more effective. It is the accumulation of all these small choices that begins to make the difference.

In attending to the presence of God's life in us, we can be intentional about two things. First, we can discover and enjoy the ways in which God's life is coming to us. Second, we can clear away the things that dam the current.

DISCOVERING AND ENJOYING GOD'S LIFE

By its very nature, the choice to pay attention to the presence of God's life in us is more a passive, yet receptive, attitude. We're not trying to generate our own life or enthusiasm for God. We're simply looking for the ways God is already surprising us with life.

This attentive, quiet spirit is a profoundly important antidote to the spirituality of achievement that afflicts so many churches today. In a spirituality that focuses on what we do, the onus is on us to create the dynamism of our spiritual life by trying harder or doing more.

This is the basis of the unending "challenge" to be more committed, more faithful, more devoted. It is the bane of much sincere preaching—a bottomless pit of expectation in which people's spiritual struggles can always be blamed on themselves.

A more receptive attitude enables us to relax a bit, let go of control, and embark on an adventure of discovery.

This attitude invites us to let go of control and follow the current of

God's life. We do not determine the flow. Rather, we "go with the flow." We learn the art of paying attention. We discover rather than produce the ways in which God's life is flowing in us.

Silence and solitude are valuable ways to sharpen our wits so that we can see the movement of God in our lives. Taking time for silence can be the spiritual equivalent of time spent tracking an animal or watching for birds. We create spacious times to be attentive to all the little sounds or marks we wouldn't typically notice in everyday life.

The ancient method of *Lectio Divina* is reading Scripture and other devotional writings in a way that allows truth to soak into us. We read the text slowly until one word or phrase strikes us. Then we stay with that morsel, turning it around and praying with it as long as it is alive to us. Then we move on again, slowly.

We can take a passage—for instance, Ephesians 3:16-19—and begin to open up more and more deeply to God's life at the core of our being. In this section of Scripture, Paul said,

> I pray that out of [God's] glorious riches he may strengthen you with power through his Spirit in your inner being, so that Christ may dwell in your hearts through faith. And I pray that you, being rooted and established in love, may have power, together with all the saints, to grasp how wide and long and high and deep is the love of Christ, and to know this love that surpasses knowledge—that you may be filled to the measure of all the fullness of God.

I invite you to notice three things in this passage. First, this life-giving connection takes place inside us. Second, we are rooted in love, a whole universe of love. And third, in the love of Christ we are filled with the fullness of God.

Now take some time to pray with this passage. Read and reread the passage slowly, opening yourself prayerfully to these fundamental truths about the life of God in your soul. Spend time in silence and then listen for your response to the passage.

Attend to your emotional as well as intellectual response. You might experience anything from boredom or fear to delight. Offer your response to God and then allow God space to respond to you either through a thought or an inner awareness.

Can you hear this passage over and over, until it becomes as soothing as a creek running nearby? Can you be enveloped with the truth that you are loved by God at the core of your being? Slowly, this process of attentiveness affirms the presence of God's life in you. It is a profound choice for the current.

For many people, however, the guidance given in Colossians 3— that is, to let God's Word dwell in us richly—has been overlaid with multiple layers of guilt and condemnation. These people can no longer hear Scripture as a fresh, living word from God. Over time, they have developed almost an allergic reaction to the Bible.

In such cases, it would seem wise to me for that person to start with his or her lived experience—practical everyday life—and then go from there. The person might be assured of God's love by being alone in nature or by attending to the love people have for their own children.

This may seem overly accommodating. But when I begin to doubt its validity, I am reminded that this is nothing more than reenacting the model of Jesus' life.

Jesus came to us in our need, rather than making us come to Him. If we pay attention to the Incarnation, recognizing that Jesus emptied Himself for us (Philippians 2:5-11), we won't be so harsh with others who can't come the way we think necessary.

If you experience this kind of reaction to Scripture, I invite you to go outdoors into the created world. There in the sensuous experience of nature, you can breathe deeply. You can accept yourself as part of the complex web of creation. You can allow creation to call forth the presence of God within your soul.

It feels something akin to what I imagine the psalmist meant in Psalm 42: "Deep calls to deep." In a very simple and powerful way, creation often calls forth the life of God in us. In the simplicity of creation, there is no complication, no institutional barriers, nothing but God calling to God.

This simple step, allowing oneself to be caressed by the goodness of a crocus in the snow or the soft moss hiding the trickle of a small spring, often awakens people to their own goodness and to their desire for God. It brings an awareness that God is within them, just like God is present within the created world. As part of the dance of creation, they can begin to feel their own steps in the grand rhythm.

When we begin to be rooted in love again, we can reopen Scripture with new eyes. We can see beyond the ways we have read that focused only on guilt and condemnation, and Scripture will come alive again.

Another way to awaken to God's love might be to recall a time when you felt a deep, unshakable love for your child, or remember a person who offered that kind of love to you. Allow this experience to draw you toward God as an "icon" of God's ongoing love for you. Let it be your prayer.

Relish the moments when you experience love. Pay attention to the ways you resist letting yourself emotionally rest in that kind of love from God. Those places of resistance can then become a prayer for healing so that the life can be free to flow.

One person I know finds this kind of love from a sibling with Down's syndrome. His brother simply accepts him and enjoys being with him without any expectation at all. The "handicap" has become a gift—an icon of God's love.

As we become familiar with the truth that we are held in love, we can pay attention to the ways in which God's life might already be coming to us. One way of doing this is to think about what it is we look forward to—something that brings us great anticipation or joy.

A game of squash? If so, then feel the goodness of God in the lightning speed of a smash and countersmash. Think of it like Eric Liddell in the movie *Chariots of Fire* when he spoke of feeling God's pleasure when he ran.

Perhaps for you the anticipated moment is a few minutes alone by the window, or coffee with a friend. Allow all of these times to be sacred. Relax and attend to the goodness of God's life inside you. Allow God into those moments, and above all let God welcome you into those moments as well.

One woman who came to me suffered terribly with physical disabilities. Her plight was compounded by feelings of needing to be a perfect mom. She had no time, no place, no energy to pray. Her whole life seemed to be a blur of requirements, of things that she must do for others while coping with her pain.

When I asked what she enjoyed and looked forward to each week, she said that she loved to swim. It wasn't hard on her back, and she enjoyed the feeling of being enveloped by the water. During the quiet moments of doing those boring laps, she experienced a few minutes of pure freedom. For a brief time she had nothing to worry about or feel responsible for.

I invited her to allow that time to be a celebration with God. Here at least, she was in touch with herself and with God. She could luxuriate in the freedom from responsibility, luxuriate in the water that caressed her body. She could imagine God surrounding her and invigorating her like the water. She could allow it all to be her prayer. It could be a very tactile way of experiencing the goodness of God's presence.

This suggestion was a revolutionary thought for her. She fought it for a long time, wallowing in the demands of performance and perfection. It seemed strange to "pray by swimming." But gradually she opened up to receive life instead of trying to make it happen.

We have been so programmed to think of prayer as the words we say rather than something we experience with God. Many times there are no words, just the presence of our desire to be with God and the trust that God is present with us.

This woman's heart was right. She was conscientious, but she needed some place to start again. She needed to get in touch with the way God was already bringing life to her. The pool gave her that opportunity. She didn't have to add it to her schedule. She didn't have to crank up some extra discipline. She simply discovered God in her everyday experience and celebrated the find.

There is an inexhaustible list of ways you can begin to discover and celebrate the presence of God in your life. One woman I know discovered that a warm soaking bath at night was a time for her to be with God.

The "how" is not so important. The attitude of anticipation and discovery, rather than an attitude of control and responsibility, is the crucial thing. We want to keep the focus on the current rather than on the particular way we go about attending to it.

When you've made simple discoveries of God's presence with you, then you can go back to Scripture and find fresh meaning and have your experience of God reinforced and refined. But until you have some connection, Scripture often just remains words.

CLEARING AWAY THINGS THAT DAM THE CURRENT

The second way to make choices to go with the current of the river is to deal with the blocks that dam the current and keep it from flowing freely through us and out into life.

This emphasis is not so passive. It's just plain, hard work. Challenging the layers of fear and shame that inhibit the flow addresses the old reasons why we placed those blocks there in the first place. This can be painful to face. It calls for healing that we may never have wanted to admit we needed.

We get used to the numbness of a squelched life. We don't even know how these blocks keep us from enjoying the life of God in us. Instead of a river, a trickle becomes normal.

Last summer, my friend, Gord, and I canoed part of the Elk River in southeastern British Columbia. We had already fished the river in spots and decided that, before we left, we would like to canoe the whole stretch.

Record floods that spring had done some amazing things. New channels had been cut. Massive boulders that had created deep pools the year before were now miles downstream, and large spruce trees were scattered everywhere.

The water level was low, and the littered riverscape was the only thing that made the trip at all dangerous. We needed to be careful of hidden debris and logjams that let the current through but could pin a canoe or a dumped canoeist in no time.

It was an idyllic afternoon, and we lazed our way downstream. At one place we came to a huge logjam. When we went to investigate, we discovered to our chagrin and laughter that the river ended right there. It braided off to the west and to the east, but there was no real flow. It just kind of spread out into the surrounding lowland.

We had to go searching for the river! Finally, a hundred yards downstream we found a part of the river that had branched off above the logjam. This was a new experience for both of us. We had lost canoes and paddles and life jackets before, but never the river itself!

So it is with many Christians. There's plenty of life to be had, but it's been dammed up and diverted in a thousand rivulets.

We block the current of God's life in us by the defense mechanisms we've learned to use as coping strategies in the face of life's difficulties. Fear, guilt, shame, or resentment cause us to hide, to dam the current of passion within, and refuse to enter the dance of life.

These issues of unresolved or false shame and guilt come from distorted expectations of who we should be. Instead of believing we should be what God is creating us to be through the flow of His life within us, we think we should be something else. We've come to believe we should be something our parents, society, or we have convinced ourselves we should be. Because we're not rooted in the truth of God's loving presence in our lives, we always feel alienated and not good enough. Our identity is rooted in something outside of us. When we're cut off from our innermost life, we get into an endless round of failed attempts at life, which compound the discouragement and the shame.

In a very real way, these blocks are nothing more than passion turned in on itself. The very intensity of the fear or shame is a measure of our passion, but it has been distorted into a protective mechanism rather than released into life.

These emotions are often interrelated. We can't always separate them out into neat distinctions, but we do know that we experience a loss of flow, a diminution of the passion of God's life.

Many people have lived with these blocks in very deep ways. Guilt is a given. And when they get past the guilt, they uncover a whole substrata of shame that has paralyzed them for years.

Shame makes them feel that the life they were given by God is unacceptable, not even presentable. They have nothing worthwhile to offer others. They may as well keep their mouths shut. In hiding from life they think they're doing the world a favor.

While they may feel safer this way, they inadvertently dam the life of God that wants to flow through them and become a gift to others.

What specific steps can a person take to clear away the blocks? What small choices can we make to move into a more free-flowing experience of God's presence through our lives and out to others?

For me, the movement has largely been to practice receiving God's love in the middle of my life experiences—in the midst of its goodness and its mess. It's one thing to know that God loves me when I'm doing well; it's quite another to know that God loves me in my weaknesses and neuroses.

That is the true test of love. When we're doing well, we never know whether God loves us because of who we are or because of how we're doing. But when we're in the middle of our struggle and we discover that God loves us there, too, then we really know we're loved.

In the end, I come to the place of being tired of the downward spiral and I sit down and say to myself, either God loves me or He doesn't. If I am loved, it means that I'm loved as is and not because I have it all together.

In that moment, right in the middle of terribly negative feelings,

I can choose to receive and believe in God's tender love for me. I can trust that God knows the worst about me and deeply loves me anyway.

This process is like surreptitiously sneaking around the dam to get in touch with the flow of God's life upstream. I can trust, in those moments, that God's love will break through the blocks or flow around them. The current will get through anyhow.

My spiritual director used to say, "Name the fear, own it as your own fear, and then offer it to God. You can't fix it anyway, but you can at least stop running from it, and you can give it to God."

Another practical step is to find relatively harmless places in which to practice being passionate. If we tend to "stuff" our lives because we're afraid we'll make a mess of them, we can practice safe ways of getting in touch with life. It may sound silly, but it's been a major stepping-stone for me.

I have found that the world of creation is a great place to practice being passionate. I've danced on the top of a mountain ridge. I've yelled all kinds of feelings of rage, shame, and betrayal out in the woods. The trees just don't seem to mind. They don't run away from me, and when I'm exhausted from my emotional outbursts, the grass, the willows, the flies and ants are still there, unperturbed by it all. They are an ongoing sign to me of God's unconditional presence in the midst of my struggles.

I have found "safe" friends with whom I can begin to share my experiences. As I've opened up little pieces of my fears and shame to others, it's been a revelation to realize they don't condemn me. In fact, they're touched when I'm willing to be open with them.

I have also journaled my anger to avoid exploding it on other people.

While I have spoken mainly about how I've chosen to face my blocks in safe, indirect ways, I believe that, at times, we will be called to face these things directly, even though we don't feel prepared for them.

We don't always get the choice of time and situation. We find ourselves cornered by life, and we realize that if we want to live, really live, we have to take the risk, even though we feel inadequate to the task. In those times we must simply offer our lives to God and do the best we can, knowing that God is with us, under us, before us, and behind us. God will carry us whether we're aware of it or not.

Often we discover that we can't go back anyway. We've had enough of a taste of life to realize we can't go back to being dead to our passion again. Each time we experience the joy of God's life we confirm in a small way that we can never return to the old, dried-up life again. In 1 Peter 2:2, the apostle hinted at this attitude. Even in the face of their terrible suffering, Peter said, "Like newborn babies, crave pure spiritual milk, so that by it you may grow up in your salvation, *now that you have tasted that the Lord is good*" [emphasis mine].

Lord, how do I let go when I'm so unsure
of things? I'm unsure of your will, and I'm
unsure of myself. . . . That really isn't the
problem at all, is it? The truth of the matter
is I hate the very idea of letting go. I really
want to be in control. No, I need to be in
control. That's it, isn't it? I'm afraid to give
up control, afraid of what might happen.
Heal my fear, Lord.

How good of you to reveal my blind spots
even in the midst of my stumbling attempts
to pray. Thank You!

But now what do I do? How do I give up
control? Jesus, please, teach me your way of
relinquishment. —Amen.

RICHARD FOSTER[1]

CHAPTER TEN

SECURING THE BANKS

∎

LOOK DOWNSTREAM NOW. WAY DOWNSTREAM. WHERE IS THIS RIVER flowing? What is the goal of all our passion and desire?

Paul said in the book of Romans, "From [God] and through him and to him are all things" (11:36). The goal is God. Like a river flowing to the ocean, eventually all vitality and desire returns in the great circle of love back to God.

God's life flows through us so that the beauty of God's creative and healing purposes might be accomplished in the world. Caught up in this wonderful swirling love, we offer the expression of our passion as our love gift back to God.

When we are convinced that our deepest desires come from God and are given to us in love, we can hold ultimate fulfillment with an open hand. The longing itself is good, whether or not it ever gets fulfilled!

This is the love relationship underlying the words that follow immediately after Paul's great expression of the goal of our passion. He began Romans 12 with the famous lines, "Do not conform any longer to the pattern of this world, but be transformed by the renewing of your mind. Then you will be able to test and approve what

God's will is—his good, pleasing and perfect will" (verse 2).

Every river needs a channel. So it is with the river of God's life. We are called to make choices, sometimes excruciating choices, to create the banks that will sustain our passion and keep it flowing in the right direction for the long haul.

So we must make choices for the banks as well as for the current. Anything less than this goal corrupts our passion and pollutes our world. We need to look at the reasons for creating healthy, appropriate banks for our lives. Then we can explore the kinds of choices that can help to make this happen.

GOOD REASONS FOR DISCIPLINED CHOICES

Have we truly affirmed the current of God's life in us? Sometimes the deepest test of our trust in the goodness of our passion as the expression of the ever-present life of God comes in our ability to say no to what would keep our passion from being a true love gift back to God.

Once we've come to trust the flowing of life within us, we can trust that choices to forgo the fulfillment of passion are not the negation of passion. Choices for the banks, which curb and direct our passion, do not squelch or deny our life.

Saying no is never an end in itself. Life will still emerge. We do not make choices to shape or restrain our passion because deprivation is somehow seen as more spiritual. Rather, we make choices for the banks in order to experience the greater good of our desire. If we've come to treasure our passion, we don't want to settle for anything less.

Passion suffers unless it is ordered and directed. Structure keeps the river of God from dissipating and being diverted from its true goal. It holds the vigor of our passion so that we can live our lives with power and integrity. It honors the long-term vision of seeing our desire flow back to God in love.

There are three major reasons to say no in the present. We may need to say no to curb the evil tendencies we all struggle with inside. We may need to say no so that we don't hurt others. And we may need to say no because the way we want to express our passion may be premature.

Curbing Our Own Evil Tendencies

The most obvious reason for ordering our passion is that we'll run amok if left to ourselves. We have the uncanny ability to distort our good passion into hurtful and evil ends. Some people might object to that statement by saying, "If this is truly the life of God in us, then isn't it an unqualified good? Shouldn't we just live and let passion find its own way in the world? Why don't we just trust the process and go with the flow?"

This is the advice of much contemporary "spirituality." Many people today want to avoid the notion of evil and acknowledge only the good.

I would have thought we'd explored this naiveté in the free love miasma of the late sixties. Surely we discovered back then that unrestrained passion came with tremendous cost, both medically and emotionally. Surely we found out that, in the end, it wasn't satisfying.

When we look open-eyed and honestly at the brokenness in our world, we can't help but realize the current of human life is not all positive. We find no end of ways to pollute the river of our lives and wreak death and destruction. We all contribute to this evil.

We've been given the high privilege of being invited into the life of the Trinity. We share in the privileges of that life; we also share in the responsibilities.

The sooner we take responsibility for our own contributions to the pollution of the world, the better. Then we can learn to choose new ways of living so that we don't perpetuate or exacerbate the mess.

If we fail to acknowledge the goodness of our passion, we are being disrespectful to God whose life it is. On the other hand, if we fail to acknowledge our role in shaping and guiding this passion, we are being disrespectful to ourselves and the important part we play.

These days, we often blame the evil in our world on our circumstances or our childhood experiences. As one person recently noted, our culture seems to be in the business of manufacturing victims.

But let's face it. We're not pawns. We may have been hurt in the past, but we can make choices now. As they say in the Jewish tradition, we can contribute to the healing of the world or we can add to the evil— which shall we choose?

To choose for healing means that we have to get over blaming our past on others. It forces us to become honest about the evil we all harbor inside.

None of us reaches adulthood with a natural trust that God's all-sufficient life is flowing within us. We do not naturally depend on the truth that God loves us deeply and is supplying to us all the life we need. We learn to twist life to our own ends in an effort to make sure our needs and desires are met. Unsure whether the universe will be good to us, we feel driven to assuage the tremendous thirst that being participants in the fellowship of infinity has created within us.

We learn to control others — use and abuse, manipulate, wheedle, or schmooze — and do whatever it takes to get others to give us life again. We become vampires, sucking the passion out of others in order to satiate our own unending, disconnected thirst.

Many of the texts in the Epistles about immoral conduct are warnings against violating other people's boundaries. Paul offered one such list in Colossians 3:5-8: He named "sexual immorality, impurity, lust, evil desires and greed . . . anger, rage, malice, slander, and filthy language."

The unbridled expression of passion is never satisfying. When we seek to suck life from others, we're at their mercy. If we're addicted to other people's approval, we're always on edge lest they withdraw their approval and leave us high and dry.

We're vulnerable and we feel like victims. To ensure this horrible prospect never happens, we find ways to control others. We treat them like cows; we try to keep them fenced and docile, and we make sure they're always at the stanchion, ready to be milked when we need them.

When we live like this we've lost sight of God's love at the source of our life. We must find life some other way. And this craving becomes the evil that distorts our passion and harms our world.

We must learn to say no to the ways we abuse the gift from God at the heart of our passion. We learn what it means to make choices for the riverbanks — choices to order our desires so that they reach their true end, which is God's glory. We make choices to respect others and choices to curb our own evil tendencies. This is what the spiritual writers of old referred to as the "ordering" of love.

"The body is not meant for sexual immorality, but for the Lord, and the Lord for the body" (1 Corinthians 6:13). We want to celebrate our life but not simply consume it on ourselves. We want to enjoy it and express it but not become its slaves.

Respect Those Around Us
Many expressions of passion do not threaten any bond of commitment, and we would normally be free to exercise such passion as we

wish. Yet sometimes even the normal exercise of passion, in good ways, can be hurtful to another person.

We may choose to curb or restrict the exercise of our passion for the good of others. We don't want to tear the delicate fabric of life emerging in the relationships that surround and support us.

The New Testament offers some examples to illustrate times when we are called to structure the exercise of our passion for the sake of another. Perhaps the most famous of these is Paul's discussion of eating meat that had been offered as a sacrifice to idols (Romans 14–15; 1 Corinthians 8–10).

Paul recognized his freedom to enjoy a celebration with others. Yet, when the stakes were so high that a fledgling convert might slide back into idolatry because Paul exercised his freedom to eat consecrated meat, he chose to affirm that freedom by forgoing that particular fulfillment.

In 1 Corinthians Paul argues for his right to be supported as a teacher of the good news, but he chooses to pay his own way. John wrote that when we see someone in dire poverty and give them a pious blessing instead of tangible help, we've missed the point. There are times when the appropriate thing to do is to "lay down our lives" for our brothers and sisters.

This kind of saying no can be abused. It has often been one of the cornerstones of an imposed, insipid spirituality. It's easy enough to say, "Don't do it, you might offend someone." We could end up doing nothing if we followed that dictum, which was the great blanket reason offered for many of the prohibitions in my childhood.

Paul's advice in the issue of meat sacrificed to idols is brilliant and normative. First he said, "Eat anything sold in the meat market without raising questions of conscience, for, 'The earth is the Lord's, and everything in it'" (1 Corinthians 10:25).

In one fell swoop Paul takes us out of some hypothetical fear that we might offend someone. He gives no quarter to a scrupulous and paranoid avoidance of life. Life is to be enjoyed!

Second, Paul advised that if eating meat causes some wobbly, new believer to revert to idolatry, then it's better to refrain. The reason I might forgo wine is because some recovering alcoholic might revert to alcohol, not because some scrupulous Christian would be offended. Jesus clearly chose to "break the rules" to show they were keeping people from God instead of bringing them to God.

When the issue becomes significant enough to jeopardize a person's new faith, respect for the person calls for saying no, even in the face of a possible yes.

Honoring a "Mature" Passion

Sometimes we have to say no in the present in order to say yes in a fuller way at some future time. When we live through times of saying no to an outlet of passion's life and power, we experience only its raw intensity without fulfillment.

It isn't because the passion is wrong. It's because, in those moments, any expression of passion would be inappropriate, or at least premature.

We are dealing with explosive power when we deal with our passion. If we stay open to God's leading, it will become a creative and healing force in the world. Without the appropriate restraint—without the riverbanks—it can flood out immature or misdirected, wasted or destructive.

In marriage we learn to say no to competing relationships because we take a long-term view of the gift of passion and because the making and breaking of intimate bonds would hurt our own soul and the soul of the one to whom we are already committed. We live a complex web of relationships—with spouse, children, friends—that would be deeply damaged by betrayal. We say no because we believe that the deepest intimacy can only grow through long years of building trust with our partner.

Building the power of a long-term relationship is worth the choices to keep passion on track. A deeper, more powerful yes is achieved because we have said no to the indiscriminate flowing of passion that attracts us at the moment.

It's hard to learn to say no. We may want immediate gratification so badly we can taste it. But we say no so that we can say yes in a deeper way to the life that is in us.

Saying no to passion, when the desire is excruciatingly acute and the object of our desire so tantalizingly available, catapults us into the mystery of Jesus' passion and death.

If we celebrate with Jesus in His life, we also follow Him through the experience of death and resurrection. Only the power of the Resurrection gives us the courage to risk this kind of letting go.

We can fight the dying process. We can demand a particular way of gratification. But an ultimatum to life will only disappoint us in the end. Instead, we can enter into the dying process with trust. We can believe that, in Jesus' resurrection, there is always new life to come.

We can act too quickly and then we settle for the wrong thing. Sometimes the truest expressions of faith are found in the waiting. And Paul's words, "If we died with him, we will also live with him" (2 Timothy 2:11). In another place Paul said, "I want to know Christ and the power of his resurrection and the fellowship of sharing in his sufferings, becoming like him in his death, and so, somehow, to attain to the resurrection from the dead" (Philippians 3:10-11).

HEALTHY BANKS FOR OUR PASSION

If it's important to channel our passion, then what choices can we make to give it positive direction without choking the freedom and goodness that is there? Let's look at some of the choices for the banks that can help us stay faithful to the current of God's life within us.

Staying Grounded in God's Loving Presence Within

A good offense is the best defense, so the sports pundits never tire of saying. It makes for bad filler but good sense. The best thing we can do in creating boundaries for our passion is to be immersed in the goodness of God's presence.

When we are at home in our souls, we don't need to cling to a particular expression of passion with such a tenacious grip. We can afford to enter life freely when we know we're rooted in the reality of God's love.

Surprising as it may seem, the first appropriate advice in learning to tend the banks is to be confident in the stream. The choices described in chapter nine do not just open us up to passion, they provide our greatest resource in dealing with the perversions of passion we struggle with every day.

Tilden Edwards has offered an interesting way to practice this grounding.[2] He suggests that we allow ourselves to focus on the particular passion or emotion we're experiencing at the moment and feel it as deeply as possible for a period of time.

Gradually we begin to descend below the surface level. What's underneath the surface emotion? We follow the energy of the passion deeper and deeper until, finally, we're below any particular expression and are in touch with pure, undifferentiated desire. There we can rest, knowing that we are with God.

We may begin with anger at being snubbed by a friend. As we go deeper we find that the anger is fueled by fear of rejection. Lower still we discover that we have a profoundly simple longing to be loved and accepted for ourselves. Finally we get below all these feelings and experience the strength of pure desire without any attachment to a specific goal. It's the desire of God's love in us. Once we're back to that basic level, we find it easier to welcome the desire again.

In this letting go, we've followed our passion back to its Source. We have relinquished the external pull toward a particular fulfillment. We've let go of our focus on the fragmentation at the surface and have gone back to the pure headwaters upstream.

Once we're back at the Source, we can direct our passion in new ways. Anger at being snubbed can be directed toward learning to trust our own goodness in God and not needing others' attention so badly.

This is the essential purpose behind all the disciplines of abstinence. They take us back to the Source of our lives and train us to say yes to the "all-sufficiency of God."

Making Long-Term Choices that Give Structure to Life

So many people live fragmented and chaotic lives. We are a culture drowning in a plethora of options. It's one of the great curses of our age.

We're run ragged as much by the pressure of opportunities as we are by the pressure of duties. Then we wonder why our passion is so out of control. This kind of fragmentation dissipates our passion and leaves us feeling desperate and full of unresolved hunger. Disintegrated and dissatisfied, we easily slide into unhealthy choices.

A single man who works as an advertising consultant came to me, struggling with a deep-seated addiction that created shame and confusion in his life. He wanted to know what he could do to stop these sinful actions.

As we talked, he began to describe his lifestyle. Gradually a sad picture of terrible drivenness emerged. He would bury himself in his work, knowing that he was only as good as his last ad. He pushed himself to the limit to achieve his goals. He didn't eat properly, didn't take time for relaxation or even for adequate sleep. Finally it would all catch up with him, and he would go out of control and binge his passion.

What was I to tell him? He came presenting his addiction as the sin he wanted to deal with. But there was no single, simple solution for dealing with his addiction in the midst of this chaos. The addictive sin was only the manifestation of a more fundamental problem. The fact is, his underlying life structures had disintegrated. These simple overall life structures, which could have held his passion, had collapsed in front of the drivenness of his intense focus on career.

The disintegration came, in this case, from being overly focused. In another person's case, it might come from being unfocused. We may suffer from the accumulation of being busy about everything and focused on nothing. Eventually, the lack of structure leaves our life in shambles.

Somewhere along the line, the truth begins to dawn on us that our fragmented lives are not caused by making a few individual mistakes. We discover that we're adrift. Over time the structures that could have served us have rotted like an old post under the front porch.

Some long-term choices can set direction to our lives and provide a coherent structure to help bring wholeness to our passion.

We can make choices, for example, about where we live. We can choose how deeply in debt we're prepared to be and how much financial stress we're prepared to tolerate. We can determine how many hours a week we're prepared to work or how many relationships we're prepared to support.

All of these choices, and many more, tend to ground us. They bring us up against our limitations in a freeing, constructive way. When we learn to say no to uncontrolled dissipation of passion, we contribute to our own healing.

Another long-term choice we can make is that of fidelity. Fidelity is more than just stepping into a cage and promising never to step out again. Fidelity is a commitment to stay present to another person throughout each other's transformation process. It is a commitment to support the other person's growth—as well as to be faithful to one's own—and to protect the growing relationship that emerges over the long haul.

Fidelity in marriage means that we're committed to our spouse even while we explore our passion in the larger world. We make our choices based on a pre-commitment. In Ignatian spirituality this is referred to as choosing "insofar as we are free."

My exploration will be shaped and conditioned by my fidelity to

Miriam. I may learn to embrace my sexuality and be free to be a wholesome sexual being in all my relationships, but I have chosen to explore and express that in ways that respect the shape of a prior commitment. I am not free to choose experiences that violate the commitment.

Fidelity is not restricted to the marriage relationship. We learn to choose fidelity within community in much the same way. Over time, we realize that flitting from church to church doesn't take us into depth.

We can't learn to love deeply if we move in and out of a church community at the first whim of disapproval. We learn to stay present in the face of struggle and misunderstanding. We grow through fidelity and are shaped by the forgiveness and reconciliation process required over the long haul.

Long-term choices can also include choosing to say no to the fears and shame that torture us into conformity and paralysis. In her book, *The Artist's Way*, Julia Cameron writes of self-criticism as one of the chief blocks to creativity. She likens it to an addiction.

I can easily become hooked on self-criticism. Once I get started I spiral downward into depression and creative paralysis. Like an alcoholic who can't afford the first drink, I can't afford the first destructive self-criticism in my creative growth. I have sometimes said to God, I really do want to grow, but I'm no longer willing to listen to the internal critic that sabotages everything I do. So, if You want me to grow, You'll have to find another way!

Respecting Ourselves and Other People

As we learn to value the current of God's life in us, we recognize that this same current flows in others as well. Our relationships are part of a Trinitarian mystery that honors both union and uniqueness.

Our commitment to Trinitarian love means that we will respect both our own dignity and the dignity of the person with whom we are in relationship.

We have no right to usurp another person's life for our own pleasure. We do not have to steal other people's lives to ensure that we have some life ourselves.

Walter Brueggemann describes the second tablet in the Ten Commandments as a line drawn in the sand to protect the dignity of each person. These commandments keep us from oppressing others and call us to offer them dignity in how we treat them.[3]

We have come to be rooted in the goodness of our own passion, therefore we can offer that grace to others as well. The trouble is, we lose our center. We get overextended. We're too busy, too distracted. We become alienated from our inner source of life by constantly being outside ourselves. Then, like Augustine said, in our desperation for life we look for life from outside sources instead of from the God of our heart. We find it all right, but at someone else's expense.

In these choices we learn to say no and yes. We can move from exploitation to respect, from greed to generosity, from neediness to offering our gifts.

Creating Room for Surprise

One other way we can learn to tend the riverbanks of our passion is to make room for surprise. By creating space in our lives, we open up our little universe to the possibility of something new.

Life can become so controlled, so predictable, that it leaves no room for change. Yet one of the great characteristics of the presence of God is the element of surprise.

God surprised Abraham with a child. God surprised the first-century world by being born in obscurity. We can prepare for that surprise in our own lives by creating some open spaces. By learning to say no to a crammed schedule and a predictable way of doing things, we can open up space for new shoots of life and growth to emerge.

Henri Nouwen used to talk about the difference between structure for enterprise and monastic structure. Structure for enterprise is the way we organize ourselves to accomplish things. Monastic structure creates and protects space for things to grow. It guards the sacred center of our lives from being trampled by life.

The classical disciplines of solitude, silence, and fasting are examples of this kind of choice. They create room for us to focus more intentionally on God. They also create room simply to be.

In that restful state of being, who knows what might emerge? The thought is scary enough to keep many from trying it at all! But when we think of it like Christmas, like Jesus being born in a stable, we can begin to open up to the possibility of an unexpected gift. If we create room— if we simply create some room!—we may just be surprised by the gifts we receive.

Accepting the Goodness of Unfulfilled Desire

The entire process of learning to tend the banks of our passion hinges on a central conversion of heart. Our culture lives and breathes consumerism. The entire economic structure of our society is based on awakening desire and then cultivating the demand for its immediate gratification. We're caught at the very point of our passion.

It's possible to challenge that monolithic idolatry in our culture. We can learn to affirm the goodness of passion and choose at the same time to forgo its fulfillment. In so doing, we learn to accept the goodness of unfulfilled desire.

This is such a simple thought, but it is revolutionary in its implications. If our commitment is first of all to the passion of God's life in us, then we're committed more to the passion than we are to any particular fulfillment.

It seems like an oxymoron to validate the desire and to validate the choice not to satisfy that desire. No person whose life is shaped by consumerism can think of unfulfilled passion as a good in itself.

Yet, this is the truth of it. As Gerald May said, this longing is our deepest treasure, "our best gift, our most treasured possession."[4]

It's possible to come to terms with our desire and befriend it. Desire itself is good! It is a sign of God in us.

Often our passion rages uncontrollably because we think of it as enemy rather than friend. When we can treasure our longing as a sign of the Spirit's presence in us, then we can open ourselves to a new level of freedom as to how and when we experience fulfillment.

Dr. James Houston has said, "We learn to value the quality of admiration." We can love the goodness of many things without having to consume them.

The affirmation of unfulfilled passion takes us into transcendence. It proclaims that there is more. It accepts the infinite quality of our passion.

In this light, the passages in the Psalms and Lamentations about the importance of "waiting" begin to sparkle with life. In the face of the complete collapse of all that he had believed in, Jeremiah trusted in the continual emergence of fresh mercy. He said that the Lord's compassion never fails. "They are new every morning; great is your faithfulness." Then he added the radical words, "I say to myself, 'The LORD is my portion; therefore I will wait for him' . . . it is good to wait quietly for the salvation of the LORD" (Lamentations 3:23-26).

I will pour out my Spirit on all people. Your sons
and daughters will prophesy, your old men will
        dream dreams,
your young men will see visions. Even on my
servants, both men and women, I will pour out
        my Spirit in those days.

JOEL 2:28-29

CHAPTER ELEVEN

DARING TO DREAM

■

UMAN BEINGS ARE DESTINED TO DREAM. WE HAVE THAT UNIQUE, MYS-terious ability to live beyond the present. We hope for what has not yet appeared. It's one of our richest blessings and one of our deepest curses.

Our dreams expose us. They picture the things we hunger for. They lay bare the real intentions of the heart. They hold the power for evil or for good. Dreams can be the shoots of faith that grow toward wholeness and healing or the bitter fruit of our inner brokenness.

Jesus said, "No good tree bears bad fruit, nor does a bad tree bear good fruit. . . . The good man brings good things out of the good stored up in his heart, and the evil man brings evil things out the evil stored up in his heart. For out of the overflow of his heart his mouth speaks" (Luke 6:43, 45).

We dream and then we act. Our dreams shape our actions. What we long for in our dreams eventually fleshes out in our behavior.

Because our dreams become the passions that drive us, we dream with anticipation and with care. When we nurture a dream over a long time, we're pumping into our spirit veins the very fuel that will drive our choices.

Passion and dreams, perhaps as much as any other part of our lives, are the road on which we walk the long journey of spiritual growth into intimacy with God. In opening our dreams to God we come to one of the places we are most vulnerable and, therefore, one of the places of greatest intimacy. We learn to embrace the passionate goodness of our dreams and the deep transformation that is inevitably part of the package.

If we look at our dreams closely, we can see in them a deep and important example—a case study—of the way we deal with passion in our spiritual growth. We face the same fears, the same kinds of choices, and the same experience of the presence of God that we experience in other areas of passion.

ARE OUR DREAMS LEGITIMATE?

God dreams.

Look at the many passages in the prophets in which, with a transparent heart, God speaks of dreams for the earth, for the people of God, and for all humankind.

It's easy to overlook the dream when it comes from such an authoritative place. God knows everything and can do anything. It doesn't quite seem like the same kettle of fish as our dreams. But from the perspective of longing and opening the deepest desires of the heart, the picture changes dramatically.

God pours out a deep, passionate longing for the healing of the world. Dreams of justice and shalom. There is no shortage of ways in which God shares with us a deep desire for future wholeness.[1]

If dreams come from the wellspring of our passion, and if that wellspring finds its source in God, and if God dreams, we can safely conclude that, at heart, our dreams are wonderful! They reflect the emerging of God's life into the world of our lives.

The fulfillment of a dream lay at the heart of the promise to Abraham. Sarah, past childbearing years, was going to bear a child. The impossible was going to come true.

Imagine the utter shock and incredulity that must have jolted Abraham in that moment of promise. Could it be that he would see the one great dream of his life come to fruition after all? Would the hemorrhage of disappointment finally be stanched?

Other people in the biblical record dreamed. Joseph dreamed of becoming the leader of his household and having his brothers bow to him. David dreamed of building a temple for God. Micah and Joel and Isaiah dreamed of a healed world.

You may dream of finding a life partner. Of seeing your children grow up into healthy, passionate adults. You may dream of being the best sculptor in the world . . . or at least the best in your neighborhood! You may dream of being a great preacher. Or of being a good, trustworthy friend.

Was Abraham's dream for a child a good thing, or was it a selfish wish to satisfy his own desires? Did he want a child in order to fulfill God's will, or did he simply want a son to carry on his name?

God wanted a child for Abraham and Sarah to fulfill God's redemptive purposes in time and space. Even though God had promised to make Abraham a great nation, I doubt Abraham could have known the full extent of what that meant. Was it necessary that Abraham know how to distinguish between his own longings and the deeper significance God had in mind?

Does God mind if we carry a passionate dream, even if our heart motives are a mixed bag? How many of us can truly fathom the motives behind our dreams? And how many of our dreams, even the most "spiritual" ones, are fully pure?

In Abraham's case, it seems clear that these distinctions didn't really matter. However complex his own motives were, Abraham's dream for a child coincided with the movement of God in history. And Abraham lived the dream in one long, ongoing story of purification.

Good for Abraham! But what about me and my dreams?

Whether we're in "the ministry" or in used car sales, we all have dreams that are the beginnings of passion. The dream may be a church with the greatest program in the city, or it may be at least one sale today.

If I dream of a nice house and a happy family, is that legitimate? If I dream of having a black Porsche and spending my winters on the beach in Tahiti, is that legitimate?

In sales, the gurus encourage us to believe in our dreams to help us be successful. "We are limited only by our ability to dream," we're told.

In the church we're encouraged to dream of great numerical growth in our congregations. We're encouraged to believe that God will move mountains in response to our faith dreams. At the beginning of the modern Protestant missionary movement, William Carey preached his "Deathless Sermon" in which he coined a famous line,

"Expect great things from God; attempt great things for God."

It's difficult to know how to deal with our dreams. What is legitimate and what is simply the product of our ego and our jumbled motives?

A dream for something "spiritual," like evangelizing the world, doesn't guarantee any less ego attachment than any other dream. The ambiguous reality of our inner motivations may be enough to make us fearful of dreaming at all.

We hesitate to believe Psalm 37. "Trust in the LORD and do good; dwell in the land and enjoy safe pasture. Delight yourself in the LORD and he will give you the desires of your heart" (verses 3-4).

But the conclusion is simple. Our dreams come from God and are intended to be a gift to the world. Like other expressions of passion, if we deny or suppress our dreams, we are cutting off the flow of God's life.

Denying the passion of our dreams because they might lead us in the wrong direction and take us away from God sabotages the journey of discovery and purification. Like all other passion, we affirm our dreams in the face of 101 ways in which the dreaming will have to be deepened and transformed.

In the end, the question is not whether or not to dream, or whether our dreams are spiritual enough. The real question is how do these dreams express God's life and how can we live well with them?

GIVING SHAPE TO OUR DREAMS

What can we dream that will be consistent with the truth of our passion without being simply the product of our own distorted ideas?

What would the passions of the Three-in-One God look like if they were expressed in wholesome ways in our world? If suddenly everyone lived out of the truth of their own individual passion and lived respectfully toward everyone else and the creation in which we live, what kind of shape would this life take?

Scripture gives us some hints. It reveals that Trinitarian dreams are fleshed out in the prophetic material, in Jesus' ministry, and in the exhortations of the Epistles.

In the Hebrew Scriptures, the prophets speak of "shalom," a sense of well-being and integration. They dream of a community of people living in harmony and respect, who are looking to Yahweh as the center and giver of life.

They envision shalom as the affirmation of each person's unique place. They dream about a time when "every [one] will sit under . . . [their] own fig tree" (Micah 4:4). They also dream of an integration and union, a time when "the leopard will lie down with the goat, the calf and the lion and the yearling together" (Isaiah 11:6).

Within this respect and integration they anticipate a time of peace, a time of redirecting our activities from violence to fruitfulness. They promise a time when people "will beat their swords into plowshares" (Micah 4:3, Joel 3:10).

In the Gospels, Jesus invited, and still invites, the marginalized people to dream. His actions and His teachings bring hope and possibility to people whose lives have become victimized or devalued by others.

He proclaims a reversal of values. Those who experience poverty may still find their place in life. Those who have access to power will learn to be servants. We will learn to wash each other's feet and thereby respect each other within the bonds of union.

The Epistles show us dreams of a community of people who offer the gift of their love for one another as a model of what God has done for them in Christ. Paul spoke of a unified body of gifted people in which each person is respected and the more hidden people have as much value as the more prominent.

After a list of things to put off, like discarded clothes, Paul encouraged the Colossian believers to put on some new clothes that expressed the "real you"—actions that befitted the deeper truth of their passion. He said, "Clothe yourselves with compassion, kindness, humility, gentleness and patience. Bear with each other and forgive whatever grievances you may have against one another. Forgive as the Lord forgave you. And over all these virtues put on love, which binds them all together in perfect unity" (Colossians 3:12-14).

Paul's list suggests a dream in which it's possible for people with very different experiences, very different external characteristics and expressions, to sit down together in harmony and respect. It seems to imply that these people were not nice little correct, passionless clones. From the evidence we get in the Epistles, these believers were very alive and sometimes not so together!

They faced all the quarrels and sins that are part of human experience. They had to dream a new way that enabled life to remain juicy and passionate yet respected self and others. This dream is at the heart of the apostles' instructions about how to behave as Christians living in community with one another and with others who are not yet awakened to faith.

These all point to a Trinitarian lifestyle—a respect for personal differences and a communal experience in which those differences are offered as gifts for the sake of the whole community.

The shape of our dreams can be as wide as God. We must not be afraid to dream. God's life emerges through them. As we affirm God's presence in our dreams and allow them to be purified and deepened, we develop the strength of character to act in the world in a way that pleases and glorifies God.

Do you dream of going back to school? Ask God to deepen the dream as an expression of the Trinity. Think about this dream as an expression of your courage, potency, sensuality, and wonder. Let it be a dream of passion.

At the same time, ask God that you might be able to hold your needs and wishes with honest integrity. Ask that you might be considerate of the needs of those around you in your dreaming. Ask God to deepen the dream as you attend to its pulsing power. Maybe it's pointing to something even more profound than what you originally planned. Maybe the issue isn't school or getting qualified. Maybe the issue is learning to trust God with your life. Maybe the dream is calling you to stand up and ask people to take you seriously rather than for granted.

Whatever the case in your particular circumstances, the dream will lead you to trust God if you treasure its goodness and let go of the need to control it.

HOW WE EXPERIENCE THE PURIFICATION OF OUR DREAMS

Affirming Our Dreams

So what do we do with our dreams? Joseph Campbell told us to follow our bliss. But what is our bliss?

I'm afraid that for many people today, Campbell's words are permission to do whatever they want. We can all rationalize what we desire at the moment to be the true dream of our hearts. Many parents raise their children to believe they should fulfill every desire, as though the frustration of being told no will do permanent psychological damage.

For others, the pain of unfulfilled dreams is too much to risk. They close their hearts to dreaming.

When I was growing up, we were taught not to dream or desire. Rather, we were to empty ourselves so that we could respond to the call of God, whatever it might be. It was a sin to want, because wanting would be a sign of our will instead of God's will.

Desire raged inside us but was never acknowledged or honored. It became easier to pretend. We learned not to desire, to block it and get on with life.

One of the exercises Julia Cameron suggests in *The Artist's Way* is to list some other lives we would like to have chosen. The exercise seeks to spark the choices that remain open to us and that might clear away the blocks and allow God's creative freedom of expression.

The first time I went through the process, I simply couldn't do the exercise. My complete block surprised me. I couldn't say anything about the future or the possibilities that were still open to me. I was so terrified that I could physically feel my fear.

My feelings didn't improve when I came to the chapter on money. The question of choice was asked again in another way: "If money wasn't an issue, what would you want to do or be?" Again I couldn't answer the question.

As I gradually listened to my fear, it became clear to me that for years I had used finances as an excuse to avoid choosing. As long as I didn't have much money I could always excuse my lack of choice by saying I couldn't afford it. Poverty (relatively speaking!) is a wonderful umbrella for lethargy of the will.

Dreaming confronted me with two intolerable scenarios. It either meant admitting I was doing things wrong now (which I couldn't bear to face), or it meant contemplating new choices in which I would risk disappointing or hurting those around me. Fear of change and growth kept me paralyzed.

No wonder I couldn't dream. I felt totally trapped. Life could buffet me at will. I could respond to life, but I couldn't choose. If I chose to spend time alone, it might hurt my family. If I chose to be less intense about my job, I would disappoint the people in the church. If I spent money to buy good binoculars for birding, it would take away money from choices Miriam might make to enjoy life.

I had cornered myself—no room to move, no room to dream.

Sometimes we don't dream because we fear that the things we desire most strongly will be taken away. Loss of our dreams becomes the way we prove we're fully committed to God and haven't made our dreams into an idol.

If we think of God as vindictive, we may feel that whatever we fear the most (having to give up dreams of marriage and family or career) will be the very thing God calls us to do. It's better not to dream.

While this image of God is absurd, it's often a very strong subconscious reality. We would rather not admit to this kind of thinking, yet we stay just a little suspicious of God and refuse to get too close. If we do, we inwardly fear that our desires and our dreams will be smashed into tiny shards.

The beginning of the healing of our dreams is to recognize that dreams are an expression of passion. We live somewhere between the gift and the dream. Passion springs up in our lives as a pure gift from God. And dreams are the intimations of where the passion is headed. They are our desire for life yet to come, passion projected into the possibilities of what might be.

Dreams are the artwork of our souls . . . pottery sculptures of desire molded out of the still malleable clay of future possibilities.

The past may have hardened into grotesque patterns. Sometimes the present seems already too stiff to work with. But the future is still unformed. We can still dream—beyond the brokenness of the present—dreams of wholeness and abundant life.

Like all passion, we affirm the basic desire or energy that underlies the dream. At any given point, our dreams may be skewed in all kinds of selfish, distorted directions dictated by our warped experience of passion. But if we listen to the dream with an open heart, we will deepen our desire for God in our lives.

The healing comes in acknowledging that underneath the short-sightedness and lack of discernment lie hints and indications of the life of God. That tiny sprout is to be nourished and held with an open hand. We will find its purification in allowing the stream to run clean and full again. When we remove our focus from fixating only on the object of our dream and focus instead on the gift of God's presence in our dreams, we often experience a new freedom and joy.

I have often witnessed the joy of seeing people "seduced" into growth in the best sense of the word. As they discover how good their life is, rooted in the life of God, they are set free to dream again. It's surprising and wonderful to see how creative and generous these people can become. They get out of old, unproductive ruts and allow their true dreams to emerge.

One friend, Donna, went back to school at great expense, both emotionally and financially, to get her speech arts diploma. She got honors in her work.

For a while she taught speech to children. But gradually she became aware that the dream was deepening. What she really loved was to introduce the children to books. She loved the stories.

So she learned to be a storyteller. Her life gradually took on focus and richness of purpose as she held to the dream and let it speak to her of how God was yearning to be expressed in her life.

As people are set free to be passionate about life, often they choose something unexpected, something truly fresh that becomes a wonderful gift to the world. As they find small ways to say yes to the life inside them, their whole countenance brightens, and they begin to move into a sense of power and freedom.

My counselor once said to me, "Jeff, suppose that by miracle of miracles you were to walk out of this office and discover that you loved yourself. What difference would it make in your life?"

Here I was—forced to dream once more! But as she probed, I began to see that I wouldn't become a narcissistic psychopath after all. It would bring a new sense of balance and harmony into my life. I could see myself clicking my heels for joy. I could envision myself being more confident to enter into intimate relationships, and I could see myself bringing joy to others.

I've used that dream many times to keep me going in the right direction. I've allowed it to shape me and fuel my choices to accept myself.

Sometimes we experience transformation in the courage to continue to follow our dreams in the midst of discouragement, failure, and countless other reasons to quit. The great missionaries like William Carey, J. O. Fraser, Adoniram Judson, Jim Elliot, and a host of others are wonderful examples of people who lived their dreams in the face of overwhelming obstacles.

Their determination to be true to their passion caused them agony of soul. They had to face their own deep questions—sort out what was their desire and what was God's. What were they to hang on to and what were they to relinquish?

Many people experience this same growth as they begin to say yes to the goodness of their lives. As they begin to lean into the new freedom of life that is theirs in Christ, they face huge muskegs of tradition and habituated relationship.

Family background and the roles they've learned over years act like a great suction to keep them stuck. They've always been responsible; how can they choose to let up on the old responsibility messages now? They've always been quiet; how can they choose to speak up now?

People don't want us to change because they'll have to change, too. The rules in the relationship are changed when we change and grow. If we've been living as a doormat, it's challenging to begin to live out the truth of our dreams. Those who have enjoyed using us as a doormat will not want to lose what they have.

Gradually, however, we become convinced that the dream is good, and that it's worth choosing, even if it means bucking the current and swimming upstream. Like salmon homing upriver to spawn, we can experience our dream as the call of our soul to respond, regardless of the hardship or opposition.

A wonderful communion with God emerges when we follow the dreams at the heart of our lives. We've learned that we can celebrate moments of fulfillment without demanding that we hold in our own hands the power to bring fulfillment. We've also learned that unfulfilled desire is good in and of itself. We can offer the dream—the anticipation and the waiting—as our love gift to God.

The Death and Resurrection of Our Dreams

The other side of the picture is that transformation also comes through the death—and resurrection—of our dreams. For some of us, it takes work to learn to dream again. For others the blood, sweat, and tears come in loosening their grip on the dream and allowing the presence of God's life to deepen and shape the dream into something that is God-like.

Those who have finally been given permission to dream often hold their dreams most tightly. The possibility of having their dreams dashed or left unfulfilled, when they've finally risked dreaming, seems too cruel. So, once they begin to dream they run the danger of gripping their dreams too tightly and refusing to let God purify them.

Our culture is possessed with dreaming as a substitute for living. No wonder motivational speakers are the new gurus of society.

We dream of the time when we've gotten our education, when we can get a new car, when we can stay at home and raise children, when we're retired. But mostly we dream about when we'll have more time.

We parent for the future, planning our child's schooling, music lessons, and career before our children have had time to enjoy being children. Our culture has overdosed on dreams as a narcotic to blind us to the chaos of the present.

To live well with our dreams will require the courage both to dream and to allow these ethereal, fragile dreams to be purified and shaped to express God's life in us.

Quite naturally, our dreams begin with a distinctly self-oriented flavor. We dream about the things we think will ensure that our needs get met.

We dream about a better job because we think this will give us the respect we need. We dream about financial success so that we'll have the security we need. We dream about someone who will give us the intimacy we need.

We haven't yet come to trust that the God who cares about us is the same God who is present in our passion. We don't yet see that God wants to deepen our dreams. God wants our dreams to fuel actions that express the flowing love of the Trinity in our world.

As we grow, we're called to deepen our dreams so they better express God's desire for wholeness for ourselves and others. In this clarification and purification process, we experience the pathway of Christ's passion. Hebrews 12 tells us to follow the pattern of Jesus, who on the basis of His dream of the "joy set before him," endured the cross.

There are several ways we may experience the death-resurrection cycle in our dreams. Sometimes we're forced by outside circumstances to open our dreams to be deepened and transformed. And sometimes we have to make the choice to say no to a particular fulfillment.

"Death" Imposed on Us
We face transformation when we have to let go of dearly held things that have embodied our deep longings. Sometimes we have to let go because life has simply taken away the object of our dreams. It is a deathblow to the very thing we thought was the sign of God's life in us.

Death of our dreams is a very common and often misunderstood part of spiritual growth. Even the best dreams often have to die before they are realized.

How many deaths did Abraham experience along the way while he waited for the fulfillment of his dream to have a son? Joseph, Moses, David, and other biblical characters faced the terrible night of death in regard to their calling.

This death experience happens when a marriage breaks up or when we realize our spouse and children are not the people we had hoped they would be. The dream for a nice home, a happy family, and a secure place to be—a safe haven of family life—goes out the window.

Circumstances beyond our control, like the birth of a handicapped child, call us to let go of the way we thought our dreams for our children and our old age would turn out.

It happens when you lose something that has been a big part of your life—a job, physical prowess, a dream for the future.

Bonnie, a dear friend, has had to live through the death of her dreams. An infection ripped through her leg and destroyed tissue. She was given massive doses of antibiotics to treat the infection, but because of the antibiotics she lost most of her hearing. A treasured part of her way of experiencing the world is gone forever.

Bonnie has always been involved and in the middle of things. Now she misses out on conversations and group discussions. She often feels on the fringe. She's had to face the death of her whole orientation to life.

This "death" created deep struggles in her relationship with God. She agonized over how her life could be good again. She was grieving the death of her dreams. Could she face into the "No" to her usual ways of living and find a deeper "Yes"? Could she experience resurrection as God deepened the dream? Could her life become a gift again?

When the dreams that embody our longings for life are taken from us by circumstances outside our control, we feel victimized—crucified at the hands of "fate," or God, or the people around us.

What are we to do? We can let go of our dreams and settle for something less. We can get bitter. Or we can, over time, go back to the Source of our desire and allow our passion to be transformed and deepened.

John experienced the death of his dreams when his ministry got destroyed by other people. As the director of an active nonprofit agency, he was falsely accused by a coworker of manipulating the books. Eventually he was forced out of the director's role.

It's one thing to contend with the blind circumstances of "fate," but to be crucified by the machinations of a fellow-worker, who through political savvy has gained the upper hand, is truly terrible.

One man I know had a dream to start a home for victims of domestic violence. He bought an apartment building and helped get a core of people to make the dream come true. He dreamed of seeing the center become part of a community outreach.

Through political maneuverings, the whole project was steered away from its community moorings to become a bureaucratic institution. It seemed like a cruel and unnecessary death.

Pastors have often experienced crucifixion at the hands of powerful parishioners. And conversely, the countless hours invested by a dedicated parishioner can be written off unceremoniously by a new, aggressive pastor who imposes his dream on the congregation.

There are so many chances to let our lives be coffined by bitterness. It would be tempting to let go of dreaming in total disillusionment.

The transformation comes in opening to passion again in the midst of this kind of defeat. It comes in holding on to the dreaming but turning the page to a new chapter. It comes in refusing to be bitter and refusing to shut off the re-creative energy of God in our lives. It comes in waiting to see how the life of God will flow anew. As we let go of thoughts of payback that dominate our minds and close off creative thinking, we're freed to discover a new and deeper possibility.

That is the truth of resurrection. If my passion is not going to live in one particular fulfillment, then how will it live? I don't yet know. But I've come to trust one thing—it will live!

There would be no death and resurrection if we could predict the outcome of the death and know ahead of time what the resurrection will look like. The painful thing about death is that we can't predict when or how the resurrection will come. We have to trust that God is good, even though we don't know the outcome of God's dealings with us.

We Choose the Dying Process

When our dreams are overflowing with desire, who will be there to make sure the banks stay intact? Who will ensure that our passion doesn't become a monster in the world?

Sometimes we must be the ones. We're called to lay down our own lives, so to speak.

Anyone who has fallen in love with someone else's spouse knows what this means. Love becomes flamingly intense. Life is juicy and meaningful again. There is the possibility of a grand passion, a great love. It may come our way only once in a lifetime. Everything seems so good, so possible.

The temptation is enormous. And the rationalizing we can do to justify the choices we want to make is almost endless.

"I've never felt so alive before."

"I refuse to go back to that old death again."

"There is something monumental here, a cosmic experience."

I've heard people use all these rationalizations to avoid choosing their own death.

Eric worked for years to set himself up for an important job contract. It would be a chance to have huge influence and would bring financial independence. He was right there; he could taste it. Then, at the eleventh hour, he found out the contract would force him into compromising situations he could not morally tolerate. He tried twisting in every possible direction, but finally he chose to let go of the job.

Sometimes we simply have to choose our own crucifixion. In such cases there's no other alternative but to say, "Yes, this is my passionate desire. Yes, I feel like my whole life is at stake here. And no, I will not choose to follow fulfillment in this way."

Our natural tendency is either to insist on the particular expression of passion or die to passion altogether. It seems utterly too painful to let go of the thing that seems like heaven yet keep our hearts open to let God fill us with passion.

We have to trust resurrection. We have to open into a deeper, more profound expression of God's life that wouldn't have been possible otherwise. We would have shortchanged ourselves by insisting that this destructive expression of passion be fulfilled.

We have to trust that by choosing the dying process, we're not choosing the death of our passion but the death of that one, distorted way of expressing it. We have to believe, in those fiery moments, that God is not against our passion but for us and for life.

THE OUTCOME OF OUR DREAMS

Fidelity to God, in the transformation of our dreams, produces character. We become strong, substantial people. The purified passion that fires our dreams becomes the muscle and bone of our action. Dreams die. That's the reality. But God's life continues to bubble forth.

Consider Joseph. He could have aggrandized himself with dreams of power and respect. Instead, he embraced the dreams he had been given but surrendered to the crucifixions along the way. His dreams turned out far differently than he could have originally imagined. He traded in his own small interpretation of the dream for the large interpretation of God's creative purposes for Israel and the world.

Through the fidelity of long choices, God comes to birth through us. We fulfill God's dream that we become God's workmanship, created in Christ Jesus unto good works, which God has dreamed in us from the beginning (Ephesians 2:10).

Paul's understanding of this transforming process is captured in the Greek word *hupomone*,[2] sometimes translated "patience" or "endurance." It's a picturesque word that carries the idea of sticking with something under pressure and persecution or opposition.

Between the Source of Life and the fulfillment of the dream in communion with the Triune God lies the long journey of choice. We choose to stay under pressure, to remain in the furnace of transformation, by holding to the dream and choosing the purification.

It is in this long process of myriad choices day after day—choosing for life, for communion, choosing to be true to the presence of God flowing in us—that character is built.

Character is the consistency of choice through both promising times and hard times. It is the fruit of godliness. In C. S. Lewis's fantasy novel, *The Great Divorce*, people arrive in heaven from their hellish busyness as shadowy, thin beings. Everything about heaven is hard at first.

The beautiful waterfall hurts because the droplets of its spray are hard against these weak, phantasmagoric shadow people. Even the grass of heaven cuts their feet. If they're going to stay they will need to become substantial people.

Lewis understood that we have to grow into substance. By choosing, over a long period of time, for the life of God in us, we become substantial beings. Our shadowy, insubstantial dreams are gradually shaped by God into powerful visions and actions.

When people encounter us, they realize they've come up against a person of substance. Over the course of time, the choice to remain faithful to the life of God has called us to learn when to say yes and when to say no.

We have strength because we have purpose. We've chosen to live out of the passion of God's life in us and we've learned over time not to deviate from that purpose.

It's painful to watch someone have to give up on a dream that has charted his or her life for years. I've seen people agonize over these choices. They're afraid there will be no resurrection. They can't trust that if they go through the death process they will experience a newness of life they could not have predicted.

I don't want to minimize the difficulty of choice nor the powerful struggles we will face. At times we will feel desperation and futility. Our longings will be as raw as an open wound. No one knows the full force of temptation until he or she has said no right up to the end.

But I also want to encourage you that there's something simple but profoundly fruitful here. It isn't all a heroic assault on the mountain.

Amazingly, we survive. Our very survival makes us stronger. It reveals to us our grit and the grace that has come to us.

We become more deeply rooted in the life of God. We become stronger in our choices and, without our knowing it, the river of life flows into our thirsty world.

LIVING PASSIONATELY

■

God dwells in His creation
and is everywhere indivisibly present
in all His works. This is boldly taught
by prophet and apostle and is accepted
by Christian theology generally. That is,
it appears in the books, but for some reason
it has not sunk into the average Christian's
heart so as to become a part of his
believing self. Christian teachers shy away
from its full implications, and,
if they mention it at all, mute it down
till it has little meaning.

A. W. TOZER[1]

CHAPTER TWELVE

LIVING PASSIONATELY IN CREATION

■

A RECENT CONFERENCE FOCUSED ON THE URGENT NEED FOR EVANGELICALS to deepen their understanding of spiritual formation. We talked about the need to get beyond a shallow spirituality of performance and experience real transformation of soul and body.

The conference was held on the eastern edge of the Rocky Mountains. Deeply etched canyons, dramatic rock spires, and dark evergreens surrounded us with an imposing, almost confrontational presence.

Throughout the weekend we listened to thoughtful lectures, shared deeply about personal spiritual growth, and worshiped together. We were busy, thoughtful, and interactive. But for all practical purposes we could have been in downtown Manhattan. We were active in our heads, and occasionally in our hearts, but we weren't active in our bodies. Not once did we acknowledge our surroundings. We didn't take time to offer thanks for the glory that enveloped us or pray for the health of the earth. We didn't go outside or take time to listen or be present in any way to the creation around us. A few of us purposely sat on one side so we could see the hills from the window.

I came away wondering about it all. I do not criticize the organizers.

The conference was inspiring, and a disconnection from surroundings is certainly not unique to this conference.

But why would nearly three dozen spiritual leaders reflect on the importance of deep spiritual formation without even raising a question about our encapsulated spirituality? Why would we be so full of words and so "out of body"?

What's missing in this picture? If we were consciously in tune with the passionate presence of God, would that not somehow overflow into praise and wonder, into sheer enjoyment of the created goodness around us?

If our spirituality integrates the whole of our experience, surely our understanding of discipleship must encompass our experience of the world around us.

A. W. Tozer's statement at the beginning of this chapter may be a bit of a jolt. Does God really dwell in creation? Is God "everywhere indivisibly present in it all"? Tozer has articulated the church's understanding throughout most of its history. If we're to take the statement seriously, we must open ourselves to our relationship to the earth as part and parcel of our spirituality.

Embracing the creation as part of our growth into intimacy with God calls us to address two important questions. First, in what way is God present within creation? Does that imply some kind of pantheism?

Second, what difference does it make to our spirituality if God is truly present, although not confined to, creation? If God is present, can we meet Him and experience intimacy with Him there?

The answer we give to these questions reveals much about our relationship with God. If we believe that God is passionately alive in the burgeoning world around us, then we miss a great opportunity to experience intimacy with God by failing to attend to God's presence. If a Trinitarian relationship of passionate love is the ground of all being, then we participate in the life of the Trinity by being intentional about our relationship to the world around us.

IS GOD PRESENT IN CREATION?[2]

As soon as we ask the question, "Is God present in creation?" we find ourselves somewhere on a continuum. Pantheism (God is encompassed within creation) occupies one end of the continuum and deism (God is entirely separate from creation) occupies the other. Because of the present new age scare, pantheism seems to be the greater evil at the moment.

It's important to distinguish between the idea that God is present within creation and the idea that God is encompassed by creation. Pantheism maintains that God is the sum total of creation and nothing more. There is no "God beyond." No Creator, and therefore no external reference point.

If God doesn't exist beyond the creation, then nature itself is God, and the forces of nature become the final norm for life. Such a view may make us attentive to creation, but in the end it lacks any hope of salvation. There is no God to intervene in the affairs of this world. We are caught in the repetitive cycles of nature and are pawns to its power.

Christianity has always rejected the notion that nature was God or that there was no God beyond the natural world. However, we sometimes back so far away from pantheism that we come dangerously close to deism.

Deists focus on the separation between God and the natural world. God, a deist would say, made the world, wound it up like a clock, and left it to its own devices. Again we're left without a God who cares — a God who comes to us in our historical situation and saves us.

Somewhere between these two obvious errors we have to say that God participates in creation but isn't confined to its limitations. What, then, is the nature of God's participation within the creation?

Does God simply act on creation as an external force, or is He actively present within creation? That is the question we must answer.

Scripture stresses the intimate relationship between God and the creation. God is the Creator but not a machine operator. Let us take a brief look at some of the evidence.

The entire worldview of the ancient Israelites was significantly different from ours. We've been formed more than we realize by the philosophical dualism of our Greek heritage. We make big distinctions between mind and body, the material and the spiritual, the earthly and the heavenly.

The ancient Israelites had no split between their spirituality and the earth. Humans were of one piece — body and spirit together — and the world around them was the only arena they knew in which God was alive and actively present.

In Psalm 139:7, we discover that wherever we go, God is present. "Where can I go from your Spirit? Where can I flee from your presence?" the psalmist cries. Nowhere! is the final answer.

Everywhere he turns God is there. He lives in the immediate presence of God everywhere.

In Psalm 104, God, the Creator, clothes Himself with light and then spreads out the heavens like a tent (verse 2). The image obviously relates back to the creation of light (Genesis 1:3). Light, the very essence of the material world, is God's clothing. The clouds, says the psalmist, are God's chariot, and God rides on the wings of the wind (104:3).

God's providence is no less intimate. When God takes away their breath, the animals die. When God sends forth His Spirit (that is, breath[3]), they are created. In so doing, God renews the face of the earth (104:29-30).

Breath, to the psalmist, was a very intimate gift—the gift of life itself. God breathes His life-giving spirit into creation and it burgeons with life. It is parallel to the original creation story in which God breathed into Adam the "breath of life" and Adam became a living being (Genesis 2:7).[4]

The New Testament carries forward this same understanding. In Colossians we read that Christ "is before all things, and in him all things hold together" (1:17). The world has life and coherence "in Christ," not outside of Christ. Paul said that God put us on earth with its limitations so that we might seek after God and reach out for Him, "though he is not far from each one of us. 'For in him we live and move and have our being'" (Acts 17:27-28).

Finally, the Incarnation—God manifest in the flesh—is the great revelation of God's presence in creation. God took on flesh and blood and clothed Himself with created material. This was the ultimate, archetypal expression of God's presence.

Yes, God is present in creation, but He is not limited to creation. As the Creator, God has chosen to create in such a way that His life is the life of the world. It's hard to conceive of any other possibility. Would we be prepared to say that the life within creation is something other than God's life? Hardly. Creation is breathed into existence by God and is held and sustained in God. God's life is the environment, the womb of all created life.

St. Augustine asked how God can come into him when even the heavens cannot contain God. He argued that nothing that exists could exist without containing God. So, too, "I should be null and void and could not exist at all, if you, my God, were not in me. . . . Or is it rather

that I should not exist, unless I existed in you? For 'all things find in you their origin, their impulse, the center of their being.'"[5]
Providence is not the action of God as machine operator. God is not detached from the creation, flipping switches and turning the dials that make it all run. Grace is not God's gift separate from God's presence. God's grace and God's providence are nothing less than the gift of God's presence, given to us so richly.

WHAT DIFFERENCE DOES GOD'S PRESENCE MAKE?

What shape, then, does our passion for the earth take? What is our vision and dream?

We can dream about exploiting the earth for our own benefit, or we can dream about living within the rhythms and limitations of the earth for the benefit of all. Does it make any difference in the transforming of our souls?

Even at the purely human level, we no longer have the luxury to ignore the importance of passion to our spirituality. Corrupted passion, alienated from God and indulged without restraint, has brought us to the brink of ecological ruin. It is polluting the earth like a flood of untreated sewage.

We've treated the earth like an oversized pantry. We consume its resources as unthinkingly as we would wolf down a bag of chips during the Super Bowl. We've polluted the air and the rivers and raped the forests with a flood of greed. This is passion gone terribly awry.

If we don't embrace this rampant, raging flood and learn to live with it in more healthy ways, we will die. Human survival alone makes it imperative to learn to live well with our passion and develop a positive discipleship with regard to the earth.

We can blame big business or whoever "those other people" might be, but the unspoken disconnection from creation that characterizes much of our discipleship must also contribute to this crisis. If we can worship, teach, discuss, and carry on all the normal experiences of spirituality without reference to creation, we must bear some responsibility for the crisis we now face.

Thankfully, many people are becoming aware of the great damage the unrestrained greed of our consumer culture has unleashed. They've begun to long for a more balanced way to live with God's creation.

Rather than seeing the earth as something to be consumed, many people are beginning to see the earth as something to cherish.

This is commendable. But as Christians, we can take it much further. Rather than looking to nature as the new (renewed) God, the ultimate value, we can explore a Trinitarian dream for creation. We can envision the earth created and sustained within the life of the Three-in-One God. We can embrace the earth in all its complex goodness as an integral part of our experience of God.

When we include the created world in our intimacy with the Trinity, we can freely receive the gifts God has to offer us. In return, we can gladly offer our gifts back as a response of love.

This relational intimacy is what the early church was so careful to maintain. In the Incarnation, we see the Trinity as a relationship of vibrant love—the ground of all reality, the essence of being. If all existence finds its being in a relational God, then we are part of a relationship with the created world that is vibrant and rich. Our experience as embodied, earthly people is part of our surrender to God.

We can also turn it around and say it another way. Our desire to be independent of the rhythms and seasons of the natural world is a fundamental part of our rebellion against God. Our craving to dominate and consume the world is part of our sinfulness.

A humble submission to the presence of God within the created world lies at the heart of our submission to the Lordship of Christ. The issue of our passionate dreams for creation is nothing less than an issue of obedience—a place for us to incorporate spiritual disciplines to nurture and structure our intimacy with God through a loving relationship with creation.

The quality of relationship we sustain with the earth will be, in large measure, decided by our dreams. If we dream of the earth as the answer to our needs, we will consume it at will. On the other hand, if we dream of the earth as a good creation—an expression of the storm of love in the Trinity—we will treat it with honor and care. We will enter into life-sustaining community with the earth and all living things.

SEEING SIGNS OF THE TRINITY IN CREATION

Creation is the most astounding expression of lavish attention to particular detail. It's also the most profound web of interrelated life we know. It is the Trinity on display.

Creation displays an immense variety within the very humblest of life forms. There are, for example, approximately eight hundred species of caddis flies. That's a stupendous variety.

Caddis flies happen to be a major source of food for trout in North America. But eight hundred separate species? That can only be conceived as a wildly prodigal display of variety. Fortunately for the fly fisher, they're similar enough to be imitated with a few flies.

For years we accepted the vast diversity within the natural world without thought. In a wilderness continent where we had to carve out space for our homes and farms, we got used to the idea of limitless variety and availability. There was plenty of wood from the place we got our last log. We could carve up the land at will. There was more than enough space for our garbage.

But the earth is more than abundance and variety. Now we're being compelled to pay attention to the connection between things. Because of the threatened existence of so many varieties of life, we've begun to discover that all of creation is tied together in a web of existence we now call our global ecosystem. We're becoming aware, for example, that the clearing of the forests in Central and North America threatens the destruction of songbird habitat.

Other human-engendered hazards have also played their part. Pets kill millions of birds each year. And surprisingly, the lights left on in office towers at night have played havoc with the navigation system of migrating birds, leaving thousands disoriented and eventually dead.

These human factors have all combined to bring the population of migrating songbirds to a place of critical danger. This past year it was noted in the *Calgary Herald* that the songbird population has dropped by 50 percent since the mid–1960s.

Broad links between habitat and survival like this are commonly known. Countless lesser-known but equally telling examples abound of the incredible and unexpected webs of interdependent relationships within the natural world.

Darryl, for example, threw a potluck picnic to celebrate the completion of a new house on an acreage outside Calgary. He had worked hard getting a junior oil company off the ground, and now buying the acreage was his "reward" to himself and his family. He cleared some land and built a beautiful sprawling house with windows opening to the Rockies.

Wanting to clean up the place that fall, Darryl worked hard to cut down all the dead trees and chop them up into firewood. He anticipated long evenings in front of the fire; he didn't realize that he was breaking an intricate circle of life on his property.

The thought never crossed his mind that some birds like Pileated Woodpeckers and Northern Flickers depend on the dead wood for food, drilling holes in the trees to forage for insects. These holes become the nesting spots for other birds like Nuthatches and Chickadees. By clearing out all the dead wood, Darryl was destroying the habitat for these birds to nest. He was interrupting a very simple life chain that many species depend on.

All of this incredible variety, held together in a myriad intricate strands of relationship, beautifully expresses Trinitarian life. If we take seriously that creation is more than our food pantry, which we can raid at will, or our sandbox to play in however we please, it will affect how we live with creation.

The early church insisted on a doctrine of the Trinity to emphasize the fact that *relationship* is at the heart of all reality. In Western Christianity, this emphasis was eventually lost, and reality became objectified: Land was no longer something to have a relationship with, it was a commodity to be speculated on and exploited for profit.

If we see the natural world as an expression of the Divine life, if we let the love of the Trinity fill our hearts, our dreams for the created world will move from exploiting nature to shared communion with it.

In the "receiving" and "giving" of Trinitarian communion, we enter into true relationship with the earth. We can move from exploitation to shared life, from management and control to intimacy and love.

Confined now to our paved streets and insular offices, we easily lose sight of this possibility. But from the ancient days when the tribes of Israel identified with tracts of land, down to the Alberta farmer who has simply loved the soil all his life, people have shared a deep and powerful intimacy with the earth.

As we deepen our sense of communion with the life of God, manifest in the earth, we affirm the current of God's life and receive its gifts. We also give back to the earth the gifts we have to offer as we attend to the banks of the stream and find healthy boundaries for our passion.

WHAT WE RECEIVE FROM THE EARTH

What do we receive from the earth that can create gratitude in our hearts as we live in relationship to its complex life? The earth gives us at least four great gifts: life, love, the gift of our bodies, and an appreciation for the ordinary.

We Receive Life

At the most basic level, we receive our sustenance from the earth. The air, water, and resources of the earth are God's gifts to us.

We breathe, eat, and sleep in the womb of nature. This is the way we were made. We can't separate ourselves from the earth and its well-being.

It's easy for us, with our technological know-how to think that our life is independent of the earth.[6] When we dream of our independence and superiority, we use the earth however we wish. When we think we're detached from the earth, we forget that we're embedded in its life and its seasons.

Accepting our God-given life through the created world affects our prayer. We begin with a very simple receiving. We breathe and are thankful to the Creator for giving us life through the creation. We look around us and are filled with love for the incredible bounty of God's gifts. We bow in submission to the Creator by accepting the life that comes to us from nature that surrounds us like a womb.

Imagine, for a moment, what it would be like if everyone (even all Christians in North America) dreamed this dream together? Imagine how differently we would experience the world if everyone lived in humble submission and gratitude for its gifts of life to us. It's hard to conceive of such a dream, but we can add our little strands of love and gratitude to God as part of the web of communion we experience in creation.

We Receive Love

Nature is one of the great, uncomplicated expressions of God's love to us. Sitting on a log in the woods, resting at the edge of a meadow, or staring at the endless sea, we receive a quiet, unconditional acceptance from outside ourselves—from God through His creation.

Often people come to me and say they don't feel loved by God. It's no wonder. Disconnected from the earth, we're cut off from one of the primary ways God showers us with love.

How can people deal with that terrible sense of alienation and aloneness?

More "telling" will not do anything for them. It might help them to read John 3:16 one more time, but chances are the verse will just bounce off their consciousness like a deflected arrow. If they don't get some charismatic experience that overwhelms them with a sense of love, what are they to do?

One of the suggestions I've found helpful is to invite people to get out into nature and experience God's love through the created world. I invite them to let creation surround them and offer them a sense of quiet acceptance.

A friend of mine finds that she prays best when she's digging in the garden. It's not that she prays better words. Surrounded by the earth and the plants, she has a deep sense of healing and re-creation. Lovingly tending her plants becomes a form of communion with God, whose life is shared.

The earth lets us experience the sense of Trinity in very simple, uncomplicated ways. We begin to feel truly unique, accepted for who we are as distinct persons. At the same time we feel at one with all life around us. Paradoxically, we feel more ourselves and at the same time more in union than we've felt for a long time.

When we're alone, surrounded by the desert or the forest or our backyard, we can be ourselves. We don't have to wear masks in nature. We don't have to try to interpret the complex motives of others. We don't have to prove ourselves. All the baggage from our relationships that pollutes our personal images of God can, for the moment, be laid aside.

In the silences of the earth's wild places, we can simply exist as we are because we're given the dignity of presence. We experience a deep rest that we might call a rest of our very being.

It doesn't matter whether we're smart or strong, whether we've failed or whether we're famous. Our accomplishments do not matter in front of the chattering squirrel that announces our presence from his perch on the spruce branch. The squirrel would announce the president of the United States or the least known person on the face of the earth.

A Christian leader, I'll call him Thomas, once came to talk about the tremendous pain he was suffering through the breakdown of a significant relationship. Everything in his body and soul cried out in the agony of aloneness and abandonment. After hours of sitting together and hashing through his dilemmas, I suggested we go for a walk by the Bow River. Calgary has one of North America's premier pathway systems along the river's banks.

Thomas didn't want to go. When I asked why, he replied, "I don't really like to go outdoors. I don't enjoy it; it doesn't do anything for me."

As I reflected on this later, I thought to myself, *How easily we miss one of the most simple and profound ways God wants to love us. No wonder modern people struggle with feeling loved. No wonder we easily feel alone and abandoned. We're removed from the earth.*

Sometimes physically getting outside is too difficult or awkward for people. No matter! It can be wonderful to pray by a window, a cup of coffee in hand, and look out at the goodness of the earth nearby. Surely there's a poplar tree or a lilac bush we can gaze at. We can take five minutes to quiet our hearts and open our souls to God's love by looking out at the world He has given.

The Earth Grounds Us in Our Bodies

Creation brings us back home to ourselves and restores our center. I don't think it's an accidental juxtaposition when the psalmist said, "He makes me lie down in green pastures, he leads me beside quiet waters," and then adds, "he restores my soul" (Psalm 23:2-3).

We are from the earth—from the dust, as the old graveside rite somberly says. When we embrace the earth as an expression of God's life, we are brought home again.

We're given back our bodies. Our bodies are not foreign to us, they are not a physical hindrance that keeps us from the spiritual world. Our bodies are the dwelling place of God (1 Corinthians 6:19).

God is more than creation; we are more than our bodies. Yet our bodies are our vessel for the life of God flowing into creation. The goodness of the earth reminds us of the goodness of our bodies. Coming home to the earth brings us home to our bodies.

When the earth is seen within the Trinity, all its seasons and rhythms become signs of God. Day, night, fall, winter, menstruation, birth, death— all become sacred places of discovering God's presence in our lives.

If our spirituality moves us away from our sensuality, we will live disconnected lives. We will never live at home with ourselves or with the earth.

When we live disconnected from our bodies, we end up being

nervous and afraid. Fear and anxiety can easily lead us to become violent toward ourselves and—finally—toward creation and toward others.

There are many ways for us to pray about our connection to the earth. Tilden Edwards taught me one helpful way. He suggested praying with our feet. Sometime, when you're alone, you might want to try it. Plant your feet firmly on the ground and gradually imagine them becoming solidified in the earth. Allow your being to flow down through your feet into the earth and back again into your body. Then walk slowly—very, very slowly—planting your feet deliberately and paying attention to each step and how it feels to be grounded in the earth.

Talk to God about the goodness of the earth and the goodness of your body. Ask God to bring you back home to your rightful place, to restore your soul within the environment He has created as your birthright.

When we learn to live at home with our bodies and with our passion, we end up being healed and becoming a healing influence in the world. When we begin to see that the earth (including our bodies) is as good as God said it is, then we reap the benefit of that great reconciliation. By embracing the earth, we become grounded. That frees us to enter all our other relationships from a healthy, more secure place.

The Earth Restores Our Sense of the Dignity of the Ordinary
What does it mean to open up to the created world again? These days, trying to describe it feels a bit like trying to describe snow to someone in the tropics. Many people live so far removed from direct contact with the earth they no longer know what they're missing.

Grandiose experiences are easy to talk about. We ogle sights like the Grand Canyon or the Oregon Coast. Our calendars are filled with pictures of spectacular mountains and thrilling sunsets. We're tourists of the magnificent.

But as wonderful as these sights are, they're not our primary links to the earth. They titillate us, but they don't necessarily ground us. They may only fuel our addiction to bigger and better experiences.

The small, ordinary encounters with nature ground us in ways no magnificent experience ever could.

The sprig of foxtail grass outlined with morning dew, or the droning buzz of a cricket in the early evening are so ordinary they may get lost in the rush. Yet these everyday experiences surround us, embrace us, and create a sense of gratitude and union.

For example, it's hard to imagine how good it is to live close to the rhythms of night and day when we hole up in an office all day and then try to avoid the night by turning on lights everywhere. There is no great circling rhythm in that life, only the incessant nagging of our Day-Timers.

It's too easy to take the convenience of the light for granted and to continue at breakneck speed with what we feel compelled to do. We miss the daily rhythm of listening to the night fall quietly around us.

How can we begin to know the deeply settling experience of the evening unless we purposely choose, for a few moments at least, to leave the lights off and watch the daylight fade?

It's fascinating to watch a pair of red-breasted Nuthatches work their way down a spruce tree, conversing in quiet tones to each other while they search for insects. But who has the time to spend a half-hour doing nothing but quietly watching when so many other things seem more important and clamor for our attention?

Is that not the very question? What is important? Is it more important to have our lives grounded in the environment for which they were created, or deny that environment and live increasingly disintegrated lives in a world of our own making?

These ordinary experiences of nature teach us about beauty and respect for the simple things. Taking time to experience the importance of the ordinary is one of those overall structures we can choose to channel our passion in healthy ways. We learn, through the unexpected dignity of the ordinary, a respect for the dignity of all the other relationships in our lives.

WHAT WE OFFER THE EARTH AS OUR GIFT

In the Trinitarian cycle of uniqueness and union, we receive the dignity of being rooted in the presence of God's life around us. We also offer ourselves with joy, surrendering to the oneness the Trinity creates. Within the communion of this wide prayer, we can dream of what we can give as well as what we've been given. Let us look at two particular things we can offer the earth as examples of a wide field of dreams we can explore.

We Can Offer a Submission to the Earth

One of the great gifts of creation we can offer as part of our Trinitarian communion is submission. The earth teaches us humility. Through humility we find our place within the created order. We learn appropriate banks for our passion.

The tendency, which has been expressed so violently in our own culture, is to bypass submission through technology. We live climate-controlled lives. We go from climate-controlled houses to climate-controlled cars to climate-controlled office buildings. Jets, phones, faxes, e-mail, and the Internet are all good things in themselves, but they belie our ever-present desire for total independence.

It isn't wrong to want to be comfortable or to communicate long distance. But we detract from our spiritual health when we attempt to escape the bonds of our relationship with the natural world.

Perhaps technology embodies its own evil, but the historical evidence makes it seem likely that this desire to transcend the natural world has been aided and abetted by a disembodied spirituality.[7] We've attempted to bypass or transcend our bodies and the whole of nature in our spirituality.

Now we must learn to submit to what we've thrown off. We have the privilege of accepting creation as one of the great disclosures of Trinitarian life. We can choose to attend to the rhythms and seasons of life and allow the limitations of creation to be a sign of God's authority in our lives.

We Can Offer the Earth Our Care

Much recent Christian dialogue on the great ecological questions of our day has circled around the theme of stewardship. God told Adam to fill the earth and subdue it and to rule over it (Genesis 1:28).

For centuries that seemed to mean a *carte blanche* mandate to consume the earth. In the last few years Christians have begun to see God's command as a mandate to exercise wise, nurturing stewardship as God's vice-regents.

I suspect, however, that we will never understand our role as stewards within creation until we begin to love the earth passionately. The real problem with much of our stewardship is that we still see ourselves as separate from the earth. We haven't surrendered to the life of the Trinity. We respond with our analytical and managerial ability instead of responding with love.

Stewardship is not first of all about management. We can only partly manage creation. And for all that, our attempts to manage often only create worse messes. Management implies that we are better and bigger than creation and that we know what to do. Managing creation can easily be a way to resist entering into a relationship of love.

Loving the earth includes taking the time to know it intimately. It means appreciating the detailed beauty of its life. How can we say we love creation if we seldom give it a second glance?

Loving the earth as the dwelling of God also includes becoming vulnerable to its needs. Love anticipates a response greater than that of a doctor or manager. It calls for care and delight and commitment to the other's best. Then when we're called to make management decisions, we will do so from a heart of love.

When we take the time to go beyond management and submit to the natural structures and rhythms of creation, we're submitting to the One who placed us within nature as our home. Such a stance offers the reciprocity of communion. It helps us accept our own unique dignity and at the same time accept our limitations as part of a larger union.

As we come to love the earth, we sense the interplay of the whole. We learn not to misuse creation in an attempt to satisfy the cravings of our own distorted passions. We can allow love to shape new choices that help us dance with the earth in the unity and uniqueness of the Trinity.

CONCLUSION

You may be thinking, *I have enough on my plate already without being bothered about all this. Maybe when I get my act together with God and with those closest to me I'll be more interested in dealing with creation.*

As in the other dimensions of our relationship with God, grace enables the process to flow the other way. We don't get our act together first and then develop a relationship with God. We are called to open up to God, to invite Him into our lives, and then the rest of life begins to heal and grow.

So it is with the world of creation. When we open up to the creation and to our place within it, we begin to be restored in the rest of life. By learning to love the natural world, by experiencing the affirmation that is ours in the midst of creation, and by submitting to its limitations, the rest of our relationships tend to change.

As we come into harmony with God through our experience of the earth, we have a context or an environment in which to live well with all other relationships of community and intimacy. It is to those relationships we now turn.

Forgiveness and celebration
are at the heart of community.
These are the two faces of love. . . .
Community can never take precedence
over individuals. In fact, its beauty
and unity come from the radiance of each
individual conscience, in its light, truth,
and love, and free union with others.

JEAN VANIER[1]

CHAPTER THIRTEEN

LIVING PASSIONATELY IN COMMUNITY

■

AL HAS BEEN CHURCH-HOPPING FOR OVER A YEAR. WHEN HE MOVED TO Calgary, he began attending the nearest church of his denomination. It happened to be a large, high-fashion church. He was almost ashamed to drive his old Honda into the parking lot.

Despite joining a few programs, Al never felt at home. He was lonely in the crowd. Another large church, noted for its Bible exposition, attracted him. Then he switched to a church that puts on a sizzling worship experience.

Al is ordinary in every sense of the word. Not especially bright or successful, he simply wants to belong. He hungers for a community that recognizes the importance of the individual. He wants to be with people who can honestly share the joys and struggles of their faith.

Is this Al's problem? Is he stuck in his own personal image of what the church should be for him? Perhaps he wants the church to take responsibility for his loneliness. Then he can blame the church when his feelings of loneliness don't go away.

Or could this be a church problem? Have churches become so institutionalized that people are lost in the crowd? Can the church truly embrace Al's uniqueness as a person, or is he important only as a boost to the statistics and as a supporter of the program?

Over time we learn that Al's situation, replicated innumerable times in our churches today, encompasses both. Al needs to take responsibility for his own struggles. He cannot expect the church to "rescue" him.

But the church also needs to look at its choices. Is it focused on itself? Is it modeling the flowing love that respects both union and uniqueness? Is it truly an expression of the Trinity?

Are people there for the church or is the church there for the people? The question takes us to the heart of the paradox of Trinitarian passion.

When people are there for the sake of the organization, the church easily slips toward becoming autocratic and oppressive. When the church is there for the people, the people can become passive and consumeristic.

God's life is relational to the core.[2] The life of God-the-Trinity has planted in our souls a hunger for community.

Our deepening intimacy with God enables us to enter the world of relationships from a new place. Rooted, and at home with our desire, we are free—within the love of the Trinity—to give ourselves generously to others.

This is to be the defining characteristic of the church. We are to be signs, living icons, of the Trinity in the world. Jesus put it this way: "By this all [people] will know that you are my disciples, if you love one another" (John 13:35). Later that same evening, Jesus prayed, "May they be brought to complete unity to let the world know that you sent me and have loved them even as you have loved me" (John 17:23).

Imagine having the passion of the Trinity flow like an artesian well in our church life. Imagine living in a community of people both "self-possessed and other-oriented."[3] Imagine a church that calls people beyond themselves yet honors the unique journey of each.

How would this dream shape our church experience? How would it shape our church structures and policies? How would it affect our choices as individual members?

Can we sustain our passion for community and let God shape our churches into the image of the Three-in-One God? It won't be easy. It flies in the face of our cultural experience. But the fruit will be the sign of a new world—a world of God's love in our tired culture.

THE NATURAL TENDENCIES

In the struggle of the storm between the desire for oneness and the need for difference, churches often get caught on one side or the other.

Institutionalism

When all the differences of denomination are accounted for, the single most influential image of God on our Western church life may be the Greek notion of God as the Absolute One. This view of God is symbolized in our churches by the senior pastor or the priest.

One person presides over the entire life of the church. Even multi-staffed churches often reflect more a managerial vision concerned with a delegation of responsibilities than a Trinitarian vision of communion.

When we perceive God as One instead of a Trinity of Persons-in-communion, the focus shifts from relationship and vulnerability to status and power. Our experience of God and the church can get caught in a hardening hierarchy. Submission can become the dominant relationship. Combined with exclusively male images of God, this can degenerate into an unhealthy patriarchy in which power and position are more important than people.

The church becomes preoccupied with authority and acceptability. It loses the fragile focus of intimacy and concentrates on the clamorous question of stability. The mystery of mutual respect and mutual passion gets lost in the face of a need for control.

Churches with an authoritarian bent often unwittingly ride roughshod over people to keep the institution intact. We have fragmented over doctrinal splits. The words and the distinguishing dogmas of the institution have become more important than who we are as persons.

We have fragmented over styles of worship and over the agendas of greed and competition on the part of the leaders. All because we would rather have uniformity than the diversity of true Trinitarian fellowship.

One woman went to her pastor and said, "It isn't doing us any good to listen to more Bible teaching. Everything is in nice, proper order on the surface. But underneath, many of the women are suffering terribly. Their husbands are dictatorial as 'head of the home.' Their marriages are a sham, and the women have no sense of worth. Some have tried to raise this issue to their husbands and to the church, but they have no voice."

The pastor softspokenly replied, "God's grace is sufficient, Brenda.

His ways are best. These women need to confess their sins of pride and discontent to God. They will find peace in surrender."

When you strip away all the spiritual language, this pastor was really saying, "People are here for the sake of the church."

In a charismatic church, the pastor became obsessed with a vision that all of the members should become faith healers. This agenda became the focus of church life. Finally, one member confronted the pastor. "Your idealism is admirable, but people aren't even being good here. You're trying to make everyone into spiritual superheroes. It would give you a good name. Meanwhile people are backstabbing and critical to each other; marriages are falling apart; and the atmosphere is harsh, competitive, and oppressive."

Almost by definition, the church and its leadership exert a pull away from genuine Trinitarian communion. They gravitate naturally toward conformity — toward submission to church structure and program. After all, for the paid staff at least, this is the sphere of their influence and the focus of their career. If the institution isn't stable and successful, their reputations, and perhaps even their jobs, might be in jeopardy.

Churches that succeed in numerical growth tend to be the churches with successful programs. Programs must be administered, and program administration requires institutional structure.

So the temptation to let the institution dominate mounts. If the institution fails, everything ceases. Decisions must be made on the basis of what will continue to keep the institution running smoothly and successfully, not on the basis of personal need.

We say that the church is people, not buildings or programs, but that's a very difficult truth to live out. Pragmatically, we often choose in favor of the institution.

Elizabeth O'Connor wryly remarked that churches don't usually support individuals finding their own way. She wrote, "If the church were true to herself, she would help all people to discern and be faithful to their call. In such an effort, however, institutions probably recognize a threat to their own structures."[4]

Individualism

The uneasiness of church leaders toward personal passion is not without foundation. It is exacerbated by the obvious evils of our individualistic culture. Catering to individual desires in the church, especially in our society, can breed spoiled church members. It's not difficult to see the evil effects of individualism on church life. People come and go, relate to the community as they please, and generally become consumers of church.

The Canadian sociologist Reg Bibby described it as *à la carte* Christianity.[5] People pick and choose their experience from 11:00 to 12:00 on Sunday morning, much as they choose their food at the Sunday buffet an hour or so later. They slide from church to church, and program to program as it suits their spiritual taste buds or their family preferences at the moment.

Our postmodern society is suspicious of all institutions and of authority in general. It rejects the notion of any overall structure or story. Institutions that claim authority or ask for allegiance are out of order.

While we may bemoan the loss of authority in our postmodern era, we must admit, sadly, that our church institutions have often asked for it. There's been enough evidence of the abuse of institutional authority in our churches to validate large-scale suspicion.

Sexual abuse by church leaders has come into lurid focus. Gross spiritual abuse in the way churches have squelched people through guilt and tyrannical authority has been a terrible blight on the church as an institution.

Many people are now instinctively unwilling to be told what to believe or how to act. Church authority by the promotion of fear and exclusionist superiority doesn't cut it anymore. It's not enough to say, "This is what the church stands for."

Witness, for example, the huge controversy even in the Catholic church. Despite its historic appeal as an authoritative church, many of its members simply no longer accept the institutional decrees about contraception and the ordination of women.

So people have come to pick and choose. Consumerism fragments our church communities. Churches increasingly find themselves in competition. They have to advertise to the consumer wishes of the individual members much like a business has to advertise for customers.

As one pastor said in an interview with *Christianity Today*, "Any church that is going to sustain growth must put to work the best principles, marketing ideas, and service strategies."[6] The whim of the current taste in worship, teaching, and programs dictates how the church will operate.

THE DIFFICULTY OF CLEAR DISCERNMENT

If either of these two movements were all bad, discernment would be easy. If we could label the danger of institutionalism as the great sin, we could design a church focused solely on the individual. If we could argue that the contemporary suspicion of institutions was the sign of a corrupt society, we could call people to close ranks and submit to authority.

The movement toward unity is important. It reflects the Christian notion that revelation calls us beyond ourselves. Union invites us to open our hearts to a greater reality than our ideas and preferences. God confronts us in the group and asks us to make choices of fidelity, even of death to our needs and wishes, in order to be part of a larger whole, imperfect as it is.

The movement toward recognition of the individual is also important. Our spiritual growth naturally includes an individuation process. This often necessitates letting go of the accepted understandings of the group for a time.[7]

People from authoritarian churches frequently have to go through a period of skepticism and rebellion before they can come back into the church as a full adult. There can be no real intimacy as long as all the people in the church are like dependent children.

People have to experience their own life with God as uniquely theirs. No authentic vision of church life can deny or oppress this important journey.

However, in our individualistic culture, it's difficult to know when people are legitimately claiming the uniqueness of their own spiritual journey and when they're simply moving toward a narcissistic "spirituality." The real story isn't always clear.

Are people abandoning the party line because they're being honest to their own process of growth? Or are they simply reinforcing self-centered claims of autonomy? When the church leaders urge people to "get on board" and be part of the church, are they doing it because they're truly calling people to respond to God or are they building their own kingdom?

The storm of passion rages!

A Trinitarian dream that leads us away from the extremes of institutional bureaucracy and individualistic fragmentation is a radical and lonely dream in our society. We will have to withstand overwhelming pressures if it is to shape meaningful choices in our lives.

EMBRACING A TRINITARIAN DREAM

Paradoxical movements can never be resolved. How then can we nourish in a practical way a Trinitarian dream that can help us move toward true community?

Accepting the polarities. To accept the polarities between the needs of the institution and the needs of the individual is to embrace the storm. As people who accept the Trinity at the heart of our being, we can learn to cherish the goodness of each pull.

Embracing the polarities keeps us humble. We will always be out of kilter in one direction or the other. In the ever-changing landscape of church life, we will not resolve these issues into a satisfactory compromise. We'll never be certain we have it right. Our need for forgiveness and guidance will be a constant confession.

Embracing the paradox of Trinitarian passion also keeps us dependent on the Spirit. We will need discernment through the storm of a thousand and one specific decisions within the life of the church.

We can't hold the fabric of Trinitarian life together on our own. We can't keep life from exploding into fragments or imploding into a black hole. Only the flowing of God's love will keep us from institutionalism or consumerism.

We need not be discouraged by the conflict; rather, it calls us to prayer. We pray that the Spirit will be revealed in the storm in fresh ways, giving us the courage to follow. It's almost like reading Job again and finding God mysteriously present in the storm (Job 38:1).

Risking respect. The dream of Trinitarian community involves a twofold trust. The community must risk trust by offering respect. It must put its life on the line in order to honor the goodness and the passion of each person.

Each person must also risk trust by offering generosity. Each must open his or her passion and share the goodness with the community as a freely offered gift.

Both the community and the members are called to become vulnerable to the other. In this vulnerability, life is born.

Because the church leadership particularly embodies the tendency toward bureaucracy, they must intentionally commit to the value and integrity of each person. The community must continually offer concrete signs of respect and dignity to each member in order to warrant the person's trust.

That is no small order. Whatever structure we adopt, from democratic Baptist to hierarchical Episcopalian, Trinitarian passion calls us to ask the following kinds of questions. Does our church foster the development of passion in each person in the church? Do we fear the distinct life of each person, or do we celebrate it? Do we see the diversity of passion as a sign of the presence of God?

Do we allow people to follow their own path of growth, following the flow of the river, or do we dictate what questions they can ask, what choices are acceptable? Does the passion acceptable in our church embrace all of life or is it limited to passion for our programs and our ways of expressing the truth? Do we create safe places for that passion to be explored and empowering places where it can be structured in healthy ways?

A church community shows dignity toward its membership by choosing policies and decisions that demonstrate that each person is at least as important as the program. In this way we follow the pattern of Jesus' life. Jesus continually championed the needs of people, one at a time, in the face of institutional rules and bureaucracy. Every time He touched a leper or healed on the Sabbath or accepted the full presence of women, He was exercising the kind of trust the religious leaders were supposed to be offering.

I will never forget my friend from l'Arche telling me about a time when they were deciding whether to ask one of the handicapped people to leave because of behavioral problems. Round and round they wrestled with this hard choice. Finally each community member (including a man with Down's syndrome) was asked what should be done. The man with Down's said quietly, "I think he should stay."

The community pondered the statement. Without allowing themselves to be dominated by any one person they were, nonetheless, committed to respecting the voice of each person. And in this instance, they realized that God had spoken through the weakest member of the group. And they chose to allow the person to stay on for one more year.

In a church where the group respects the dignity of its members, the leadership will not call for commitment on the basis of guilt. Allegiance or submission gained by making people feel guilty or obligated is disrespectful, manipulative, and dehumanizing. The true mark of the church is love, and it is love that brings people into the circle.

In a church where passion is acknowledged, the leaders will not seek to divorce worship from our bodies and our emotions. They will not stifle it into safe, intellectual forms. Where the dignity of each individual is honored, the poor will not be bypassed in favor of the rich (James 2:1-13). That includes the materially or intellectually rich, or the one rich with the gift of persuasion and group power. Rather, in following the example of Jesus, those marginalized from power will often set the agenda.

Rugged demonstration of this trust on the part of church leaders is the basis on which people can commit themselves to community. They may commit themselves for other reasons—for their own security, for the programs offered, for the mission—but those commitments won't last.

It is especially in the gift of respect and dignity that people are able to let down barriers, explore the inner fountain of their own life in God, and learn to offer their gifts generously to the world.

This offer of respect for each person can easily be misused. A power-hungry person can seek to grab power under the guise of pursuing his own call. Some, seeking to be true to certain passages of Scripture, will conclude that women should have an equal place in the church. Some seeking to be true to other passages will conclude the opposite. Some will think we should forgive the sinner in order to avoid institutional oppression, while others will think we should throw the sinner out in the name of church purity.

The temptation to grab power in order to "save" the church can be enormous. Pools of power develop to push each agenda. The leadership must find the strength to stay grounded beyond the conflicting agendas and must continue to model respect while calling each person to hear and respect the other's side.

Admittedly, this is a vulnerable trust on the part of the leadership. It's a risky choice to voluntarily switch from focusing on power to focusing on affirming each person. It takes a great deal of awareness that one is grounded in God's love to be able to take up the towel and serve others.

But when this respect is offered, consistently and without strings attached, new webs are created. Authority isn't abdicated, it's shared—like broken bread. People become self-possessed in their own right and are invited to join in the dance of communion and self-giving.

Risking generosity. Another risk in the reciprocal flowing of love is the trust offered by each person. The passion of love arises within us. As it flows to the surface, it becomes the gift of generosity we can offer to the community as a whole.

Each person is called to become a contributing part of a loving community. Each, in the current of life he or she receives from God, has life and gifts to offer. Perhaps it's the gift of grace and forgiveness, or a cup of cold water given in Jesus' name. Large or small, the gift may be extended freely with trust that it will be accepted by the community. This is a sacred and fragile trust. It calls for courage and compassion on the part of the whole community.

The vulnerability of offering our gifts to the community is first and foremost in the act of offering who we are. We don't merely offer our gifts. Generosity runs deeper than the talents and achievements that make us feel good about ourselves. Mostly, we offer the gift of presence. We bring *ourselves* into the community, not just what we can do. This is a more profound commitment.

It is our life, shared with the lives of others, that creates the webs that form the mystery of community. This includes the things we're good at doing, like teaching and serving and evangelizing. But it also includes the ways that life flows through our disappointments and hurts when they are opened to God and brought into the flow of love.

Our spiritual gifts are more than our successes. The apostle Paul gets to the heart of spiritual gifts in his words, "Now to each one the manifestation of the Spirit is given for the common good" (1 Corinthians 12:7). The gift is not so much the activity but the way the Spirit is revealed. The Spirit is manifest both in our strengths and in our weaknesses (2 Corinthians 12:9-10).

One Sunday, a couple in the church spoke of their long saga in seeking to adopt a special needs child. Several years had gone by and now they had been offered a six-year-old child. For a complex of reasons, they couldn't say yes to this opportunity. Both spoke of their longing for a child and of the pain of what saying no to this child meant for their future. Afterward, someone thanked them for the precious gift they had offered the community over the years through their pain. They hadn't backed away from the new births in the church. They had offered, and continued to offer, themselves faithfully to the children, both in Sunday school and beyond Sunday morning. Their gift came through their wounds and not just through their successes.

Often our gifts aren't received with the same enthusiasm as we offer them. What we have to offer may be threatening, unappreciated, or simply ignored. It's difficult to remember that we're offering a gift and not a demand. We're simply sharing the life we've received. Our primary task is to share the gift in free and generous ways, not to evaluate how well it has been received. When we demand the right to share our gifts, we demonstrate that we're trying to possess the gift rather than participating in the dance of love.

Jean Vanier has spoken of coming to community for what we can get out of it and staying in community for what we can give. He said, "A community is only a community when the majority of its members is making the transition from 'the community for myself' to 'myself for the community,' when each person's heart is opening to all the others, without any exception. This is the movement from egoism to love, from death to resurrection."[8]

Vanier suggests that it takes time for a heart to make this passage from egoism to love. This is the true maturing of our passion. Through embracing our passion we've moved past the issue of whether we're given enough and whether or not our gifts are received by the community. We simply choose to offer our life to the world in ways that seem to be consistent with the flowing from within us and the need around us. In Frederick Buechner's wonderful phrase, "Call is the place where our deepest hunger and the world's deepest needs meet."

LEARNING TO CELEBRATE AND TO FORGIVE

Jean Vanier founded l'Arche, an international federation of communities for mentally and physically handicapped people. The experience gained from years of forming community with people who cannot offer the gifts of achievement and mental sophistication has profoundly changed this one-time philosophy professor.

Vanier says, "Forgiveness and celebration are at the heart of community. These are the two faces of love."

In community we learn to celebrate each other and to forgive each other. We celebrate our differences. That is what makes the community rich. Paul described community as a body with individual, interconnected parts (1 Corinthians 12). Peter spoke of our different gifts as expressing the variegated or multifaceted grace of God (1 Peter 4:10).[9] This is the essence of community life: "*Vive la différence!*"

It is a radical gift of the Spirit to celebrate and respect our differences, especially when those differences change the agenda of the group and make group life uncomfortable for us.

To speak of a spirituality of passion in this context only ups the ante. We are called, in community, to a place of vulnerability not only to differing agendas but to the passionate intensity with which they are held.

We face the clash of conflicting agendas in our worship, in our teaching, and in our response to the world. Some want a polished worship performance, some want a homey, warm atmosphere.

Some feel that the church needs strong exhortation. Others feel we should be more invitational, encouraging people to respond out of a sense of God's love.

Often there are irreconcilable differences between people when agendas clash. Can we continue to accept and respect the differences and look for a deeper unity? Can we trust that our unity isn't based solely on how we express ourselves but on our shared life?

It goes against every instinct within us to celebrate differences. We want likeness. We want to associate with others like us. We want to be with people who worship like we do, who believe like we do, who look like we do. Our churches are full of likeness. This is the root of discrimination and injustice.

If we're called to celebrate the differences, we're also called to forgive the way those differences affect us and hurt us! We learn to forgive as we become aware of our own need for forgiveness. Life in community will challenge us. It will open our wounds, lay bare our broken and hurtful places. As we bring these wounds to the light and seek forgiveness, we are given the strength and humility to forgive others.

Forgiveness is the lifelong companion of celebration. It is the sign of respect for others, and it takes us beyond differences back into unity.

We can't pretend to live this well. People often get hurt by the church. Sometimes, as in marriages and friendships, the community cannot sustain the vision and simply falls apart. We must be honest about the failures as well as persistent about the vision.

This life, as Ruusbroec so eloquently stated it, is a storm of passion. It is like lightning, a maelstrom of energy and conflicting desire. As we offer both our passionate dream and our failures to God, the beautiful broken glass of church life can often produce shards of incredible, if ragged, glory.

If your church life has become listless, try seeking to be faithful to the passion of the Trinity!

Love is the source of friendship. There can be love without friendship, but friendship without love is impossible. With love there is always reason which may keep it pure, while affection [passion] keeps love sweet. But the foundation of spiritual friendship is the love of God. To this divine love, all human love points. This, then, must be the foundation on which we build.

AELRED OF RIEVAULX[1]

CHAPTER FOURTEEN

LIVING PASSIONATELY IN RELATIONSHIPS

■

REG HOPED TO BE A DAD SOME DAY. HE EAGERLY ANTICIPATED HOLDING HIS own child in his arms and relished the idea of taking his daughter or son fishing.

Two years after Reg and Carrie were married, Carrie informed Reg that she didn't want children. It literally turned her stomach, she said, to think about giving birth and having to mother a young child.

Carrie's mother had beaten her as a child. She had come to recognize similar personality traits in herself. Now she was afraid of repeating the same story over again.

"Why didn't you tell me this before we got married?" Reg demanded.

"Because I didn't know it myself back then."

"But what about me and my needs?" he challenged. "Isn't there something we can do to alleviate your feelings and get on with it?"

Carrie responded just as adamantly. "It's not about getting on with it. Don't you see that having children would be a disaster for both me and the child?"

Reg and Carrie worked out a compromise. They went for counseling with the *proviso* that no decision about children would be made until after they had been through the counseling sessions.

That was ten years ago. Reg and Carrie have stayed together, but they don't have children. Counseling lasted until they began to touch the deeper issues. They never did work it through to any real solution.

Reg knows he just capitulated. He withdrew from Carrie emotionally and now their relationship is one of mutual toleration.

How do we live our closest relationships passionately yet unselfishly? Marriage, parenting, family of origin relationships, and friendships are crucibles for some of our most profound, difficult, and fulfilling choices for spiritual growth. The mystery of our passion for uniqueness and for union is most powerfully desired and most deeply threatened in these arenas.

The great context that surrounds and infuses our intimate relationships is the mystery of Trinitarian love. Everything we've dealt with prior to this chapter has been preparation for living these deepest experiences of Trinitarian love.

Henri Nouwen once remarked that it takes a community of supportive people for a marriage to survive. If it "takes a village to raise a child," we have the village of the Trinity, the earth, and our faith community surrounding us.

When our primary intimacy is secure in the love of God dwelling deep in our souls, it's easier to live well in our most intimate relationships. Assured of this continuously flowing love, we enter our intimate relationships less needy and more able to offer to others the gift of love we've already received.

Reconciliation with the earth as our true home also provides an important structure for intimacy. It grounds us and cultivates gratitude and humility.

A church community that respects each person and the free offering of their gifts to others can provide modeling and social reinforcement for our own choices for intimacy.

When we live ragged, alienated lives, our intimacies absorb this fragmentation. We become defensive, and real intimacy is difficult. It's like having a heart-to-heart conversation on a busy street corner during rush hour. When we're at home with ourselves in the world, we can enter into our intimate relationships in a quieter and more wholesome way.

These larger expressions of shared love surround our intimate relationships and give them a chance to survive and flourish. They prepare us to deal with the roller coaster of love closer to home. Our closest relationships are intricate and multidimensional. We cannot hope, in one chapter, to cover the rich diversity of themes they represent. We can, however, unpack at least some of the important ones. We can consider what effect the emergence of passion has on our close relationships. We can notice potential pitfalls in responding to passion. And we can follow a Trinitarian framework to provide some helpful guidelines as we experience the unfolding of these complex relationships.

THE EMERGING OF PASSION

What happens when we seek to live out the passion of love in the relationships closest to us? The emergence of passion can be an explosive experience. It can inject renewed vibrancy and open up exciting new possibilities for growth. It can also threaten our fragile and vulnerable intimacies.

Passion wakes us up to reality and to possibility. Paul tells us to wake up and behave decently (Romans 13:11-14). It's important to behave decently, but the first order of business is to wake up from our dead patterns, our claustrophobic dependencies, our ego-centered demands. We must wake up from the ways we have feared our passion or indulged it for our own self-interest.

It's wonderful to wake up and smell life! To feel the juice of passion running in our veins. God is with us. We are alive, the world is good!

Wonderful as it is, the awakening of passion can also present a stark contrast to the ways in which we are not living passionately at present.

Emerging passion faces us with challenge; it provokes choice. But if we stay faithful to the current of God's life, we will find new gifts of intimacy in deep and wonderful ways.

Passion Can Expose the Poverty of Present Relationships
When we open up to passion, one of the first things we may begin to notice is how shallow our present relationships can be. When passion emerges, it feels as though someone blew the horizons away and made life large and mysterious, full of flavor and new discovery. Why have we lived so long in dull routine?

In the flush of opened vision, our present relationships may feel mundane and lifeless by comparison. Life seems to be flourishing everywhere around us except close to home. While this is almost certainly not an accurate perception of our lives, it can often seem that way.

Our closest relationships are often filled with accommodations to habit and convenience. Whether in the relationships of our families of origin, of our marriages, or of our closest working colleagues, we see the ruts, the lies, the facades, and the many other ways our relationships are stilted and devoid of real passion. We see the ways we have given ourselves away and buried our passion.

One person may discover how much of his parents' emotions he has carried all his life. Another person may be shocked to discover that she married a "safe" father figure and is now rebelling against the way he tries to exercise "parental" control over her. Someone else may begin to feel how much they have squelched their emotions for fear of a volcanic eruption if both people in the marriage were emotional.

These are difficult, often stormy, issues to deal with. The storm of passion generated by the courage to accept the full uniqueness of each person within the bounds of union often feels too threatening.

We would rather live a truce of mediocrity than choose for something significant. We learn to keep quiet; we learn not to rock the boat. We hide the truth of who we really are and what's really important to us. And an emphasis on "victorious living" can whitewash this slow death.

Passion can open these routine places and fill them with vigor again. But often, at the beginning, it seems to simply widen the gap between how we want to live and what we are presently experiencing.

Passion Pushes Us to Choose
It's easy for our closest relationships to insulate us against choice. The dynamics become unwritten but exquisitely understood contracts. We learn to bring into the relationship only those things that are mutually agreeable and to withhold the rest of ourselves.

Passion pushes us to make choices. Once we've become alive to passion as the presence of God within us, the old pattern of entrapment and accommodation makes us want to revolt. The prodding toward choice may, in fact, help to explain one of the great reasons why people keep passion under wraps.

Will we allow our newly found life to rock the boat enough to make us deal with deep issues in our marriage? Or will we fade away and maybe leave the marriage—emotionally, physically, or in both ways? The challenge of choice seems unacceptable, so the passion we so crave begins to dry up instead.

This is where Reg and Carrie ended up. The conflict around having children shut them down. Rather than opening up their passion to God and to one another in honest, nondemanding ways, they clammed up. Rather than allowing God to be revealed in the struggle, deepening them and shaping their passion in more powerful ways, they chose accommodation.

How do we handle these conflicting experiences? We want to honor our present relationships. At the same time, we would sometimes rather roll up the present, stick it in the closet, and start over.

If one cares about following God and making good, healthy choices, passion is frightening. In exposing the facade of these relationships, passion threatens their survival. This seems wrong. If passion is good, how can it threaten a marriage?

When God or Christianity gets separated from passion and identified only with one side—only with keeping the peace of union—any challenge to the relationship seems to be a challenge to God. When the first priority of Christian spirituality is to keep from rocking the boat—peace at any cost—passion seems to be of the Devil.

This oppressive understanding of spirituality can deeply affect our close relationships. Parents, for example, can put tremendous pressure of "Christian" obligation on their children. They can teach the child to equate God's will with pleasing them. This distortion can paralyze a child and keep him from experiencing personal growth and development.

A man named Phillip came for spiritual direction. He was in his forties. He was the only surviving child, and his mother had loaded her grief on Phillip.

She wanted to be the center of Phillip's emotional attention. Any choices Phillip made to develop a sense of independence were interpreted as a betrayal, and she complained bitterly that he was selfish. She quoted Scripture verses that always somehow implied that Phillip should give up his plans so that he could care for her.

Phillip believed that his passion for a unique place in the world meant that he was loveless and self-centered. His desires seemed opposed to the will of God, who calls us to honor our parents.

Now, as a pastor, the emotional scars of his mother's possessiveness haunt Phillip. He has no life of his own. He can't talk about his spiritual journey apart from his church responsibilities. Everything is wrapped up in caring for others.

We've talked for several months, and I've simply kept asking him the question, "Who are you—the you that God loves?" Eventually Phillip admitted he didn't know, but he desperately wanted to find out. Slowly, he's unhooking from his misconception of love and allowing himself to say no to his mother (and "mother church") when necessary. Even if it disappoints her.

Phillip is having to choose for a true Trinitarian relationship that values both union and uniqueness. He's beginning the journey that lies at the heart of each of our intimate experiences. It is in choosing rather than coasting that our intimacies are deepened.

A real danger lurks here that we need to address. These days, many marriages shipwreck on the rocks of adamant individualism. We're led to believe we can only find ourselves through unfettered freedom to choose for our immediate wants. This is the signature of a narcissistic, consumer-driven society.

Passion, we assume, requires autonomy. Real intimacy takes second place to one's own personal agenda or happiness. If the relationship restricts me or does not match my ideals for a passionate experience, I should leave. I am obligated to follow my thirst. I will find a new relationship that seems to be more suited to the present shape of my desire.

We are not autonomous individuals. Intimacy is a shared life. Within the Trinity, passion is shared, not possessed. We don't give ourselves the opportunity to discover what "being fulfilled" truly means when we stay at the surface of our immediate desires.

On the other hand, many people are sacrificed on the altar of idolatry to a static marriage institution. Relationship only hardens marriage into a truce rather than enabling it to blossom into intimacy.

Neither choice is healthy. It would be easy to say that since our culture is so self-centered we should steer clear of the slightest whiff of narcissism. We should put even greater emphasis on being other-centered.

But denial or suppression won't work. There is a good, even at the heart of narcissism, that needs to be reclaimed in a holy, more wholesome way. As in so many issues of passion, the true choice is not to shut down but to learn to choose well. For the sake of our relationships we are called to grow toward both uniqueness and union.

Like turning the light on old patterns and habits, passion clarifies the issues that are already present and suppressing the real movement of God's life in us. Passion reframes reality for us, opens us up to renewed possibility, and makes us look at our lives with new eyes.

A GIFT OF SOMETHING NEW

This is good! Passion evokes the challenge to get rid of the accumulated debris of years of habit that hinder the flow of life.

Once awakened, our passion can give us the energy to grow personally and in the intimacy of our relationships. If we're committed to passion as the manifestation of God's life in us, we will be able to interpret the wake-up call as an opportunity for deeper openness with God. Our passion can give us insight into our desires and fears and can invite us to trust in God's healing power.

If we can accept that our passion is truly God's life and not just fuel for our determination to win the argument, we can begin to go with the flow of God's life. We can use our passion to find new ways to come together again. We can find our common ground and celebrate the gifts we share.

Like center stripes on a long road, choices will continually face us if we're to grow up in our intimacy with others. As one friend quipped about marriage, "It's a serial monogamy in which you choose the same person over and over."

Where will this take us? Maybe we can't see yet, but at least it gets us out of the trenches and opens us to new possibilities. As we accept the goodness of our own life and realize that our life is God's gift within us, we can offer the same to the other person in the relationship.

Passion clarifies the issues that need to be addressed and offers the gift of God's healing presence. We can honor God's presence and trust its ongoing flow in the relationship.

Maybe the Red Sea will part. Maybe we'll experience enough manna for one day. Maybe Jesus will come to our weakest places and offer healing and courage to live again.

Maybe we'll be able to bring the other person quietly to Jesus and ask Jesus to be with them in the places they're unable to deal with at present. Maybe we can "let them down through the roof" to be present to Jesus' healing love.

LEARNING TO CHOOSE

Maggie struggled with her marriage to Cal. She knew she was marking time in her own life to keep peace in the marriage. It wasn't satisfying to her, and she felt she wasn't able to provide much satisfaction for Cal either.

Maggie chose to express the life that was in her by taking art classes.

This new choice to explore her passion through painting did not provide an income. She had to do it at night, which meant she had to sacrifice some of her opportunity to "be there" for Cal and the children. This provoked a change within the family pattern.

Could the family accept this new growth? Could they learn to support it as an expression of the Spirit in Maggie's life and a part of her gift to the world? Or would they resent her choice and label it as self-centered?

Could Maggie hold the choice with an open heart to God, or would she feel the family's resentment and begin to harden into defensiveness and determination to do this at all costs? These were the struggles she had to work through as she began to pray about the life that was emerging from within.

How do we respond to the explosion of passion that wants to transform our present relationships? What options do we have when we're faced with choice?

Put the Lid Back On. One option is to suppress our passion. Many times I've watched people catch a glimpse of what it might mean to open up to the storm of passion. Life becomes vibrant again. But the threat it poses to the status quo is too much. Frightened by their own shadow, they crawl back into the safety of denial.

Lived honestly, this choice is perfectly healthy. We may not yet be ready for "very much reality."

If we keep our hearts open to God's healing, if we remain honest to our fears—and open to God's life in us—we can trust that He will lead us. We can only face the things we're ready to face.

In Isaiah's beautiful image of restoration, God "tends his flock like a shepherd: He gathers the lambs in his arms and carries them close to his heart; he gently leads those that have young" (Isaiah 40:11). God won't ask us to go faster than we're able. Especially when we're surrounded with tenuous new life!

As our hearts remain open to the transforming work of the Spirit, we'll gradually find ways to face our fears and to trust, one step at a time. We'll begin to find small ways to risk within the framework of commitment.

However, if we simply refuse to respond to life, this option can become soul destroying. We can't say a continuous no to God's life without suffering the consequences. Our own souls, and the soul of our marriage, cannot survive the desert of dammed up life.

Escape. A second option is to look elsewhere. The choice to embrace passion often precipitates the temptation to avoid our present relationships and start over in a new one that sparkles with mystery and attraction.

The recent revival of the notion of "soul mate" has borne much of this baggage. It's often a well-worded rationalization for escape. Soul mates are wonderful. But we often shortchange soul, using it to describe our immediate longing.

A new person seems like a soul mate in light of the poverty of our present relationship. The amount of work necessary to see our old relationship open up to real shared intimacy can be staggering. We've built up walls so high, and we're so set in destructive patterns, that it seems hopeless. But the choice to escape into a new relationship is almost always an avoidance of true intimacy, a substitute for real soul passion.

Grab for Power. Sometimes one partner in the marriage decides to open up to passion and the other reacts in fear. This stalemate becomes a flash point in which the cracks already present in the relationship develop into full-blown breaks.

If one person is truly unwilling to change and grow, we might have to admit that the marriage no longer exists. There may come a time when, quite apart from using passion as a weapon, one person simply will not choose growth. In that case, the refusal to grow is a refusal of the relationship.

But life isn't always that straightforward. Sometimes the partner who claims to be choosing for passion is really choosing to grab for power in a gridlocked relationship. It's a way to get the upper hand in a relationship between two entrenched people.

"I want a passionate relationship, what's the matter with you? Why are you so controlling and fearful?" It sounds noble, but it isn't helpful. It only increases the entrenchment and makes the choice to look elsewhere seem eminently reasonable. After all, who wants to live in a marriage where there's no room to grow and celebrate passion and life?

Trinitarian passion is not framed within a power struggle! If our choice for passion is to be authentic, we must abandon the power struggle. We must begin to trust the mystery of community and believe that the transformation we need is found in the framework of our present relationships. The transformation may spring forth in resurrection through what appears to be the death of our dreams.

Stay in the Storm. The other option is perhaps the hardest. That is, choosing to watch our passion grow within the crucible of our closest, most vulnerable — and maybe our most tumultuous — relationships.

I say: *Choose the storm!* This is risky business. The storm is part of our spiritual growth, yet it's heated enough and potent enough to rip apart the tenuous strands of love.

A Trinitarian spirituality accepts a storm of love between people. Conflicts aren't necessarily a sign of spiritual immaturity. The storm is a natural expression of the craving for uniqueness and union by two different people at the same time. Can we live the storm with love and grace? Can we look for the signs of God's presence? Can we celebrate love in the face of the storm?

It seems to me that the affirmation of the storm in intimacy has been largely overlooked in our spirituality. This has produced tragic results. Life is sometimes stormy! If our spirituality rejects conflict as wrong, Christianity gets pitted against life and becomes a tyrant.

Our spirituality isn't so much revealed by the storm as by the way we deal with it. When we believe that only tranquil relationships are evidence of spiritual maturity, we misinterpret passivity and a more phlegmatic personality as being spiritual. The expressively passionate person becomes the ogre. Within a spirituality of passion, the test of authenticity comes in the way the passion is embraced and transformed.

The storm will call us to affirm the current in our lives at times when it would be easier to give up. The storm will also call us to attend to the riverbanks, to let go of what seems so important to us and trust that the death and resurrection process will ensure that life will still come to us.

In the choosing, it's important to realize these storms are more than we can deal with on our own. We're like the disciples in the boat crossing the stormy Sea of Galilee. They were beyond their own resources.

We don't enter into the mystery of passion because we can figure it out and hold it together on our own. That would be folly. Jesus was in the boat with the disciples, even when He seemed oblivious to their need. Likewise, our deepest challenge and greatest growth will be to trust Jesus' presence in the storm.

We won't always know which to choose, but we can trust that the Holy Spirit is leading us. We can trust that even though things are messy, at least we're alive!

To be serious about our passion, and to stay in our present relationships, we will need the courage to trust the Spirit, who is flowing in our lives. We will also need the courage to open up our relationships to the promise of Jesus—that by living in them, *with the presence of God,* we will experience life to the full.

Let's examine the three basic movements as they call us to move from a relationship of convenience to a relationship of courage.

MOVING IN THE DIRECTION OF GROWTH

As we live intimately with those nearest us, the Trinity reminds us to offer who we are to the relationship, to extend the same dignity to others, and to celebrate the intimacy of union in the honor of that mutual respect.

Life doesn't get much simpler than that! Nor much more difficult. However, the river continues to flow—at night, all day, under the ice, even in the late fall when it's at its lowest point. We have the rest of our lives to discern what it means to live out this dream in healthy ways.

Let's explore three basic movements as they affect and transform our most significant relationships. I will often speak directly of marriage, but these movements apply to any close relationship. The movement toward real intimacy is at the foundation of our personhood. We discover our full selves in relationship as we extend the webs of love to others.

We Learn to See and to Reveal Our True Selves

In their book *The Art of Intimacy*, the Malones, a father and son team, make an important distinction between closeness and intimacy.

Closeness, they write, "is a very intense personal awareness of the relationship you have with another."[2] It's the feeling we get when we agree with someone, when someone is like us, when we share space and emotional warmth together.

Intimacy is often confused with closeness. We think we're intimate when we're close. That may be true, but the desire for closeness may also become a trap. It can gradually force us to deny ourselves and to live a lie in order to maintain the illusion of warmth and togetherness. This produces an unnatural "truce" in which our true passion is sacrificed for the sake of peace.

According to the Malones, intimacy is distinguished from closeness. The word *intimacy* is derived from the Latin word *intima*, meaning "inner" or "innermost," and carries the idea of being in touch with our inner selves.[3] It does not focus on the feelings of warmth or the awareness of similarity. Intimacy is the art of bringing our true selves into the relationship.

Intimacy is the choice to offer ourselves openly and honestly to another person. That means offering the parts of us that admire and are in agreement with the other person as well as the parts of us that are at cross-purposes with the other person.

One recent example of this in my own marriage has been my gradual admission to Miriam of my struggle with self-hatred. I've lived around the edges of chronic depression during much of my adult life.

When I first began to speak in those terms to her, she found it hard to understand. It wasn't the Jeff she knew. She knew me as caring and attentive, if somewhat quiet.

The intimacy of this self-revelation has been a difficult thing for her. Yet it is especially around my passion that I've often battled these feelings of depression. My passionate, creative side has been so fragile — so tentative — that for years I've been unwilling even to admit to it, let alone share it. I couldn't bear the thought that the tender shoot of life I treasured so deeply and trusted so little might get stomped on.

In the isolation this hiddenness creates, I have felt misunderstood and unwanted — and finally depressed. So the cycle goes on repeating itself in self-fulfilling prophecies through many experiences in life.

If Miriam is going to truly know me, I need to offer the intimacy of who I am, inside, and not just who I am as a nurturer of others. I have to take the plunge and start communicating. I choose to trust that the ups and downs it creates will deepen our dependence on God and our intimacy with one another. I choose to trust that it will widen the flow of the Trinity in both our lives.

As we've worked through the initial concerns, Miriam has come to a whole new appreciation of why I make the decisions I do and what I face in offering myself to the world. She's learned to care for me in a deeper way without having to deny, take responsibility for, or fix my vulnerable places.

We Offer Respect as an Ongoing Gift

What we want for ourselves we need to offer generously to others. If I want to bring *who I am* into the relationship and have my self honored, I need to offer the same to those closest to me.

It has become increasingly clear to me that if people lived by the Golden Rule, "Do [and be] unto others as you would have them do [and be] unto you," we could vastly reduce the amount of conflict suffered in our culture. I now take this as a given and tell all prospective brides and grooms the same simple message.

Fidelity to our vows calls for fidelity to the growth and changes that occur as each partner's life unfolds over the years. It's a gift of respect offered again and again, in spite of the pain of growth and change.

If we can accept the storm as part of our spiritual experience, we can keep from taking the conflicts so personally. If we believe in the presence of God in the other person, we can trust they will handle the storm. If we believe in God's presence in us, we can trust that God's life will hold us both.

This willingness to be present in the unfolding of intimacy, without malice or defensiveness, frees us up. We continue to believe in our partners and to offer them the dignity and acceptance they so desperately fight for in the first place.

When the strands of trust are broken, the differences between people become intolerable. They begin to see the other person as the enemy who embodies everything threatening to their desires and, sometimes, to their very personhood.

It's a tremendous risk of faith to trust the Spirit and thereby continue to offer the dignity of respect to your partner in the face of hurt and fear. We're scared to death that the other person's agenda will cause us to lose what little we've claimed as our own.

Only in trust can we bring who we are, gently and persistently, into the relationship and ask to be recognized and respected. Only in trust can we offer the same respect to others as they risk bringing their true selves to us.

How do we offer this respect? Perhaps the most respectful thing we can do for others is to give the simple gift of listening as they reveal who they are. Heartfelt listening forces us to abandon our own agenda, at least for the time being, and to offer enough respect to others to attend to what they are saying.

Listening in order to deepen appreciation is one of the great values of groups like Marriage Encounter. They invite people to speak lovingly about their own experience and ask the partner to listen lovingly and attentively to what is being said. The goal of Marriage Encounter is not to solve the marriage problems but to deepen appreciation of each other and thereby deepen intimacy.

At times we've all nodded distractedly when someone is talking while we're trying to concentrate on something else. Miriam wants to organize her life, including the house, just as I sit down to watch a hockey game on TV. In the middle of the same old conversation that never seems to go anywhere, Bill offers a quiet clue to what he's really feeling. But Trish is so tired of the conversation she just wants to get on with her work.

These are the times we can offer respect. We can set aside our own agenda and listen attentively to the other person.

Respect naturally includes appreciation of another's gifts. The apostle Paul usually began his letters with tender expressions of how much the believers meant to him and how much he appreciated their choices to trust and follow God. Even in the first letter to the Corinthians, a church full of conflict and immaturity, Paul was able to be thankful for the rich expressions of faith they manifested.

Respect also includes an attitude of care for the other person's weaknesses. Many of the conflicts in intimate relationship flow out of our wounds. When we're able to hold another's wounds with compassion, we offer them the space to grow and change. Respect enables us to fulfill the dream of the New Testament that we clothe ourselves with compassion, kindness, humility, gentleness, and patience, bearing with each other and forgiving each other as Christ forgave us (see Colossians 3:12-13).

We Celebrate the Goodness of Uniqueness Within Union
Some people celebrate more easily than others. It doesn't always come easily to me. Perhaps that's why I see celebration as such a wonderful achievement!

The ability to celebrate the richness of life together is the fruit of a long, continual process of offering mutual respect. We grow through the vulnerability and joy that come from surviving our fears and wounds by continually re-entering the relationship and asking for the dignity of being received with respect—and offering back that same dignity. Celebrating the storm and opening to God in the midst of our passion creates new energy and possibility. We don't have to remain stuck. We begin to watch with fascination as the swirls frame and reframe our lives in creative ways that get the flow going again and give us something to offer those we love.

Last fall, in studying Jesus' responses to people in the book of Luke, I was struck by His encounter with Zacchaeus (Luke 19:1-10). Here was a man who seemed able to be lavish in the moment, a man of grand gesture.

At first I couldn't relate to what I considered to be Zacchaeus's hyperbolic generosity in response to grace. It felt as though he was just playing to the crowd one more time.

As I prayed the passage, identifying imaginatively with the narrative, I began to realize that Zacchaeus's response may not have been overdone at all. It might have been consistent with who he was all along. Flamboyant generosity had been perverted into flamboyant greed until he was brought face to face with Jesus.

Zacchaeus, as I imagine him, lived pretty close to the surface with his responses. When Jesus encountered him, a dam broke deep inside. He experienced a huge reshaping gestalt as he allowed the real extravagance that was part of his person to flow out in generosity.

I'm not suggesting we have to match Zacchaeus's flamboyance. He was only being true to the personality he'd been given by God. But I would argue that Zacchaeus encourages us to believe that Jesus can also touch us in ways that are appropriate for us. I would encourage you to consider that your way of celebrating can gradually shine through.

CONCLUSION

Celebration builds new webs—new strands—of love in the midst of seeming disconnection. Often there will be no answer to a particular struggle. Both sides have legitimate concerns. Sometimes the only thing to do is to lay aside the disagreement and celebrate the relationship. Perhaps by refocusing on the goodness, the insurmountable argument may be mysteriously transcended.

As we let Jesus enter the storms of our intimate relationships, we can move from self-protection to generosity. We can afford to make a splash with the goodness of our lives. We can find, in the passion, new and creative ways to bring life to those we love. And we can celebrate together the sense of God's presence in our lives.

What if God and I danced?
And we tumbled, doing flips
and got up and wrestled
until one of us said
"Uncle!"
And we leaned back to back
staring into the evening
pressing against each other and
savouring the warmth
between us?
And what if God took the initiative
and sent me flying down
the sloping grass or tied
my shoelaces together while I
snoozed,
And we played hockey
and I creamed God into the boards
to get even for all the times
I had the puck stolen and was left
spinning while he deked past me
and scored into the open net?

JEFF IMBACH

CHAPTER FIFTEEN

LIVING PASSIONATELY WITH GOD

■

IN THE EARLY YEARS OF THE FIFTEENTH CENTURY, A RUSSIAN ARTIST NAMED Andrew Rublev painted an icon of the Trinity. We don't know much about him, but his work has become famous. For millions of worshipers, Rublev's *The Holy Trinity* has become a doorway of devotion into the mystery of Trinitarian love.[1]

Rublev depicts three people sitting around a table, enjoying a meal together. They are the three "angels" who appeared to Abraham and Sarah and ate with them.

The scene opens to the viewer, and there is a gap at the table. An empty place. As we gaze at the icon, a realization dawns: *The empty place is reserved for us!* You and I are invited to join the table, partake of the meal, and enjoy the fellowship of love.

Through the course of this book we have explored the exciting adventure of opening up to the river of God in the passion of our lives. We've seen the ways this roiling love brings us out of a dead spirituality of performance and calls us into life. Gutsy, messy, holy life.

The storm of passionate love in the Trinity shapes and animates the intimacy we enjoy with creation, within the church, and with those closest to us. How does it also affect our intimacy with God?

What does it mean to be passionate with God? How do the themes of union and uniqueness help us to enter into our love relationship with God in holy and passionate ways?

As we contemplate what it means to be included in the fellowship of the Trinity, we will be learning how to grow up in love and be fully present at the table. We will learn to accept our place, to act on our privileges and responsibilities, to surrender into union, and to celebrate our dignity. And finally, we will learn to live from the heart.

LEARNING TO ACCEPT OUR PLACE

God invites us to join the exchanges of loving intimacy as full adults, on an equal basis. This mind-boggling truth is the great message of Christ's self-emptying (Philippians 2:1-11) and of our union with Christ in glory (Ephesians 2:1-10).

In Jesus, God meets us at our level. In Jesus, we are raised to the heights of heaven to God's level.

Being brought into such a profound place of fellowship with God takes some getting used to. It's not what we would think. We do not naturally embrace it or act on it.

For many of us, spirituality has been largely shaped by images of power. We sing and pray to God as the Almighty King, the Victorious Warrior, the Judge of all the earth. Our God is an awesome God.

These are wonderful, necessary images. They reassure us that we're not the victims of fate. To change the image slightly, God is at the helm, bringing history into a safe harbor.

Without the balance of a Trinitarian vision, though, these images skew our vision and hamper our intimacy. They focus on God as separate from us. God is in control; we aren't. God is the King; we aren't. God is above us; we are below. All this is true—but by themselves they foster a hierarchical image of God that can keep us from experiencing real closeness with Him.

I can't help but believe this dominance of hierarchical images of God has been a significant reason why so many have talked about intimacy with God yet have felt so little intimacy in their own experience.

The coming of Jesus into our world changed all that. Yes, God is the Powerful One. But God is also the Intimate Three. Both emphases must go together. We can't redress a lopsided preoccupation with Transcendence with a lopsided preoccupation with Immanence. Rather, we seek the wholeness of the mutual indwelling of the Trinity. During a class I was teaching, a man raised the question of God's power in the world. "How can I have an intimate relationship with God if God is all powerful?" he asked.

I walked over to where he was sitting. Towering over him, I said, "Pretend for a moment (a brief moment!) that I am God." Then I knelt down so that I was eye-to-eye with him and said, "Because God comes to you like this."

Perhaps I should have asked him to stand and added, "Because in the fellowship of the Trinity, we are raised by grace to be with God— 'seated with him in the heavenly realms'" (Ephesians 2:6).

Rublev's depiction of the Trinity dramatically reminds us that there's a place for us at the table of Love. We're invited to be part of the feast. Love given and love received.

FULL PARTICIPATION

What does it mean to come to the table of love? What is our status? Do we come as servants, as children, or as full adults? Scripture reveals that we come as full adults, as friends.

Paul's writing gives us a clue. He said that before Christ came, we were like underaged children. We had no more privilege than a servant. However, Christ came to free us so that we might be adopted into mature status, "that we might receive the full rights of sons" (Galatians 4:5).

In Ephesians we read that "God raised us up with Christ and seated us with him in the heavenly realms in Christ Jesus" (Ephesians 2:6). Later in the letter, Paul prayed that we "may be filled to the measure of all the fullness of God" (Ephesians 3:19).

As we noted earlier, Peter opened his second letter with the staggering revelation that God has given us "very great and precious promises, so that through them [we] may participate in the divine nature" (2 Peter 1:4).

John spoke of coming into joint participation with eternal life. "We proclaim to you the eternal life, which was with the Father and has appeared to us. . . . We proclaim to you what we have seen and heard, so that you also may have fellowship (*koinonia*, "joint participation") with us. And our fellowship (*koinonia*) is with the Father and with his Son, Jesus Christ" (1 John 1:2-3).

We have been invited into full relationship, as full as Creator and creature can experience.

I remember having to go to bed, as a child, just when the conversation was getting good. To a young boy who thought himself eminently mature, being sent off to bed was humiliating. It was a taunting reminder that my self-estimation wasn't generally shared.

The unspoken subtext was almost palpably apparent—when you grow up, you, too, can become part of the adult discussions. At the time, the promise of future inclusion wasn't particularly consoling.

Spiritual adulthood doesn't imply sophistication. We will always remain childlike. But it does assure inclusion in the deepest and fullest ways possible.

We move from cowering under authority to relaxing at the table. From being told what to do to being part of the consultation. As an adult, our contributions are valued and our opinions matter. We're brought into the heart of things.

We share in the flow of loving fellowship. When that kind of inclusion and respect doesn't happen on a human level, we feel patronized and disrespected. When our vision of God doesn't include a table of fellowship, we can feel left out or banished from intimacy.

WE'RE CALLED FRIENDS

Jesus emphasized an even greater dimension. "I no longer call you servants," He said, "because a servant does not know his master's business. Instead, I have called you friends, for everything that I learned from my Father I have made known to you" (John 15:15).

We aren't just adults maneuvering through a polite cocktail conversation. We're friends.

Parent-child relationships can easily falter in the tricky transition to full relationships as adults. Often parents hang on to their power, unwittingly dominating and controlling their children and keeping them from becoming free adults.

In conversation with a woman who was concerned about her daughter's marriage breakup, I cautioned her about how much advice she gave and how much she felt responsible for her daughter's situation. She objected, saying that she had a responsibility to be involved. I replied, "You wouldn't have wanted your mother following you around and giving you advice about your life. You made your decisions on your own and informed your mother afterward."

There's no question of status with friends. Friends are peers. True friendship means that friends share on an equal basis.

This inclusion into adult friendship is stunning, even for those who have been believers a long time. Within the fellowship of the Trinity we are treated in the same way God treats Jesus. Jesus' revelation of the Father is so full, and we are included so openly, that we share in God's heart.

LEARNING TO ACT ON OUR PRIVILEGES AND RESPONSIBILITIES

The Privileges of Adulthood

It's a mark of true friendship and intimacy when someone opens up to another person. When someone shares from the heart, you thank him or her for honoring you.

When Miriam shares openly about her life with cancer, people say they feel privileged. They're grateful they've been included, that Miriam thinks enough of them to share the details of her struggles and growth. She also feels honored when they listen.

It's our privilege to receive God's heart. We may not hear a voice, but we do share a passion for life and love. This is God's greatest gift to us. This is why the choices for the current and for the riverbank are so important. We are cherishing God's flowing love in our hearts.

As participants at the table, we can learn to listen. The disciplines of silence and solitude become ways to offer the gift of our presence so that we can receive the throbbing of God's heart.

Being friends at the table also means that we can offer our hearts back to God. Our jumbled experiences are received, even solicited. We can join the flowing love and speak our piece.

We bring all of who we are, including our struggle to live passionately, into the conversation. We share our inabilities and our weaknesses, as well as our successes. In the intimacy of love we discover a renewed assurance of our place and renewed power to act faithfully in our world.

For example, sometimes in prayer we focus on asking God to lead us. We pray fervently, affirming that we're willing to do whatever God tells us to do. We struggle with knowing God's will.

The next time you ask God for guidance, imagine your prayer being offered around the supper table with God. Can you picture God talking things over with you rather than simply telling you what to do? What would happen if, while you were in prayer asking for guidance, a voice spoke audibly to you and said, "I don't know, my daughter (or son). What do you think you ought to do?"

The image is humorous and trite. It could even be construed as grossly inaccurate. But it does help us to touch the enormity of the privilege that is ours at the table of love.

God's will is not a narrow ridge with cliffs dropping off either side. It's not a maze we must negotiate as though we were rats in an experiment, while God watches to see how well we do.

God's will is a shared life, an intimate dialogue. We become partners together with God to demonstrate the life of love as it shines through the tint of our unique character.

An imagined scene in which God solicits our participation might seem to diminish God or denigrate His sovereignty. But if we choose, such an image can be a wonderful picture of God, so comfortable and so in control, that there's no need to become authoritarian.

New teachers are often the most authoritarian in the way they handle students. They may have a great deal of knowledge, but they aren't yet comfortable with the material and with their role.

When Amy was just starting to teach high school history, she felt completely overwhelmed by her responsibility. She would stay up half the night to prepare for the next day's class. She knew her stuff, but with history there's no end to what you could know. Anxious and unsure, she kept a very tight rein on the class. She discouraged discussion and held strictly to the material at hand.

A seasoned teacher, in contrast, has heard all the questions and explored the paths. She's able to relax with the dialogue, engage the students, and let them share in the solution.

I see that same comfortableness in the way God lives with us. God is neither unsure nor on a power trip. He's comfortable enough being God that we can be included as full participants in the conversation.

The Responsibilities of Adulthood

There's another side to this image of being a grownup. It means we have to do things for ourselves. When we reach the stage of independent living, for example, we have to buy our own car, find our own apartment, and keep all the bills paid.

My daughter, Nikki, recently purchased her first car. She thought the task of perusing ads and making phone calls would never end. But she took it on, and in the end became very good at it.

Sometimes it seems like life was easier when we were children and we automatically hopped into the back seat of our parents' car. Maybe we didn't like the back seat, but we didn't have to be responsible for all the other things that go with ownership. We didn't have to face the agony of finding a car that wouldn't turn out to be a lemon. Someone else shouldered the cost of keeping the car insured and in good running order.

Becoming an adult with God calls us to participate in the fellowship at the table. It calls us out of hiding.

To be fair, it can be a frightening thing to open up to God. How can we be in the presence of the Infinite without either capitulating or shutting down?

Capitulating is a common response. People just give up on the dialogue and on their God-given dignity and cower in front of God, who seems so far beyond them.

Sometimes they back away from full intimacy with God out of a false sense of humility. They feel they have no right to speak their mind. It's true that we don't have the right, but we've been given the privilege of full communion. We can learn to trust in what we've been given.

Shutting down is another common response. Some people feel fear when they think about being in the presence of God. Their fear creates defenses that keep them aloof and prohibit them from entering into the exchanges of love that are the mark of the Trinity.

People who have felt victimized by their religious past are called to come out of hiding and take on the responsibility of being full adults with God. They may need to hide for a time to let go of false or distorted images of God, but eventually the fellowship of the Trinity calls them away from the sidelines and into the flow of reciprocal love.

Trinitarian love invites us to surrender to love without capitulating our personhood. It encourages us to accept our uniqueness without shutting down. In short, Trinitarian love invites us to grow up and become "self-possessed and other-oriented."

If we descend with our minds into our hearts and stand before God in prayer, as the orthodox tradition says—not capitulating or hiding—we will discover two essential movements in our relationship. We will feel the assurance of being respected as unique beings, and we will

know the longing for union that drives us to offer ourselves completely
and unabashedly to God and to others.

Learning to Celebrate and Surrender
Three years ago Miriam and I stayed overnight at a bed and breakfast
in southern Alberta. The next morning ten strangers gathered around a
sumptuous table. Conversation began tentatively at first, but soon the
course of the conversation became clear.

One man, an affluent doctor from Atlanta, completely dominated
the meal. His presence, his voice, everything about him simply took
over the entire room.

Is that what intimacy with God means? Does God bully us into
believing He has the right to force Himself on us, force our openness
and allegiance whether we want to give it or not? Do we just get taken
over like the North American native people did in the crush of European
expansion?

Changing the image, are we just squatters on the land of the
Almighty Landlord, or do we have any place of our own that is
respected and will not be bulldozed by the next development?

If I am God's friend, how does that affect my prayer and my openness to Him? Can I truly act on the fact that I'm brought in as a full
participant? And if so, does that mean I'm allowed to help decide how
the relationship goes? Does God's personality simply fill the room and
push me into the corner, or can I claim some room to breathe and speak?

We Can Celebrate Our Dignity
Intimacy with God guarantees room for each person's uniqueness. This
truth may seem self-evident, but it has enormous significance.

In any adult relationship there is no real union without preserving
the dignity of both persons. When one of the persons loses his or her
unique identity, the relationship becomes unhealthy. We call it a symbiotic relationship—or worse, an abusive one.

A symbiotic relationship may work between a mother and child
for the first few months of life. But eventually both mom and daughter
get tired of it if they're normal!

An ongoing symbiotic relationship has no integrity because there
is no separation, no distinct identity. So it is with God.

We are offered identity and personhood within the love of the

Trinity. As we grow in accepting the dignity we're offered, we can also grow in offering that uniqueness back to God as our contribution to the richness of union.

If we're honest, there are times when we do not feel an incredible craving to surrender to God. Sometimes we want to set limits on the intimacy, find some kind of boundary that will preserve our space and leave us intact.

One woman I know was sexually abused by her pastor father. He represented God to her. She grew up thinking that God was going to violate her, too. She shrank from intimacy with God. It took her years to come to terms with the fact that God was not like her earthly father and that she had the right to come safely to the table.

Are we wrong in this desire for space with God? When we crave our own distinctiveness, does it mean we're unspiritual or immature? Is it a sign of our rebellious nature?

The short answer is no! These desires are a natural part of Trinitarian life. How we handle them makes the difference.

If we pull away from intimacy with God to escape and to assert our own independence, then the choice to pull away becomes sin. But when we pull away in order to re-enter the relationship with deeper intimacy and fuller union, we illustrate the central truth of the Trinity.

Consider Mary Louise's story.

After a brief silence, Mary Louise lifted her head and started to smile. "You aren't going to get me to give God all the control," she said.

I laughed. We had learned to trust each other with this kind of banter. I knew something of her past. Raised in a rigidly fundamentalist home, educated in a religious boarding school, and sexually abused in the family and at school, she knew all about religious expectations.

"Who said anything about control?" I retorted. "You're the one who brought up the idea of control, not me. I'm talking about intimacy, about opening up and allowing God to love you. Control doesn't sound much like intimacy to me."

"Yeah, well, if you don't deal with control issues you'll never have intimacy."

"So how are you going to deal with them?" I asked.

"Sometimes when I pray," Mary Louise said, with tears beginning to fill her eyes, "I tell God He can come in the door but He has to sit in the chair and keep quiet. I know it sounds stupid, but I don't want any of this omnipresent, omnipotent stuff. That's too scary for me.

"I tell God I would like to learn to be open and intimate with Him, but I don't want Him violating me. Between church, school, and family, abuse is all I've ever known. Others have always felt they had the right to do with me whatever they pleased."

Mary Louise's comment was courageously honest. She almost physically cowered when she said it, but she said it anyway.

Yes, we can hear the abrasive tone in Mary Louise's words, formed like a scab over wounds that are still tender. But we can also hear the honesty of true intimacy.

There may not be an overwhelming feeling of closeness, but Mary Louise's statement is a revelation of what's going on in her soul. It's her truest response to intimacy with God without either capitulating or shutting down in the relationship. She's already much more intimate with God than she realizes.

Can we be this open with God? This kind of honesty is rare for most people. They wonder how we dare talk this way to the King of the Universe.

We can be aware of the danger of spiritual rebellion. We can recognize that there's a pull in us to become independent of God, to refuse to be part of the river of love. But we can also be assured that God is completely respectful. God is patient. We will never be ignored, run over, or abused.

People who come for spiritual direction often have to work through their fear of authentic intimacy with God. Like Mary Louise, they're afraid to take their place as full participants in the divine friendship. They think it's wrong to assert themselves, because their religious background gave them no permission to do so. They believe they became God's victims and they still can't say no.

In these situations I encourage people to do what they must to create space in their prayer experience. They haven't been sent to bed while all the decisions for the next day are made in hushed tones by the adults.

They can rant and rave about their past and they can tell God how afraid they are. They can sit in silence. It doesn't matter. All I ask is that they stay in the conversation and keep their hearts soft to the possibility that God might love them in a healthy, respectful way.

William Barry, co-author of the classic book *The Practice of Spiritual Direction*,[2] uses the story of "The Little Prince" to illustrate this stance of respectfulness on God's part.³ When the Little Prince came to earth, he wanted to get to know a fox. The fox said that if the Prince wanted to get to know him, the Prince should sit down over there and watch for a long time. Then gradually they could begin a conversation. Personhood is formed in the relationship of love. The God who is Three-in-One is offering the dance of respect and union. God will never violate our personhood. We have the right, within a relationship of love, to ask God to go slowly, to respect our wounds, to stay distant enough to demonstrate respect for our dignity as persons.

God does not merely tolerate our uniqueness. That's the genius of the Trinity. Within the union, which no one can fathom, the distinct personhood of each of the three members is celebrated. It is this affirmation of uniqueness that gives the union its striking beauty, its flowing passion. This respect gives us the courage to surrender gladly and fully into God.

We Surrender into an Unfathomable Union
As we accept our place at the table, we become free to surrender to the flow of love. All the work needed to learn how to stand on our own two feet in God's presence now makes sense. We have something to offer, wholly and unreservedly, in the swirl of intimacy.

Our uniqueness is not an end in itself. Uniqueness is for the purpose of surrender. We surrender what we have.

The famous hymn "Jesus, Thou Joy of Loving Hearts"⁴ expresses the ongoing longing of our endless desire for union with God.

We taste Thee, O Thou living bread,
And long to feast upon Thee still;

We drink of Thee, the fountainhead,
And thirst our souls from Thee to fill.

Many of the great spiritual writings in church history are laced with this same passionate, all-consuming thirst for union. A. W. Tozer, an evangelical prophet steeped in the mystical tradition of the church, wrote a book entitled *The Pursuit of God*, which is a panegyric to the longing for union.

St. Augustine began his *Confessions* with the words, "You have made us for Yourself. And our hearts are restless until they rest in You." Then, after describing his tortured journey to faith, he burst into praise:

You shone upon me; your radiance enveloped me; you put my
blindness to flight. You shed your fragrance about me; I drew
breath and now I gasp for your sweet odour. I tasted you, and now
I hunger for you. You touched me, and I am inflamed with love of
your peace.[5]

Trinitarian love creates a satisfaction that cannot be superseded and a
thirst that will never be quenched. We are drawn to surrender to love. Our
love is caught up in God and we experience moments of intense surrender
and union.

The next moment we feel the dissatisfaction of a never-ending yearning to surrender even more deeply.

Longing will always be present and will always be honored. The fellowship of the Trinity enables us to accept the longing, which becomes a
sign of God's presence, even in the darkness and the desert.[6]

At the climax of thirty days of silent retreat, the Spiritual Exercises of
St. Ignatius brings the retreatant to the point of full surrender, culminating
in the prayer,

Take, Lord, and receive all my liberty, my memory, my understanding, and my entire will—all that I have and call my own.
You have given it all to me. To you, Lord, I return it. Everything is
yours; do with it what you will. Give me only your love and grace.
That is enough for me.[7]

This is surrender into unfathomable union. In the mystery of the
Trinity it is also the moment of birth into fruitful assurance of our own
unique and free place at the table.

As we live this flowing of love with God, we will gradually learn to
live in the midst of paradoxes that would otherwise immobilize us. I would
like to close this exploration of intimacy with God by suggesting some of
the ways our spiritual adulthood may be reflected in the way we live.

We Accept a Deeper Affirmation of Our Passion and a Deeper Cleansing of Our Motives

Learning to live with God in the depth and width of our passion will
gradually make us more confident and at home with wide swings of
desire. We will be able to embrace God and embrace life with a sense

of assurance, through long practice, without being paralyzed by fear that we'll be bowled over by our next overwhelming passion. We will have learned to enjoy and celebrate desire. We will also realize that saying no to desire is not the end of the world. There will be no need to shut down passion in order to live in a way that is pleasing to God. Rather, in living with God through the ups and downs of desire, we learn what it means to live out God's will in the whole of life.

At the same time, because we become more accepting of our passion, we will also be more willing for the purification of our motives. Knowing that God embraces the whole of our lives frees us from the need to be defensive.

We do not need to demand our own way. Instead, as we come to know the goodness of our passion, we long to have our passion cleansed and purified so that it more truly reflects the life of God from which it comes.

As we grow, we become more aware of the subtleties of our self-deception. This makes us desire God to purify us in ways we wouldn't have expected. And as we grow, we become more trusting in the grace that is bigger than we dreamed.

Like running water, God's life will not be stopped. If life doesn't come to us one way, it will come to us another. The spring of living water won't fail us.

We Learn to Trust Our Deepest Intuitions and Allow Scripture to Shape Our Hearts

Many people these days, especially those outside the Christian tradition, emphasize the need to trust ourselves and our intuition. "Go with your gut and you'll know what to do," they say. As with much of this kind of spirituality, it's a good idea with an inadequate basis. In a self-help spirituality, going with one's intuition may be nothing more than going with one's preference.

I don't mean to criticize the way in which this emphasis has freed many people from being driven by guilt or external expectations. But it lacks sufficient foundation to be a long-term solution. Unless we're assured that God is at home in our souls, we have no basis for this inner trust.

Christianity calls us to live out of our relationship with God. We are caught up in love as we experience God's presence and God's grace. Then we are called to live out this love in brand-new territory every day.

Paradoxically, as we learn to trust our inner intuition we continue to learn how to bring that inner call into dialogue with Scripture—not Scripture as a rule book but as the story of grace. We discover in deeper ways how the story of our lives matches the stories of Scripture. We bring our questions to Scripture to keep the interpretation open, and we allow Scripture to question us to keep us open, to reveal God's truth to us in new ways. Scripture and inner trust revolve together like a gyroscope to keep the ship of our experience on an even keel.

We Discover That We Are Not Alone
As we learn to accept our spiritual adulthood, we also come to accept the limitations and complexities of life. When we were small, we thought every story should have a happy ending. Often in our intimacy with God, we can't understand why God doesn't intervene to make things turn out right. We struggle with sickness and death, with broken relationships that seem so preventable. We grieve the rape of the environment and the ongoing oppression of the poor. As adults, we come to accept that fixing everything is not always the answer. We find there's more to life than solutions.

Etty Hillesum wrote a remarkable chronicle of her spiritual unfolding under the shadow of the Holocaust. Her story is called *An Interrupted Life* because she voluntarily chose to go to the camps and eventually faced death with her fellow Jews.

Etty knew that praying to God to spare them from this unprecedented tragedy was not going to fix things. God was not going to intervene. What would she do? Would she get bitter? Would it be the end of her theology, the collapse of her trust?
She wrote:

> One thing is becoming increasingly clear to me: that You cannot help us, that we must help You to help ourselves. And that is all we can muster these days and also all that really matters; that we safeguard this little piece of You, God, in ourselves. And perhaps in others as well . . . we must help You and defend Your dwelling place inside us to the last.[8]

When things are relatively smooth for us, it's easy to be critical of such a statement. We're often guilty of being critical of people when they're going through terrible times. But anyone who has faced the insolubility of death or of degenerative disease or of institutionalized injustice will know what Etty means.

We learn, as adults, that we often have to act alone. No one is holding our hand or doing it for us. We're not being rescued. Like the Israelite midwives of old, we act anyway in our small way to keep our trust open and our humanity from shriveling.

Philippians 2:12-13 says it well: "Work out your salvation with fear and trembling, for it is God who works in you to will and to act according to his good purpose."

Sometimes all we're able to do is create a space for God. Sometimes the whole range of passion seems to be taken away from us. Yet we can at least create space for God, knowing that God has created space for us at the table of Love.

We can offer our silence, our helplessness, as the space in which God can live. As Jeremiah mourned the destruction of Jerusalem and the whole cycle of worship in the temple, he concluded, "The LORD is good to those whose hope is in him, to the one who seeks him; it is good to wait quietly for the salvation of the LORD" (Lamentations 3:25-26).

We will come to recognize that solving our problems is not as important as continuing to create space for God in the world. God will not always rescue us, but we can always be the sign of incarnation in the face of crucifixion.

We Become More Free to Offer Ourselves to Others
As we open ourselves to loving God with all our heart in all the wide experiences of life, we're moved to be generous with the life we've received. We no longer need to cling to life to keep us secure.

This is the true meaning of self-sacrifice. As sharers in the gracious gift of love, we're enabled to extend that love to others. A generosity is born that can be astounding in its bounty. We become the woman who washed Jesus' feet and anointed them with expensive perfume.

The apostle John wrote so movingly about this sacrificial generosity. "This is how we know what love is: Jesus Christ laid down his life for us. And we ought to lay down our lives for our brothers [and sisters]" (1 John 3:16).

In a world of contract negotiations, it's hard to imagine the bold generosity of laying down our lives. In a world of numbing bureaucracy it seems better to hold on to them tightly.

In a narcissistic society, we don't know much about open-hearted sacrifice. How do we know when to take up our life and when to lay it down? When are we to care for ourselves and when are we to care for others?

There's no simple answer to these questions. We're invited to look to Jesus as our model. Knowing that He was loved and that He came from God and was going to God, Jesus could gladly offer His life for us. Trusting that the flow of life would bring resurrection even out of death, Jesus could choose when to take up His life and when to lay it down.

One thing is certain: Self-sacrifice cannot be prompted by guilt. Guilt cannot provide the flowing of life necessary to sustain the sacrifice over the long haul. The fragrant generosity of sacrificial love can only emerge from the Source of love—God. We are given our place. We are assured of our dignity. From that place we can afford to risk offering ourselves to the world.

Generosity is born out of love. When we are loved, passion and all, we become lovers. When we discover that we've been gifted, we are enabled to give. All that we are and have comes from the flowing of love, and we become partners in the flow.

We learn to revel in the passion of love and to offer it generously to our world.

Teach me to seek you,
for I cannot seek you
unless you teach me,
or find you
unless you show yourself to me.
Let me seek you in my desire,
Let me desire you in my seeking.
Let me find you by loving you,
Let me love you when I find you.

ST. ANSELM[1]

WILL THE RIVER FLOW IN YOU?

■

ALMOST A MILLENNIUM AGO, ST. ANSELM CAPTURED THE HEART OF OUR passion with God in two powerful, encircling phrases — "Let me seek you in my desire / Let me desire you in my seeking." The first phrase opens us up to passion, the second keeps our passion focused on God.

We seek God in our desire. Our desire is the haunt of God. St. Anselm reminds us that our desire is good. We can embrace our passion and expect to find God there. We can look for God in our lonely longing, in our dreams for intimacy, in our most desperate cravings to be known and respected. Our life is part of the eternal flow.

But St. Anselm didn't stop there. He reminds us that life is more than passion for passion's sake. We desire God in our seeking. Our goal is not simply to live juicy lives; we want God. We want to live God's life; we want to love God with all our hearts; we want to enjoy God thoroughly.

We want to be grateful for every minute of friendship with the Trinity. We want the fruit of our passion to flow back to God in gratitude and praise. We have tasted that God is good, and now we want God more than anything else. We want to be all flame.

Through years of opening our hearts to God again and again, we grow into an ever-deepening confidence that there is no split between passion and

God. Our life is from God, through God, and to God. It is all of God.

Miriam and I have a favorite spot on the Elk River in Southeastern British Columbia. Someone has collected enough rocks to make a small fire pit, but there are no amenities. Right at the spot, the river makes a ninety-degree turn. So we can look directly downstream and see snow-capped peaks or we can turn to the right and look upstream toward the mountains across the valley.

Surrounded by meadow behind us and a mix of spruce and quaking aspen on either side, we can sit by the river and watch it flow by. We can sit there for hours without seeing another person.

Watching the river can be mesmerizing. Sometimes, after sitting for a while, Miriam will comment, "Where does all this water come from? It just keeps flowing and flowing! You'd think it would have to stop sometime."

But the river never stops! It never runs dry.

Like the Elk River, God's life is a constant stream within. It is an artesian well springing up to eternal life (John 4:14). It is rivers of living water emerging from our inmost being (John 7:38). This is God, our Life and our Hope.

Perhaps while reading this book you've become aware of God's presence in your life. You want to respond to God, but you're still afraid. You're tired of the split between your soul and your image of spiritual maturity.

You may realize how you've been preoccupied with making sure the banks are in place. You've given little attention to the current of God's life. Now you want to open up and enjoy the flow.

Perhaps your marriage or your friendships have come into clearer focus. You see how important it is to balance the Trinitarian emphasis on union and uniqueness. You want to be able to accept yourself and to give yourself freely to others.

"But how do I do this?" you may ask. Most of us continually revert to seeking the answers outside of ourselves. We want to avoid growing up into our spiritual adulthood.

You are asked to get into the water and learn with God. Scripture will teach you; God's inner presence will urge you; other fellow pilgrims may give you encouragement and companionship. But the journey is uniquely yours. This life is not about conforming but about learning to express God from inside out in your own particular circumstances. It will be a journey of deepening trust in God's faithfulness and mercy.

What will be your confidence? What assurance can you have that will see you through the powerful and uncertain experiences of loving God and living passionately?

Thomas Merton once began a prayer with similar uncertainty. "My Lord God," he prayed, "I have no idea where I am going. I do not see the road ahead of me . . . nor do I really know myself, and the fact that I think I am following your will does not mean that I am actually doing so."

In the same prayer he returned to a grounding place, even in the midst of confusion. "I believe," he prayed, "that the desire to please you does in fact please you." He concludes with the lines, "Therefore I will trust you always, though I may seem to be lost and in the shadow of death. I will not fear, for you are ever with me and will never leave me to face my perils alone."[2]

Many times I've been glad Merton was honest enough to say what I feel! I'm often painfully aware of my own inadequacies and the potential for self-deception. If the flowing of the river were up to me, I would be lost.

But my fears and feelings of uncertainty are not the final story. I consider Merton's prayer to be one of the most profoundly optimistic prayers I know. It honestly names the worst case, the times when we feel lost and afraid, and reassures us of God's ongoing presence.

When we're in love with the Infinite, we should not be surprised to feel at a loss sometimes. We're not lost, we just don't have our spiritual life neatly packaged. Our intimacy with God will be a constant journey into unknown territory. But God will be there.

Merton's prayer puts the emphasis back on God where it belongs in the first place. It reminds me that I'm not a city engineer trying to manage the water flow. I am not managing passion, I am seeking to be faithful to God and open to God's life in the middle of my passion.

Earlier, we said that God's will is not some precarious ridge we have to cross . . . a maze we have to run. Sometimes, in the swirl of living, we get so caught up with our own choices that our understanding of God's will fixates on our responsibility. We focus too much on how well we're doing rather than on God's presence.

"How can I know for sure that I'm making the right decision?"

"Will I make a mistake?" "Will I ruin my chances for God's best for my life?" These can be important questions if asked within the confidence that God is with us and in us. Without that confidence, they are paralyzing questions.

When I first began taking daylong prayer retreats, I was plagued with such questions as, Have I prayed long enough? Should I journal now or am I avoiding prayer by journaling? Can I take a walk? Is walking part of my prayer or do I have to come back to my room and pray? These questions sound silly now, but they nearly put me off solitude forever. They made me ready for a spiritual director!

We need to come back to the assurance that God is more deeply involved in this than we are. This is God's life and God's purpose, a river of life within us. We didn't start the flow and we will not provide the current.

Perhaps now, looking back, we can say that even the image of a path may not truly express the goodness of God's presence in our lives and in our choices.

God's will is a river. God wills that the loving intimacy of the Trinity flows through our lives and out into the world.

There is a great difference between a path and a river. A path is static; a river is dynamic. A path is passive; the river will find a way. As the Neville Brothers sing, "You can't stop running water."

We are to work out our salvation, Paul says, not because we're being tested by God to see if we do it perfectly, but because God is already at work in us (Philippians 2:13).

A river is irrepressible. Indomitable. Within the overall contours of the riverbed, the river will find its course through the changing seasons of spring runoff, summer clarity, and winter ice. It will overcome obstacles, find new channels, and continue to flow.

Its twisted journey becomes part of its rich character. Only canals are straight. In the end, the twists and turns, the boulders and rapids all contribute to the river's enchanting beauty.

By the grace of God, the life of the Trinity keeps coming to us; it is always available to us. If we have dammed it out of fear, we can open up again to the current. If we have distorted it through our lusts and poor choices, we can choose again to relinquish control and open up to God's sufficient presence.

God's life keeps coming to us in the places of exuberant joy and fearful uncertainty. Surely this is rock-bottom good news! Paul's letter to the Philippian church bubbles with an irrepressible sense of joy. In the face of imprisonment, competition from self-aggrandizing preachers, and the squabbles of church members, Paul had learned that God was sufficient. His prayer for them in the passion of their own experience can be our prayer of trust.

"[God] who began a good work in you will carry it on to completion until the day of Christ Jesus" (Philippians 1:6).

God started this torrent. And God will complete the flow.

Notes

Chapter One: The Risk of Growth

1. Abbé de Tourville, *Letters of Direction* (Wilton, Conn.: Morehouse Barlow, tr. 1939), p. 24.
2. C. S. Lewis, *Mere Christianity* (New York: Macmillan, 1943), p. 49.
3. James Nelson, in his book, *Embodiment* (Minneapolis: Augsburg, 1978), for example, seeks to offer a spirituality of sexuality. In the process, however, Nelson ends up abdicating values for the sake of passion, concluding that nearly anything is okay if our hearts are right. We might agree with much of what he is trying to express, but an accommodating spirituality ends up just as unhelpful and insipid as fundamentalist legalism. "Vapid" is the word one prominent liberal used to describe his own tradition of accommodation.
4. See Dante's description of the goodness of desire at the core, even of our sinful impulses, in *The Divine Comedy: Purgatorio*, Cantos 17 and 18.
5. Dallas Willard, *The Spirit of the Disciplines* (San Francisco: Harper & Row, 1988), p. 75.
6. Willard, p. 80.

Chapter Two: Becoming "All Flame"

1. Henri J. M. Nouwen, *Bread for the Journey* (San Francisco: HarperSanFrancisco, 1997), reading for May 9.
2. Ironically, this is a phrase coined by the early Jesuit missionary, St. Francis Xavier, and widely used by Evangelicals to call for commitment.
3. Robin Lane Fox, *Pagans and Christians* (London: Penguin Books, 1986), p. 341.

4. Thomas Merton, *The Wisdom of the Desert* (New York: New Directions, 1960), p. 3.

5. Benedicta Ward, trans., *The Sayings of the Desert Fathers* (Oxford: A. R. Mowbray, 1981), p. 103.

6. See, for example, Gregory of Palamas, *The Triads: Classics of Western Spirituality* (New York: Paulist Press, 1983).

7. See Galatians 2:20.

8. James Houston, ed., *The Love of God: Classics in Faith and Devotion* (Portland, Ore.: Multnomah Press, 1983).

Chapter Three: Jesus' Invitation to Fullness of Life

1. St. Augustine, *Confessions* (Middlesex, England: Penguin Books, 1961), p. 111.

2. Teresa of Ávila, *Interior Castle* (Garden City, New York: Image Books, 1961), p. 29.

3. Colin Brown, ed., *The New International Dictionary of New Testament Theology,* vol. 1 (Grand Rapids: Zondervan, 1967), p. 729.

4. Anthony de Mello, *The Song of the Bird* (New York: Image Books, 1984), p. 2.

5. See Igumen Chariton of Valamo, comp., *The Art of Prayer: An Orthodox Anthology* (London: Faber and Faber, 1966), p. 63, where, for example, Theophan the Recluse is quoted as saying, "The principal thing is to stand with the mind in the heart before God, and to go on standing before Him unceasingly day and night, until the end of life."

Chapter Four: The Three-in-One Source of Our Passion

1. This updated English version of Donne's sonnet is found in *The Norton Introduction to Literature,* 2d ed. (New York: Norton, 1977), p. 668.

2. There has been a very important revival of interest in Trinitarian theology in recent years. It has included a return to the Trinitarian revelation of God in the work of our salvation and an understanding of the relational nature of the Trinity as the heart of all existence.

   This Trinitarian renewal is a very exciting move. It seeks to recover a theological base that is truly Christian, one that expresses a more Christian view of God and personhood than what we have inherited from Western theology and the Enlightenment. While I am familiar with this growing renaissance, I have purposely tried to stay away from a technical discussion of Trinitarian theology and present what I feel to be most germane to the topic of this book.

I would recommend the article by Christopher Hall, "Adding Up the Trinity," *Christianity Today* (28 April 1997), as a good starting point for further reading.

3. Colin Gunton, *The Promise of Trinitarian Theology* (Edinburgh: T & T Clark, 1991), p. 3.
4. Karl Rahner, *The Trinity* (New York: Herder & Herder, 1970), p. 11.
5. A. H. Strong, *Systematic Theology* (Westwood, N.J.: Revell, 1907), pp. 326-330.
6. See Louis Dupre, *The Common Life: The Origins of Trinitarian Mysticism and Its Development by Jan Ruusbroec* (New York: Crossroad, 1984), p. 11. Dupre comments that the Eastern Church assumes that the mode of our knowledge of God, namely through a revelation in Christ, signifies something about God Himself. The revelation of God as Triune in the baptism of Jesus is as important as the baptism itself. We see a relationship of love revealed as the basis of our salvation.
7. *"ousia"*
8. *"hypostasis"*
9. *"perichoresis"*
10. Colin Gunton, p. 8, expresses the thought this way: "It was the function of the *homoousion*, the teaching that the Son is 'of one being' with the Father, to express an ontological relationship between the Son and God the Father. While the precise meaning of this word in its historical context is the subject of much debate, the kind of function that it performs can be pointed to quite simply. It is to establish a new ontological principle: that there can be a sharing in being."
11. Gunton, p. 10.
12. Jürgen Moltmann, *The Trinity and the Kingdom* (Minneapolis: Fortress Press, 1983), p. 23.
13. Catherine LaCugna, *God For Us: The Trinity and Christian Life*

(San Francisco: HarperCollins, 1991), p. 1.
14. Julian of Norwich, *Revelations of Divine Love* (Garden City, New York: Image Books, 1977), p. 180.
15. A happy phrase used by Dr. James Houston.
16. John Ruusbroec, *The Spiritual Espousals and Other Works* (New York: Paulist Press, 1985), pp. 176-177.
17. John Main, *Moment of Christ* (New York: Crossroad, 1986), p. xi.
18. John Ruusbroec is not as famous as many of the spiritual writers of the church—Augustine, Thomas à Kempis or Teresa of Ávila. He was an Augustinian monk who lived in the fourteenth century. He did not live a flamboyant life. For most of his adult life, he lived quietly in the forests of what is now Belgium. However, by insisting on a dynamic Trinitarian spirituality, Ruusbroec achieved a spiritual synthesis that many say has never been superseded. So powerful was his vision that Evelyn Underhill called him "one of the greatest if not the greatest mystic of the church." Evelyn Underhill, *Mystics of the Church* (Cambridge: James Clarke & Co., 1925), p. 148.
19. This is the *"homoousia"* of Nicean theology.
20. Ruusbroec, p. 110.
21. Ruusbroec, p. 262.
22. Ruusbroec, pp. 176-177.
23. Ruusbroec, p. 263.

Chapter Five: Embracing the Goodness of Passion
1. Samuel Allen (Paul Vesey, psuedonym), "To Satch" *Poetry of Relevance*, ed. Homer Hogan (Toronto: Methuen Publications, 1970), p. 45. Used by permission from the author.
2. Annie Dillard, *Pilgrim at Tinker Creek* (New York: Harper & Row, 1975), pp. 33-34.
3. The Pulitzer prize-winning novel by Carol Shields, *The Stone Diaries* (Toronto: Vintage Books, 1993) is an exquisite portrait of a woman who, like many women of her day, lived a very narrow, "unfulfilled" life. Yet Shields is able to show that even this woman's life was significant and full of wonder.
4. Henri J. M. Nouwen, *The Inner Voice of Love* (New York: Doubleday, 1996), p. 14.

Chapter Six: Passion's Dangers

1. The emphasis is mine in each of the following passages to indicate the translation of the word.
2. See Richard Foster's book, *Money, Sex and Power* (San Francisco: Harper & Row, 1985).
3. James Houston, *The Heart's Desire: A Guide to Personal Fulfillment* (Oxford: Lion Publishing, 1992), p. 53.
4. An unfortunate KJV mistranslation of 1 Thessalonians 5:22. The NIV translation reads, "Avoid every kind of evil."
5. Clara Pinkola Estes, *Women Who Run with the Wolves* (New York: Ballantine Books, 1992), p. 8.
6. Estes, pp. 214-215.

Chapter Seven: Choosing

1. St. Augustine, *Confessions,* p. 238.
2. Houston, ed., *The Love of God,* p. 151.

Chapter Eight: The Storm in Our Lives

1. Madeleine L'Engle, *Two-Part Invention* (San Francisco: HarperSanFrancisco, 1988), p. 103.
2. This wonderful phrase is borrowed from Walter Brueggemann in *Interpretation and Obedience* (Minneapolis: Fortress Press, 1991), p. 165.
3. A cassette tape by Dr. James Houston from the course "Experiencing the Trinity: The Focus of Christian Spirituality" by Drs. James Houston, Edwin Hui & James Torrance, Regent College, purchased from Regent College, n.d. Vancouver, Canada.
4. See Gregory of Palamas, *The Triads Classics of Western Spirituality,* note 2, p. 117, in which the translator defines *apatheia* as follows: "freedom from the tyranny of the passions: an interior liberation that is the goal of monastic *ascesis.* It involves a state of stability in the virtues (*not* insensibility), in which one is no longer dominated by such impulses as anger, lust and fear, but has acquired the inner peace that frees one to love."
5. The reader can consult any history of Christian spirituality for a further explanation of these terms. Or, if courageous, the reader can read Charles Williams, *Descent of the Dove*, which may include the best explanation of all.

6. Charles Williams, *Descent of the Dove* (Grand Rapids: Eerdmans, 1939), p. 58.

7. Williams, p. 57.

Chapter Nine: Enjoying the Current

1. David Fleming, *The Spiritual Exercises of St. Ignatius: A Literal Translation and a Contemporary Reading* (St. Louis: The Institute of Jesuit Sources, 1978), p. 23.

2. Dallas Willard, *The Spirit of the Disciplines* (San Francisco: Harper & Row, 1988) pp. 22-23.

3. Willard, p. 156.

4. Willard, p. 153.

Chapter Ten: Securing the Banks

1. Richard Foster, *Prayer: Finding the Heart's True Home* (San Francisco: Harper San Francisco, 1992), p. 56.

2. Tilden Edwards, *Living in the Presence: Disciplines for the Spiritual Heart* (San Francisco: Harper & Row, 1987).

3. Walter Brueggemann,. *Interpretation and Obedience* (Minneapolis: Fortress Press, 1991), p. 148.

4. Gerald May, *Addiction and Grace* (San Francisco: Harper & Row, 1988), p. 1.

Chapter Eleven: Daring to Dream

1. See, for example, the wonderful passages of comfort and restoration in Isaiah, the promise of forgiveness and healing in Hosea 14, and the great passages in Micah about "the last days."

2. William Arndt and F. Wilber Gingrich, *A Greek-English Lexicon of the New Testament and Other Early Christian Literature* (Chicago: The University of Chicago Press, 1957), pp. 853-854.

Chapter Twelve: Living Passionately in Creation

1. A. W. Tozer, *The Pursuit of God* (Harrisburg, Penn.: Christian Publications, 1948), p. 61.

2. I can only give a brief introduction here of the topic of God's presence in creation.

3. The Hebrew word for breath, spirit, and wind is the same word.

4. See Genesis 1:30 where the same phrase refers to all of the animals.

5. St. Augustine, p. 22.
6. Thomas Berry, *The Dream of the Earth* (San Francisco: Sierra Club Books, 1988) has a very penetrating analysis of this movement to independence and how it has been exacerbated by Christian history.
7. See Berry, chapter 9, "Christian Spirituality and the American Experience."

Chapter Thirteen: Living Passionately in Community

1. Jean Vanier, *Community and Growth* (New York: Paulist Press, 1979), pp. 200, 24.
2. See Catherine Mowry LaCugna, *God For Us: The Trinity and Christian Life* (San Francisco: HarperCollins, 1991) for an excellent study of the Trinity and the importance of understanding God's being as ontologically relational. She concludes, for example, "The doctrine of the Trinity affirms that the 'essence' of God is relational, other-ward, that God exists as diverse persons united in a communion of freedom, love, and knowledge," p. 243.
3. LaCugna, p. 270.
4. Elizabeth O'Connor, *Cry Pain, Cry Hope* (Dallas: Word, 1987), p. 81.
5. Reginald Bibby, *Fragmented Gods* (Toronto: Stoddart, 1987), p. 52.
6. Charles Blake, a COGIC pastor, quoted in *Christianity Today* (8 April 1996), p. 27.
7. M. Scott Peck, *The Different Drum* (New York: Simon & Schuster, 1987), p. 188.
8. Vanier, p. 5.
9. The Greek word is *poikilos.*

Chapter Fourteen: Living Passionately in Relationships

1. Houston, ed. *The Love of God* p. 244 (parenthetical explanation is mine).
2. Thomas Patrick Malone and Patrick Thomas Malone, *The Art of Intimacy* (New York: Simon & Schuster, 1987), p. 21.
3. Malone and Malone, p. 19.

Chapter Fifteen: Living Passionately with God

1. Rublev created this icon in about 1411. For a simple discussion of the value of the icon in prayer, see Henri Nouwen's book, *Behold the Beauty of the Lord: Praying with Icons* (Notre Dame, Ind.: Ave Maria Press, 1987).
2. William Barry and William Connelly, *The Practice of Spiritual Direction* (New York: Harper & Row, 1982).
3. William Barry, *Seek My Face* (Mahwah, N.J.: Paulist Press, 1993).
4. Attributed to Bernard of Clairvaux, but probably written by William of St. Thierry.
5. St. Augustine, *Confessions,* p. 232.
6. St. John of the Cross says that longing is the sign of the presence of God in the dark night of the soul when all sense of the sweetness of God's presence is gone. *Dark Night of the Soul* (New York: Image Books, 1959), pp. 64-69.
7. David Fleming, p. 141.
8. Etty Hillesum, *An Interrupted Life: The Diaries of Etty Hillesum, 1941–43* (New York: Washington Square Press, 1983), p. 187.

Conclusion: Will the River Flow in You?

1. Michael Buckley, *The Treasury of the Holy Spirit* (London: Hodder and Stoughton, 1984), p. 147.
2. John Veltri, S. J., *Orientations: A Collection of Helps for Prayer* vol. 1 (Guelph, Ontario: Loyola House, n.d.), p. 68.

AUTHOR

JEFF IMBACH currently serves as a pastor at Barnabas Christian Fellowship. He has also worked as a spiritual director for more than fourteen years and has taught numerous courses and retreats on the spiritual life. He earned his bachelor's degree from Columbia International University and his master's of divinity degree from Grace Theological Seminary. Jeff has taught religion and writing courses at several colleges and is the author of one other book, *The Recovery Of Love: Christian Mysticism And The Addictive Soceity* (Crossroads). He lives with his wife in Calgary, Alberta, Canada. They have two daughters.

GENERAL EDITOR

DALLAS WILLARD is a professor in the school of philosophy at the University of Southern California in Los Angeles. He has been at USC since 1965, where he was director of the school of philosophy from 1982 to 1985. He has also taught at the University of Wisconsin (Madison), where he received his Ph.D. in 1964, and has held visiting appointments at UCLA (1969) and the University of Colorado (1984).

His philosophical publications are mainly in the areas of epistemology, the philosophy of mind and of logic, and on the philosophy of Edmund Husserl, including extensive translations of Husserl's early writings from German into English. His *Logic and the Objectivity of Knowledge*, a study on Husserl's early philosophy, appeared in 1984.

Dr. Willard also lectures and publishes in religion. *In Search of Guidance* was published in 1984 (second edition in 1993), and *The Spirit of the Disciplines* was released in 1988.

He is married to Jane Lakes Willard, a marriage and family counselor with offices in Van Nuys and Canoga Park, California. They have two children, John and Rebecca, and live in Chatsworth, California.

EDITOR

DAVID HAZARD is the editor of spiritual formation books for NavPress. He is also the editor of the classic devotional series, *Rekindling the Inner Fire*, and writes the monthly column, "Classic Christianity," for *Charisma* magazine.

For more than seventeen years, David has held various positions with Christian publishing houses, from editorial director to associate publisher. As a writer, he has contributed numerous internationally best-selling books to contemporary Christian publishing, some of which have been published in more than twenty languages worldwide. As an editor, David has developed more than two hundred books.

For the past twelve years, his special focus and study has been in the classic writings of Christianity, the formation of early Christian doctrine, and Christian spirituality.

If you liked THE RIVER WITHIN, be sure to check out these other books in the NavPress SPIRITUAL FORMATION LINE

In His Image

Is it possible to be like Jesus in today's world?
This book examines what it means to be like Christ,
challenging readers to follow Him wholeheartedly
and be transformed in the process.

In His Image
(Michael Wilkins) $14

Love Your God with All Your Mind

Have you really thought about your faith?
This book examines the role of reason in faith,
helping believers use their intellect to further God's kingdom.

Love Your God with All Your Mind
(J.P. Moreland) $14

Follow Me

Follow Me examines the kingdom of heaven,
challenging readers to examine the kingdoms they set up
—things like money, relationships, or power—
that keep them from truly following Jesus.

Follow Me
(Jan David Hettinga) $14

Get your copies today at your local bookstore, or call
(800) 366-7788 and ask for offer **#SFL1**.

NAVPRESS
BRINGING TRUTH TO LIFE
www.navpress.org